GREYING GRACEFULLY

Planning for Retirement
and
Old Age Happiness

GREYING GRACEFULLY
Planning for Retirement
and
Old Age Happiness

Siddhartha Ganguli, Ph.D.

ALLIED PUBLISHERS PRIVATE LIMITED

New Delhi • Mumbai • Kolkata • Chennai • Nagpur
Ahmedabad • Bangalore • Hyderabad • Lucknow

ALLIED PUBLISHERS PRIVATE LIMITED

1/13-14 Asaf Ali Road, **New Delhi**–110002
Ph.: 011-23239001 • E-mail: delhi.books@alliedpublishers.com

47/9 Prag Narain Road, Near Kalyan Bhawan, **Lucknow**–226001
Ph.: 0522-2209942 • E-mail: lko.books@alliedpublishers.com

17 Chittaranjan Avenue, **Kolkata**–700072
Ph.: 033-22129618 • E-mail: cal.books@alliedpublishers.com

15 J.N. Heredia Marg, Ballard Estate, **Mumbai**–400001
Ph.: 022-42126969 • E-mail: mumbai.books@alliedpublishers.com

60 Shiv Sunder Apartments (Ground Floor), Central Bazar Road,
Bajaj Nagar, **Nagpur**–440010
Ph.: 0712-2234210 • E-mail: ngp.books@alliedpublishers.com

F-1 Sun House (First Floor), C.G. Road, Navrangpura,
Ellisbridge P.O., **Ahmedabad**–380006
Ph.: 079-26465916 • E-mail: ahmbd.books@alliedpublishers.com

751 Anna Salai, **Chennai**–600002
Ph.: 044-28523938 • E-mail: chennai.books@alliedpublishers.com

5th Main Road, Gandhinagar, **Bangalore**–560009
Ph.: 080-22262081 • E-mail: bngl.books@alliedpublishers.com

3-2-844/6 & 7 Kachiguda Station Road, **Hyderabad**–500027
Ph.: 040-24619079 • E-mail: hyd.books@alliedpublishers.com

Website: www.alliedpublishers.com

ISBN : 978-81-8424-697-1

Published by Sunil Sachdev and printed by Ravi Sachdev at Allied Publishers Pvt. Ltd.,
Printing Division, A-104 Mayapuri Phase II, New Delhi -110064

Acknowledgements

It was first the National Insurance Company Ltd., eastern India's flagship general insurance giant that requested our organisation *Learning Club* to design a few sessions on 'Reversal of Aging' for a small batch of officers including ladies who were going to retire shortly. We designed and conducted the sessions and collected enough kudos. Some of the keener session participants had also kept touch with us through e-mail for a few months. It was thus equally a good learning opportunity for us as we could know a little deeper about the attitudes of the would-be retirees towards the terminal stage of their journey through employment known as 'retirement'. Our first gratitude is towards those first few retirees who also helped us to learn. Once those sessions clicked, we started getting requests from time to time for similar sessions from different organisations as the news had spread through word-of-mouth. We were getting enriched in the process.

Three years ago when we got a request from the National Hydroelectric Power Corporation Ltd. to design a full workshop on *Planning for Happy Retirement* for a few batches of their employees at the Loktak Power Station near Imphal, Manipur, we had to take it really seriously and started developing the course material after making a study of the background of the participants. The workshop contents have evolved over time as we had to train a few batches. Since the skeleton of this book is based on the framework of the Loktak workshop material, we are indebted to the large number of workshop participants who interacted with us sharing their plans, programmes and anticipated prospects as well as problems.

Subsequently, we got the opportunity to conduct workshops on the same theme for several organisations where we met and discussed face-to-face with hundreds of employees facing retirement. That first-hand experience has helped us in developing a reliable knowledge base about various aspects of planning for retirement and old age happiness.

As usual, I have received regular emotional support from my loving wife Utpala while working on this project. Technical and secretarial help, at every step, have come from my *Learning Club* team members Ravi Verma, Niranjan Das, Pervez Alam and Prabir Roy. Pervez has taken special interest and care to prepare the outline diagrams and collect pictures to be inserted at relevant places in the text to make it interesting for the reader; and Ravi has extended help in some editorial work.

Niranjan did frequently brainstorm regarding the book's marketing potentials while I was giving the finishing touches. Prabir was always ready to cool me down with his smiling face whenever my fuse was about to be blown out—not getting the right expression at the right moment when I desperately needed it.

I am indebted to Dr. Lawrence Whalley, MD, FRC Psych, FRCP, emeritus professor of mental health, University of Aberdeen, Scotland, U.K. for his encouragement. His authoritative reference volume *The Ageing Brain* had inspired me a lot.

I shall be utterly selfish if I do not mention that I was tempted to quote the spoken or written words of several authors, poets and celebrities as I found them most relevant in certain contexts. If I wish to record my gratitude to each of them, it would take a lot of space; so in just a short sentence let me say how grateful I am to all of them for the stimulants they provided me. Same is the case with some illustrations which I collected through the Internet. I am indeed thankful to the artists and photographers of those as their artworks excellently fitted into some portions of my texts.

And, finally, I owe a lot to Sharad Gupta, Senior Editorial Adviser to my publishers, Allied Publishers Pvt. Ltd. Delhi and his colleagues for readily taking up the project to make the book available in the market so that interested people can find something really useful for their advanced age. The project would not have been successful without their continuous back-office help.

Preface

Greying Gracefully is not a cut-and-dried textbook. Nor it is a reference book which provides you with some hard data about old age homes, doctors specialising in geriatric medicine, life-medical-general insurance-banking-financial investment schemes, clubs-associations-websites dealing with old age people and other such facts and figures which would be of interest before, at the time of, and also after retirement.

Greying Gracefully is supposed to be the guide—your constant companion when you feel unhealthy, lonely, friendless and socially and emotionally down and out at certain periods of your life: when you plan to retire, when you have just retired, and also when you are in your middle old (between 60 and 70 years) and old old (beyond 70 years) age. It is meant to provide you with tested tips on how to remain healthy, cool and in good humour. It is meant to provide you with tips as to how you would become ego-detached and happy. And, it is all based on the latest data available to keep you absolutely up-to-date.

To make you convinced, a balanced mix of serious scientific concepts, useful research findings expressed in simple layman's language and live case studies has constituted the core of the text. The style of presentation has been kept lucid so that you do not find it heavy. The matter in each chapter has been subdivided into main headings (main portions) and sub-headings (smaller portions) so that you do not lose your concentration while reading. And, each chapter ends with the 'key' application tips.

I know, an avid old reader (I am 1940-born) like me would browse through the whole book in one go; or read two to three books at a time—one or two chapters in each during every reading foray. However, for general readers, the book is organised in a fashion that one can go for selective reading. The three main reasons for such selectivity could be: firstly, you're getting on age and confronting a mental and sensory slowdown which weakens your concentration and optic nerves; secondly, you're still active and there is a lot of demand on your time—you can afford to read only the portions which interest you most at this stage of your life; thirdly, you're particularly interested in the chapters dealing with the body aspects, or the mind aspects, or the brain itself, or the financial planning and relate what you read to yourself—your strengths and weaknesses, your problems and prospects, your do's and don'ts. There could be a reason or two more.

Most honestly, I would not have ventured into writing this book twenty years ago. Today the old age population in the upper half of the pyramid in our society has increased considerably with their accessibility to modern health care services. Apart from my exposure to these senior citizens whom I meet from time to time in the *Planning for Happy Retirement* workshops that we conduct and in the *Happiness Clinic* sessions that we run through our organisation *Learning Club*, I talk to them and sometimes even eavesdrop when they are chatting with others in parks, public transports, markets and social gatherings. When I ask some of them simple standard questions like: "How are you? How have you been keeping? How are things? How is it going?", most of them answer in the negative in a depressed tone: "Not well at all. Not going good." etc. Then I have to stop and listen to the stories of their unhappiness. Since I belong to that age group myself, I thought of doing something for their happiness being a happiness researcher and writer.

Writing a series of articles in a widely circulated health magazine and publishing a Bengali best-seller on Old Age Happiness have been the natural outcomes and important landmarks in my service to the senior citizen population. *Greying Gracefully* is a much bigger venture into which lot of research and thoughts have gone over the last three years. Hope my efforts will bear fruits for those who really need them for their physical well-being and mental solace.

Just a few words before I close the Preface. As I had reached almost the end of my journey, writing this book, *The Economic Times*, Kolkata edition of 13th January 2011 published the key points documented in a OECD (Organisation of Economic Cooperation & Development) report—*Health at a glance*, Asia-Pacific, 2010 on its page 11. From there, to my utter surprise, I could gather that an average Indian was expected to live only 63.7 (female: 65.2 and male: 62.3) years in 2008 while most Asians lived longer, 71.6 years. Although there has been, the report says, a significant progress made since the 1970s, when the average life expectancy of an Indian was less than 50, the picture is still most dismal. This information came to me at a time when me and most of my friends in the academic, scientific and corporate worlds like to believe that our country is just about catching up with the West or even with the advanced Asian nations. To our surprise, compared to the low longevity of us in India, those in the OECD nations live as long as 79.2 years and in Asia itself, the continent to which we belong, the Japanese live 82.7 years, the South Koreans 79.9, and the Chinese 73.1 years.

This news flash was closely followed by another item: 'Indians like to wait till they turn 61' published in the same newspaper on 18th January 2011 which opened with a paragraph reading as: "Retiring at 40 may be on the wish list of several executives, but when it comes to reality, more than 80% of the Indian population believes that a longer working life—beyond 58 years of age—is the only way of securing their post-retirement income." The findings were based on the AXA Retirement Scope Report, which interviewed 4,300 individuals of different age groups in India's eight metro cities including the national and political capital Delhi, the commercial capital Mumbai, the IT capital Bangalore, and the intellectual and cultural capital Kolkata. Over 60% of the working population and retirees, the report said, are keen on a higher retirement age of 61 years, as the news heading highlighted. About 81% of the people surveyed commented that they see old age with little savings available at hand and hence dependence on others as a big worrying factor. Commenting on the research data, Mark Meehan, chief marketing and operations officer, Bharati AXA Life Insurance, stated: "With a large part of India's population due to retire in the next 25–30 years, early retirement planning will assure a healthy and securely retired population." In terms of preparation for old age, India is placed towards the middle in terms of effective preparation (38%) for post retirement, between countries like Hong Kong (57%) and less prepared countries like Thailand (27%).

These revealing facts have given me a fresh confidence about the timeliness of *Greying Gracefully* which provides plenty of tips about what type of lifestyle is needed to be followed after you reach close to your late fifties, for living much further into your life happily not only with reasonably sound physical and mental health and fitness but also with well-deserved economic security through proper prior planning. It will give me immense happiness if this book can contribute a little to raise the level of longevity of my Indian readers even by a decimal percentage. Let's keep our fingers crossed.

Siddhartha Ganguli, Ph.D.
(Author of the best-selling books
Live Happily, Work Happily,
SUCCESS: Can be Planned and Earned, and
Conscious Management: Managing and Leading Happily
at the Workplace and at Home.
all published by Allied Publishers, New Delhi)

Contents

Contents

Introduction

It's the Right Time to Take a Stock of Your Happiness Quotient (HQ)

"If life hands you a lemon, make lemonade."
—**Norman Vincent Peale**
of The Power of Positive Thinking Fame

MEET TWO CHARACTERS FROM TWO OPPOSITE POLES

Mr North Pole: Rajeev Mehta

This is a Special Moment for Mr Mehta

It's seconds past midnight. There has been a new arrival in Rajeev Mehta's life. The new day, 10th October 2010 has just made its entry. And Mr Mehta has started his journey into the seventh decade of his life. He's 1940-born.

Although his chronological age is 70 at this moment, biologically he feels as healthy and fit as a 33-year young man (recent research has indicated that 33 is the most active and eventful year of an individual's life). Mentally, he feels as mature and wise as one who is in his early forties (remember the common adage that 'life begins at forty'!). And, imaginatively and creatively he's like a happy child who is as open and as wide as the bright blue sunny sky and as dewy and as fresh as the autumn morning air.

What about his emotions, his sentiments—like pleasure, pain, attachment, anger, fear, envy, jealousy and, worst of them all, the ego? Is he still in their company? Yes, to a certain extent, although he has been trying for the past few years not only to reduce but to totally eradicate the interferences from his selfish genes—the creaturely instincts located in the lower parts of his brain—the extension of the brain stem on top of the spinal chord which is the trunk route of the peripheral nervous system.

Today, on his 70th birthday, he's taking a firm resolution to minimise the twitters of his lower brain to a near-zero level. He's setting it as his goal to stay put and operate from his *cerebrum*—the higher structures of his brain which is the abode of the true human qualities like love, empathy, compassion, understanding, cooperation and altruism.

Mr Mehta's Happiness Quotient: A Stock-Taking

It's the right time for Mr Mehta to take a stock of his life's journey—how has his *happiness quotient (HQ)* been behaving. HQ, may we say, is the ratio between what all good things you have got from your life and what all you had desired for and expected, at any particular point of time. We'll start taking the stock from the beginning of Rajeev Mehta's working career.

In 1970, when Mr Mehta was just 30 years young, his HQ was down to 0.6. He was 40% unhappy due to the boss factor. In the Indo-American consultancy services firm where he was employed as an architect after his post-IIT training in Helsinki, Finland with the topmost Finnish architect and town planner, he had to report to a functional director who was neither an architect nor an urban planner by training; he was only a civil engineer specialised in steel and concrete structures. He was not refined enough to appreciate Rajeev Mehta's architectural ideas and they often had noisy arguments in the drawing office.

Since Mr Mehta's HQ started sliding down further, he grabbed an opportunity that came by. He left and joined an Indo-British consultancy set-up to increase his happiness level. There, he had to report to the MD and CEO directly but, although a civil engineer who had specialised further in architecture at the post-graduate level, the big boss was so busy with his own work that Rajeev had to develop himself more as a 'self-managed' designer which was certainly a gain for him as his self-confidence grew as a consequence. He had no problem in handling his architectural clients directly. His HQ, no doubt, went up to 70%.

Nevertheless, being a creative person, Rajeev Mehta wanted much greater independence. So he walked into the shoes of the junior most Executive Partner of a premier architectural practice where his boss, the partnership firm's chief executive officer, designated as the president, changed every year by rotation from amongst the five senior partners. During the first year, his HQ went up to 0.9 as he had an admirable boss who, being in his mid-50's, started mentoring him on his 34th year. When Mehta grew a year older in age, his HQ dived down to 0.4 as he had a president who used to control and micromanage him. When Mehta was 36, his HQ went up to 0.9 again as his elderly president was most understanding and cordial in behaviour. Next year, his HQ came down drastically as one senior partner died and his young architect daughter, who inherited the partnership share of her father, became the president. Since she was fresh from college and did not have any practical experience, it was difficult for Rajeev to develop a professional under-standing with her.

If you are a *'Practically Intelligent (PI)'* person (you'll find *PI* being referred to from time to time in the text), your low HQ must become a trigger for you to get motivated to raise its score. On the contrary, if your *PI* is low then you continue to live with your low HQ and suffer; and, ultimately get very badly affected with some physical or mental problem. So, take your low HQ as a signal to look around for opportunities for raising your HQ level. (1) [(1) Ganguli, Siddhartha, *Success: Can be Planned and Earned*, New Delhi: Allied Publishers, 2010; refer to Chapter 9 'An Essential Potential for *Success* P2', pp. 98–116 for a detailed discussion on 'Practical Intelligence (PI)'. In the same chapter, there are also tests available for you to cross-check your PI level.]

Seven-time Tour de France winner Lance Armstrong has often talked of how he decided to use living with cancer as a source of motivation to achieve even greater things.(2) [(2) Hogan, Kevin, Dave Lakhani, Bob Beverley and Blair Warren, *The Secret Behind the Secret Law of Attraction*, Eagan, Minnesota: Network 3000 Publishing, 2007, p.43.]

These ups-and-downs and the long working hours (9.00 am to 8.00 pm) started telling upon Rajeev Mehta's health and fitness and he had problems in his digestive and muscular-skeletal systems. He was fed up and wanted to be free from these hassles. So the moment he crossed 40, he suddenly put in his papers one day on three months' notice and, since he had plenty of earned leave due, went on leave. Within six months, he set up his own architectural practice under the style of 'Rajeev Mehta and Associates' and started operating from his own ancestral home which was spacious. Since he was professionally superb and had excellent client contacts, in a few months' time, work assignments started pouring in.

Since its inception in 1980, the firm 'Rajeev Mehta and Associates' has provided innovative architectural and urban planning, design and project management services to over 150 organisations in India and its neighbouring countries. Being his own boss in his own organisation, there was no question of Mr Mehta's retirement from his professional practice at the age of 58 or 60 or even at 65. Today that he has scored 70, which has been proposed as the retirement age for IIT professors, he is not thinking even for a moment that he ought to retire. His happiness receptacle is more than full as his HQ today is more than 1. He is happier beyond his expectations and has been **greying gracefully**. He'll never retire as he has found a mission in his life: to come up with unique—novel yet economic designs, which could be constructed with minimum cost and in minimum time which no other architect or designer has ever thought of and, at the same time, the client organisation's decision-makers and other key stakeholders would be proud of. (About this mission in life and its critical importance for being happy in the last lap of one's life, we plan to discuss later).

Mr Mehta has been the recipient of several national and international prizes and awards for his outstanding professional achievements. He is a Fellow of the British as well as Indian Institute of Architects and is a frequent writer on architectural, town planning, interior design and allied topics in Indian and foreign journals. He is also a guest faculty in several universities and architectural schools in India and abroad.

Rajeev Mehta is happily married to Ruchi who has been an excellent life partner and homemaker all along, ever since they got married in 1965. They have three successful children who are well-settled. Neeraj, the elder son is a documentary film-maker and well-settled in his own professional practice. After his B.Com and MBA, he wanted to pursue a career in film-making and both Rajeev and Ruchi encouraged him to go ahead after they had a few sessions to discuss the pros and cons—the opportunities and threats. He is happily married to Udita with two sons, 12 and 9.

The younger son, Nikunj, wanted to go for entrepreneurship right after his graduation. He had discussions with his parents regarding his own plans and eventually he set up his own small specialised logistics enterprise, taking over from his clients—individuals and firms, the worries and hassles of deliveries and despatches. He has a team of dedicated, trustworthy young men to whom he outsources his work orders. His top-class coordination and quality service have helped him to earn a good reputation in the market and the business is on the growth path. He is married to Anisha with a 4-year old daughter and they are happy.

Rajeev and Ruchi occupy the ground floor of the big house that they own in Delhi whereas the two sons and their families live separately in the same building in the two first floor flats.

The youngest of the three, daughter Rita, is a management professional holding a high rank in an Indian bank in Mumbai, married to Amarish Kumar, a young Keralite—working as a project manager in a top IT company in Mumbai. They have their own flat in a relatively new part of the metro city.

Rajeev's HQ in the family role is also high as it is not only that he has had an understanding partner and also that all his children have done well in life so far, he never expected much in return of the investment that he had made on them in bringing them up and settling them in life.

Rajeev has a rich and happy social life professionally as he has to participate frequently in professional gatherings and socially interact with people there. His friends and relations also hold him in high esteem because of his high professional achievements.

Rajeev Mehta's is an excellent case study on **greying gracefully** and **old age happiness**.

Mr South Pole: Nitin Desai

Where does He Stand

Nitin Desai, 57, is awaiting his retirement in a year's time from Gujarat state govt. service. Since he was a very good worker and there is nobody to step into his shoes and take over from him, his boss, the joint secretary Mohan Wagle has already recommended his case for a year's extension. But still Mr Desai is a heart-broken person. His HQ has been down at 0.6 for the last two years ever since two most unexpected things happened in his life.

Why His HQ is Low

His elder child, son Naren took to drugs after he just could not complete his CA Inter despite seven consecutive attempts. His younger child, daughter Shreya got entangled, at the age of nineteen, with a local youth Madan Shah who is a singer and owner of his own folk band. Shreya came to know him through some common friends, became an admirer of his musical talent, fell in love with him and, suddenly one day, went to a temple—got married and came home along with the husband to collect her parents' blessings. Nitin has not been able to accept the circumstances still although his wife Purva has eventually reconciled. Madan's parents, Vipul and Prabha, had no objections. They have welcomed Shreya as a member of their family as she came from a very respectable back ground—a few levels higher than themselves.

Nitin's high workplace HQ has been badly tarnished by his extremely low family and social HQs. He was heart-broken as the expectations he had from his son and daughter were not fulfilled at all.

All the three—HQs in the family, social and work roles are equally important for adding up to a high value integrated HQ. Nitin is far from the goal of the present book: **greying gracefully**. The *stress* of unhappiness has already taken a toll on his health and fitness. He is a frequent visitor to Dr Gopal Bhulabhai, MD to take consultation regarding his chronic gastro-enterological problems. Besides, he has also consulted Dr Suresh Deshmukh, MS (Orth), FRCS (London), FRCS (Edin), the renowned orthopaedician of Vadodara three times this year for his shoulder and neck pain. He has been using a neck collar for the last four months and goes for physiotherapy sessions three times a week.

Both are live case studies: one good and the other bad – one bright and the other dark—one from the north pole the other, as if from the south. We thought of sharing these with you before we proceeded further.

A HQ Stock-Taking Exercise for You

If you have played the first innings of your life's game and are in the middle of your middle age, it's the right time for you to take a stock of your HQ if you have not done it already!

First of all, find out approximately what would you consider as your integrated HQ—taking your work, family and social roles all together. If it is more than 1, then you are on the right track which will help you to *grey gracefully*. You are under control now and you have full control over the rest of your life.

If it is 1, even then you are doing fine. If it happens to be less than 1, then find out the main root cause of your unhappiness—is it something to do with your work role, or is it related to your family or social roles—or is it a combination of two or all the three of the roles.

Once you discover that you are in the unhappiness zone, be more analytical and try to identify and pinpoint the causative factor. For example, if you're retired already and do not have a significant work role as such, is this lack of activity that makes you unhappy and makes your HQ low?

Or, is it that you're enjoying your freedom from work activities as today you happen to be the master of your own time which was not the case when you were working and had not retired, but since your social image has fallen after your retirement because you're not doing much economically, you have become unhappy?

Or, is it some health problem—your own, your spouse's or your children's or their families', that is causing you unhappiness?

Or, is it the economic factor, that you had a sudden drop in your standard of living after you retired?

Or, is it the social factor that every day for eight to nine hours you used to enjoy the company of people in your work role and suddenly after retirement you are at home—in almost a no man's land where it is only you and your spouse and you're bored and lonely?

If you're not retired yet but would in another few months' time, can you anticipate and pre-determine what your HQ would be, and if it is going to be less than 1 then what would be the root causes of your unhappiness—can you predict from now? Once you identify the root causes of your unhappiness post-retirement, can you think and plan out remedial or preventive strategies so that you can start the implementation right away without losing time?

Read On to Get Clues

You may not have any ready answers. Most people don't have. Don't get anxious. Read on and you may find some clues. With that purpose in mind, this project was undertaken.

APPLICATION TIPS

- Read the book and its every chapter with your spouse.

- Read the two case studies thoroughly as they are, and also between the lines.

- Where do you see yourself? Are you nearer the North Pole or in the proximity of the South Pole or somewhere in between? Or, are you confused about your whereabouts? Pause and ponder for a day or two, even for a week to find out your location. Once you have found out your bearing, work out your HQ and find out the root causes of your happiness and unhappiness.

- You will have a deep and sound self-knowledge, if you can write your own case study. Find out your HQ—particularly its current status. Why don't you make an attempt? Also influence your spouse to write her/his own case.

Chapter 1

Why People Become Unhappy in Old Age: The Seven Critical Unhappiness Factors (SCUF)

"I want to shout from rooftops and explain to people that everything is good; let go off your ego, and enjoy life."
—Hrithik Roshan, Actor
(after he was released from hospital care following
a very brief but life-threatening ailment on 28th November 2010)

MEET THE SEVEN IRRITANTS

Most of the time, in old age, the causes of unhappiness originate in the mind which, in turn, affect the body—telling upon the aged individual's health and fitness.

Seven is a very special number. Amongst the most common seven things, there are seven colours—seven rays of the sun; seven days in a week; seven notes of music; and, seven resources that one has to deal with for work performance anywhere—materials, machines, methods, money, men, information and time. We had never expected to find the golden presence of seven here when talking about old age happiness or unhappiness. But, strangely enough, we bumped into the influence of seven also in *gerontology*—the science dealing with old age.

Let us meet, face to face, the seven irritants—the seven most common root causes of unhappiness which have emotional background in the elderly. We'll call them the *Seven Critical Unhappiness Factors (SCUF)*.

Factor One: The Feeling of Economic Insecurity

We broached this subject in the *Preface* as we found it of great significance in India. We mentioned about the AXA Retirement Scope report, which is the product of a massive interview project with 4,300 individuals of different age groups in Delhi, Mumbai, Kolkata, Chennai, Bangalore, Hyderabad, Ahmedabad and Pune. The report indicated that over 60% of today's working population and retirees are keen on a higher retirement age of 61 years by raising the present common standard of 58. Although most Indians are observed to recognise the importance of saving for the old age, only 29% of those interviewed had an idea of their income at the time of retirement and post-retirement. (1) [(1) 'Indians like to wait till they turn 61', *The Economic Times, Kolkata,* 18 January 2011, p.13.]

Since many employed in the organised sector—government, semi-government, public and private sector organisations, feel secure by bestowing the responsibility of building up their superannuation funds (provident, gratuity and pension funds) to their employers, they have no idea how much would be their dues when they retire. Very few of the employers also share such information with their employees on a regular basis. We also do not know whether an employee can obtain such information readily from the concerned department when asked for. This is certainly a grey area which stands as a barrier for a person to grey gracefully. When you have little information about your old age economic security and you do not want to depend on anybody else—be it your sibling or one of your grown-up and well-established children, for economic reasons, it becomes a major source of worry for you.

The remedy lies in the following steps that you ought to take from your middle age. An employee should regularly track information about the status of his superannuation funds by maintaining excellent relationship with people in concerned departments who could be authentic sources. If he gets a signal that the total accrual at the time of retirement wouldn't be adequate for him to maintain a reasonably good living standard, he should go for some additional savings and investment schemes. A self-employed professional or a small entrepreneur should take timely steps to go for public provident fund and other secure investments on a planned basis. We'll talk about the financial planning part in Chapter 18.

Factor Two: The 'Return on Investment (ROI)' Expectations

As people get on age, one major root cause as to why they become unhappy and their HQs tend to get lower and lower is because they expect a 'Return on their Investments (ROIs)' and, for some of us, the ROI expectations are very high.

We, driven by our very basic nature, expect high returns on the time, energy, money, effort, knowledge, talent, skills, habits that we invest on something—some activity or one individual or a set of people. I'll describe it as the simple *trading (reciprocal give-and-take)* attitude of modern man, the economic animal.

It happens covertly in the family and social roles (remember Nitin Desai's case in the 'Introduction' part—how he became unhappy because his expectations regarding the ROIs that he and his wife had made on their two children were not being met) and covertly as well as overtly in the work roles (irrespective of whether you're an employee, or a self-employed person or an entrepreneur-employer).

Don't we meet parents who tell their kids time and again: "We're spending so much of our time, energy and money on your education, we expect you to score high marks and come out with flying colours in the board exams"?

Don't we meet managers who remind those who report to them: "We have spent so much time, energy, effort and money in imparting training and grooming you up, we expect a high performance from you. Is it unfair on our part to expect that"?

Don't we meet employees who complain that despite their investing a lot of their time and working very hard, they have been deprived of timely promotion? They are a common species in the world of organisations.

There are also some amongst us for whom the simple *trading* mind-set gets inflated and takes the form of a *bargaining* and *profit-making* attitude based, at times, on manipulative tendencies. Don't we, on the spur of the moment at times, comment in cases where we expect much more 'gives' than 'takes': "We have done so much for you and would expect much more from you in return."

When an individual having high expectations is not happy with the ROI, he makes those low return-givers suffer from a guilt complex and instils a feeling of indebtedness as they get branded as 'debtors', in his perception, who owe something to him.

In fact, the materialistic world is revolving around the two basic economic indices—*debt* and *credit*. One who owes something to you and you're expected to get it back (equivalent amount or on a high ROI) from him is your *debtor* and one to whom you owe something and are supposed to give back to him (equivalent amount or on a high ROI) is your *creditor*.

Interestingly, in the field of physiology, there is a common concept known as *oxygen debt*. Muscles need energy when they contract and this is obtained from glucose in the blood. After fierce muscular exertion, waste products from this process build up in the muscle tissues in the form of lactic acid, reducing the efficiency of the muscle, and causing it to tire. Extra oxygen is needed to remove lactic acid from the system, so we breathe more deeply after exertion. *Oxygen debt* thus represents oxygen deficit when an organism or part of an organism has been doing work with inadequate oxygen supply as the respiratory system cannot cope with the oxygen demand of the specific activity. After hard muscular work oxygen consumption of man remains above normal for some time, until the debt has been repaid and the balance is restored. (2, 3) [(2) Ward, Brian, *The Body and Health*, London: Macdonald Educational, 1976, pp. 22-23; (3) Abercrombie, M., C.J. Hickman and M.L. Johnson, *A Dictionary of Biology*, London: The English Language Book Society and Penguin Books, Sixth Edition, 1973, p.207.]

Get the 'debt-credit' and 'debtor-creditor' concepts out of their traditional habitat of economics and accounting, stretch or pull them a little and bring them to the field of human resource, they would then get linked to the domain of *Human Resource Economics* (4) (5) (6) [(4) Ganguli, Siddhartha, "Human Resource Economics: New Insights into Man's Personal Resources", *Globsyn Management Journal*, Vol. 1, Issue 1, January 2007, pp. 19-27; (5) Ganguli, Siddhartha, *Performance Management: 'First time Right'*, Kolkata: Platinum Publishers, 2008; (6) Ganguli, Siddhartha, *Live Happily, Work Happily*, New Delhi: Allied Publishers, 2009.]

If you have provided someone with physical energy support (in the case of a physical fight) and it has not been repaid, then that person continues to be your *physical energy debtor* and, for him, you are the *physical energy creditor*. Similarly, if you have provided some intelligent advice or wisdom to somebody, he is your *mental energy debtor* and you are his *mental energy creditor.* In case of positive emotional energy (love, affection, motivation and such other inputs), we have the *emotional energy debtor-creditor* roles. In case of social contact providing and connectivity building, there would be *social debtor-creditor* roles. Then we have the *economic/financial debtor-creditor* roles, which is very common. In the field of idea generation and innovation, there would be *imaginative/creative debtor-creditor* roles. And, finally, for higher feelings like compassion, empathy, understanding, cooperation, forgiveness and altruism, we would have *feelings-spiritual debtor-creditor* roles.

Something that You ought to remember for your Old Age Happiness: In order to be happy in your old age, keep your ROI expectations as low as possible. You simply can't imagine what sort of an absolutely free mind you'll have if you reduce them to zero.

Have a sharing and sacrificing spirit. Be a giver and a donor. You have taken a lot from life and others throughout your active life. You have tried to take it back too in return, directly or indirectly, tightly or loosely. Now try your best to go for a total reversal—a 'zero take' and a 'zero return' policy. Do not make people suffer from indebtedness which is indeed painful.

Factor Three: The 'Generation Gap'

Generation gap must not matter to you if you want to be happy and want others to be happy too.

Let us consider one positive case study. Mrs. Sumangala Chatterjee, widow of Late Doctor Himangshu Chatterjee lives alone in her own house located in the extreme south of Kolkata with two housemaids. Her late husband, who had worked as a medical doctor in Africa for more than twenty–five years and used to earn a lot, left a handsome fortune for his wife who had been from the rural Bengal and was not smart enough to take up a career of her own. She also has a car and a driver, the running cost of which is being borne by her surgeon son Pulak who has just returned from abroad after having spent more than a decade and half in England and America. Although he and his wife Ruma are staying with Mrs Chatterjee at the moment, the childless couple will move to their own two-storied house which they had purchased in south Kolkata three years ago. The renovation of the old property should be complete in another three months' time. Mrs Chatterjee's elder daughter Keya is married to Samrat Banerjee who is on an international assignment and the younger divorcee daughter Kuhu is a senior English teacher in Paris earning a lot. Kuhu's daughter Kakali is studying economics in the University of Dublin in Ireland. All of Mrs Chatterjee's children and grandchildren are westernised as many metro-based English-educated Indians in their late forties and early fifties are. They subscribe to an ethos which is different from her traditional Hindu culture. But, she has, most intelligently, adjusted very well with the generation gap and does not insist that her children and grandchildren should adopt her old-fashioned culture; nor does she suffer from any complex that she cannot express herself in English and does not share many ultra-modern habits with her children. She joins them while going to movies, plays, magic shows, musical soirees and big social get-togethers like marriage parties and sightseeing, but keeps away in the background for small parties where the younger generation normally would like to steam off and behave freely as they liked.

Unfortunately, very few of the older generation people in middle and upper middle class Indian metro and other big cities are like Mrs. Chatterjee; she is really a rare find. And, this is one of the main reasons why most of the retired elderly and who are going to retire suffer from unhappiness as neither they are flexible and adaptable enough to pick up the good things of each generation nor do they have the patience to keep their mind cool and study others' good points as well as realities.

Over the past few decades, the socio-economic environment has changed radically; the nature of the media has taken a U-turn; our metro, urban, suburban—even the rural cultures have undergone and are still under-going a rapid transformation. There has been a technological explosion with the cell phones, i-Pods, MP3 and DVD players, LCD displays, flat TVs, laptops and the Internet invading the lives of the school and college-going younger generation. These gadgets are becoming accessible readily to those who can afford them—it is no longer a matter of class and a prerogative of the affluent. The drivers who take us in public or private taxis, not to speak of company limousines, also carry more than one mobile handset; some of them with double SIM cards. Motor hospitals where ailing cars had to be sent for treatment (the other day during my evening stroll at a local park I met the erstwhile owner of a renowned automobile repair workshop who lamented that he had to close down his business five years ago) are winding up as today's car owners would rather go for changing the vehicle than having it repaired so many models of affordable new and used cars and car loans are available everywhere. The economic scenario is being dominated by plastic cards of various types.

You, I suppose, are a 1940s or 1950s born. There is naturally a generation gap in all respects between you and your children—the oldest of them being born in the 1960s. They don't choose you as their role models any longer. Their choice is from amongst the celebrities—an actor, a ramp model, a best-seller fiction writer, a young political Turk, an ace sports person, a suave laptop-bound marketing executive or a rising small business tycoon.

Besides, when you were a child, what did you want to be when you grew up? The list of popular dream professions that people of your generation had was long and diverse. It included doctor, nurse, engineer, architect, town planner, scientist, teacher, professor, lawyer, police officer, manager, administrator, artist, singer, athlete...and the list went on. The common denominator of all these desirable professions was an opportunity to touch people in a meaningful way. For the younger generation today, the topmost priority for choosing a career is *money*—for some, quantum-wise and for the most, economic security—which comes from a secure job that only the government, the public sector and big brand private houses can provide. Don't you see how the best students and the best amongst the better ones run for big brand institutes like the IITs, NIITs, IIMs, XLRI, JBIMS, FMS (Delhi) and the like? A recent newspaper headline reads like this: "Week 1 of IIT placement season sees top salaries jump 172%" (7). [(7) *The Economic Times, Kolkata,* 7 December 2010, p.1].

A 2010 computer science graduate from IIT-Kharagpur has got a remuneration package offer of more than ` 1 crore from Facebook to be located in the firm's US headquarters. Such instances become the main motivating factors for the present generation youngsters. And most of them are prepared to sacrifice many other things like professional satisfaction for money. The money motivation wave, which is now at its peak, had just started gaining momentum at a slow pace when you became ready for embarking upon a career. Its speed suddenly shot up with the coming of the IT revolution in the early 1990s.

Play it cool. Let your next generation youngsters be what they want to be. Help them and give them protection if they need it. That's all. In all other respects, leave them to cope with their life on their own. You have done enough for them to give them a good academic and value base. Don't expect any feeling of indebtedness in them towards you and your spouse as their parents for what all you've done for them. You plan for your independent existence as opposed to your parents who might have had become dependent on you in their old age.

Let me share with you a very personal case study here, at this moment. The period of the case study is late 1950s and early 1960s. I had only one uncle on my father's side, elder to my father. He had a brilliant academic career—never stood second in his life up to his MA level; but he was traditional. When my cousin, his elder son cleared his CA, got a covenanted cadre post in a British firm in Calcutta and purchased his brand new Standard Herald car with his company funds for which he was entitled (car loan from banks and other agencies were not so freely available in those days as it is today), my uncle was terribly upset with him as he considered whizzing off in a brand new automobile in a middle class locality with joint family clusters in Calcutta will be some kind of a show-off of wealth—but values had already started changing even then—in the early 1960's. So, when my elder son started parking his three cars in our porch at the age of 40, four years ago from today, I never raised even a single eyebrow. I played it cool and showed grace. So also, you would have to if you are faced with similar circumstances.

Let us see how a few senior citizens known to us are coping with the family problems, related to the 'generation gap' factor causing un-happiness to them.

Ramesh Bhargava, who is 66 and is a retired CBI officer and his wife Chandra, had to face a lot of unhappiness when their daughter Ruma got married to Umesh Srivastava who had estranged relationship with his own parents. Umesh was the son of his mother's second husband. She had an elder son by her first husband who had deserted her. Umesh, 36, was an active member of a prominent political party and had some miscellaneous business income apart from what all he was getting for his party work. When his party lost its stronghold in West Bengal, he started some trading business which developed well within a year. Unfortu-nately, he has a most whimsical temperament and has no intention of settling down. He strongly feels that his wife Ruma lacks confidence and always tells her to have an independent income and livelihood. Both of them like travelling and often go out on long tours on their motor cycle. Ruma worked for a call centre for about a year and then both of them went to Sikkim to get into hoteliering. They took a small facility on lease and did good business in season—so much so that they took two more hotels on similar terms. But, now after a year, Umesh has lost interest in the hotel and tourism business. He is applying for his passport and wants to go abroad all alone as a tourist and a traveller. His idea is to earn by doing errands to raise his travel and touring costs. He does not want to take Ruma along and would like her to follow the same lifestyle independently. Nor is he keen to take a divorce. Ruma's parents Ramesh and Chandra have lost their happiness and are at a total loss as to what to do.

Madan Gopal Verma, the 72-year old retired Managing Director of a MNC and his wife Julie are most unhappy that their paediatrician daughter Shree has a live-in relationship with a Telugu IT engineer Ramana Rao in Canada and they have no plans at all of formalising it into a social marriage. Although Madan Gopal was heading an American MNC in India, he comes from a traditional UP family and has not been able to reconcile with the situation. He and his wife have given up all social activities and, being closeted at home most of the time, have started suffering from depression.

Tarun Talukdar is 64 today and performs as a folk artiste—actor-singer-dancer. On his retirement from the Information and Cultural Dept. of West Bengal Govt. at the age of 58 years, he parted the company of his wife Srimati. Srimati continued to live in the family flat until she retired from her job as the principal of a primary school 2 years ago. Tarun decided not to have any permanent address; he started moving from one place to another inside the State giving performances and doing short-term teaching assignments in rural schools and clubs. After her retirement, Srimati locked up the family flat as she was very lonely and came to live with her only child—daughter Purba who was married to a small entrepreneur. Tarun is a very happy person now being independent and having been absolved himself of all family responsibilities. Srimati, most depressed and unhappy, has been suffering from acute arthritis and also has to undergo treatment for kidney stones from time to time.

Jaipaul Jain is the retired vice-president of an Indian business house. He and his wife Aruna have three daughters, all married, and followed by a son Sundar who did his MBA (HR) from a Delhi-based institute. After a lot of searching, they got Sundar married to Lipi who has been trained in fashion design from a top institute and runs her own boutique. After one year, the marriage is breaking apart as Lipi is more interested in her boutique business rather than setting up a home and settling down in a family. She has already moved back to her parents' place. Jaipaul and Aruna both are so heart-broken that they have become hypochon-driacs—and always hungry for others' attention and sympathy. And, Sundar has taken to smoking, drinking and binge eating.

Ram Narayan and Shakuntala Subramanian are traditional South Indians. Both used to work in different public sector banks and in different capacities. Ram Narayan retired in 2002 and Shakuntala in 2005. Although they had an early marriage, their first child did not survive. Shakuntala conceived again but had to go for an early abortion. After a long gap, she delivered a girl child Puja who finished her post-graduation in history and got married only last year to Ravi Shankar. The marriage had been an arranged one and it turned out to be an excellent match. Ravi

Shankar was a physiotherapist practicing in Chennai. However, their monsoon honeymoon at Vishakhapatnam had a most unhappy and unfortunate ending. Ravi Shankar who did not know how to swim was swept away by the devastating waves of the Bay of Bengal on a highly stormy day. What would be the fate and future of the young widow— Ram Narayan and Shakuntala have no answer to this question. Puja has already gone under the care of a leading psychiatrist and she is also taking psychotherapy sessions every week.

Are the people that we have talked about *greying gracefully*? Perhaps not. In order to *grey gracefully*, they have to take a 360-degree turn. First of all, they have to learn to stay cool. Only then they will get the support of their brain to think about alternative solutions with their pros and cons.

Factor Four: The Ego-attachment Propensity

Sonu Kapoor retired from an international assignment with a fabulous superannuation package. He had also spent big fortunes, as a part of his pre-retirement plan over a period of last five to six years, to acquire and set up a spacious apartment in a fringe area of New Delhi and renovate his ancestral home in a most congested central area of old Mumbai.

What satisfaction have these acquisitions given him? Only the satis-faction of his ego—his feeling of power and prestige—that he is one up on his relatives, friends and acquaintances in terms of wealth and status.

However, since his ego is attached to his material assets, it'll be difficult for him to be happy. A little problem here and there would make him frustrated and he will feel out of control. Pangs of stress have already started having their adverse impact. Since he and his wife are dividing their stay between New Delhi and Mumbai, whenever they are away from Mumbai, slum- and street-dwellers and vagrants escape the notice of the drowsy security guards, break into their property, indulge in burgling and take away and sell even parts of doors, windows, antiques and furniture and brass and stainless steel fittings and fixtures. The same problem has not started occurring in Delhi as their daughter and son-in-law are temporary occupants of a part of the big apartment there prior to their moving out to Singapore on a two-year contract assignment. Their only son is settled in New York and has no chance of returning to India for good as he has an almost permanent live-in relationship with a Chilean girl.

The retired couple is confused as to who will take care of their house properties once they are no longer in this world. All this agony is taking place as they have not been able to practice ego-detachment which is impossible for any normal human being even at an advanced age after all our worldly desires have been almost met and materialistic expectations have been fulfilled to the brim as our ego is located in our selfish genes.

It is impossible for any individual to *grey gracefully* and enjoy *old age happiness* with a strong ego-attachment deep-rooted in the mind. You have to transcend the sense of ownership and adopt a custodian role as I have been trying my best ever since the sixth decade of my life. I'll tell you how. Please forgive me for bringing the 'I' factor particularly here; it could not be helped as it is my own case study.

There are frequent footfalls in the house that I own. I have inherited it from my father. Whenever I'm not on tour and available at Kolkata, people visit our *Happiness, Planned Success* and *Winning Child* clinics. They come from far away places, sometimes from other States too—all by prior appointment. Almost all of them would invariably have a good look, with admiration, at the well-ventilated high ceiling spacious rooms all of which get enough natural light. The other day, a young mining engineer manager of Coal India Ltd. Pawan Barua, who is from Assam and was visiting me, commented in appreciation: "It's a fantastic house, Sir. Is it your own?" I responded with a smile: "Well! I can't take any credit for this building. My father constructed it during the period 1940–42 after I was born in 1940 in our ancestral home just across the road from here.

After he, the owner, passed away, the property has come to me. I consider myself only as the custodian and take good care of it without any ego-attachment just with the same spirit as I take care of my personal resources—my body and the brain, which are also gifts from my parents. With these two absolutely personal things also, I have been trying to practice ego-detachment and self-control so that I do not become the victim of and indulge in any excesses. Even, a few years ago, I used to be controlled by my body's desires like love for good food, addiction to tea, coffee and nicotine and so on."

Pawan Barua was so culture-shocked that he could not utter a single word in response. Nevertheless, from the non-verbal mode of his communication, I could see that the level of his admiration for me had risen suddenly. He left that day but on the next day I got an e-mail from him, which read as: "Sir, yesterday while talking to you, I got answers to the questions which had been itching me for the last few months: what is happiness and how to be happy. I'm indeed grateful to you, Sir."

The Retired Morning Walkers: Are They Ego-attached

Whenever I'm in town, I go for an early morning walk in my local park, which still has a British name (for some unknown reason its name has not been Indianised by the Kolkata Municipal Corporation). And, I see the same set of people sitting on a couple of fixed wooden benches and also on portable plastic chairs and stools borrowed from the park's club tent, sipping tea and munching crispy semolina biscuits from the adjacent roadside tea stall. You'll find such pools of old people everywhere—in every park, at every lakeside, on every seashore or every bank of a river, in every part of the world, even in developed villages. These are usually mixed groups with members from different socio-economic strata in a free-wheeling, idle chatting mood. They are generally not in a hurry for anything.

When senior citizens look for company to get over their loneliness, they normally do not choose birds of the same feather—people sharing the same status. They welcome contemporaries from all levels and strata.

In the group that I meet every time, there is a retired inspector general of police, a retired public sector company general manager, a retired doctor of the Indian Army who rose to the position of major general, a retired clerk of the govt. secretariat, a retired stores assistant of a private company and the owner of a local stationers' shop. There are one or two infrequent drop-ins—seasonal birds, who are NRIs, settled in the West, after having held some small and medium level posts abroad. These guests normally coincide their visits with the onset of the most pleasant Kolkata winter.

I've never joined them in conversation beyond just exchanging pleasantries. So I have no idea if they have been able to sublimate their egos coloured by their hidden agendas which had been formed due to the way they transacted with others and the behavioural styles that they followed when they had full involvement in their pre-retirement work roles.

There is also a difference between them economically which may tend to influence their egos even today, post-retirement. Some of them had substantial amount of money by way of superannuation benefits when they retired, apart from the savings and investments that they had made and the assets that they had created; while some others who retired from small jobs and insignificant positions have to queue up every month in their local post offices to draw the interest from their post office deposits and have to depend upon their working brothers, sisters or children.

If you want to have a regular friends' circle for socialising as a remedy for your loneliness in old age, you'll not be complex- and stress-free unless you practice ego-detachment.

Factor Five: Gap in Biorhythms

This is another most interesting but extremely subtle factor that causes unhappiness during the post-retirement stage of one's life and tends to get aggravated with advancement of one's age.

A continually fluctuating tide of chemicals courses through our bodies. The amounts in our bloodstream vary from hour to hour; day to day; and as we age, vary over the years. In a healthy body, they vary in a well regulated manner—in a strictly determined sequence, producing recurring cycles of what they are described as—*biorhythms.*

These chemicals may be hormones (chemical messengers), neurotransmitters (brain chemicals) or even normal nutrients present in the blood which we have collected from our dietary or other inputs. If these substances undergo ebbs and tides in strict rotation, they produce regular cycles of physical and psycho-social behaviour, by which we time our daily activities. Minute differences in the quantities and periodicities of these chemical substances can have dramatic effects on all kinds of behaviour—less in some and more in others depending on the circumstances.

Apart from chemical biorhythms, there are electrical biorhythms which have grown over the years to become essential tools and procedures for clinical investigation and diagnosis, such as electrocardiography, electroencephalography, and electromyography.

There are also physical biorhythms such as 'hunger/need for consumption of food—consumption/satiation of hunger', 'thirst for water or a drink—satiation of thirst on consumption of water or a drink', 'activity—rest' and 'wakefulness—sleep' and so on which together constitute the *lifestyle   biorhythms.*

Then there is another subtler aspect of biorhythms like each one of us possesses some *mirror neurons* which make us mimic others unconsciously to produce the same body rhythms so that there is a mental rapport. We can also use the same approach consciously to create a harmony in the relationship with others. *Neuro-Linguistic Programming (or NLP)* according to which our verbal messages—the words that we use to express ourselves and the way we use them, can be programmed according to the neuro-linguistic propensities of the individual with whom we are communicating at a particular instant.

In a group of people, staying together—all the time like in a hostel or in the defence forces while on duty, or a good part of the day like in a school, an office or a plant or a project, biorhythms—particularly those related to lifestyle, have a tendency to become synchronised. People following the same daily, weekly, or monthly routines gradually edge their biorhythms towards a common cycle where all follow some activities like having a break or having tea or meals together.

What I want to highlight here is that in the same family, if different members have different lifestyle biorhythms for activities such as waking up in the morning and going to bed at night, meal timings and so on—particularly the elderly husband and wife, then it leads to lack of harmony; the flow of happiness is disturbed. It becomes disturbing indeed for the retiree husband who had been habituated to a set of fixed biorhythms as long as he had had a working career. Therefore, to minimise the retiree's unhappiness causing him stress, the wife must extend her understanding and cooperation and ensure what lifestyle biorhythms would suit him best. The younger family members also must try to adjust with each other and also with the elders as much as possible. Maximum number of them must thus try to have the same lifestyle biorhythms.

Factor Six: Gap in Expectations

The retiree might have had some dreams about his retired life and but had not shared them with his spouse. For example, he would have dreamt of devoting his time to singing or playing a musical instrument or writing or painting or gardening—some activity which was very dear to his heart but he could not indulge in it as long as he had an active work role.

However, if he was not the type of person to devote his time in some *Self-Engagement* or *SE* type of activity where he alone was involved in some intellectual or creative work, he would have dreamt of spending a jolly good time with his peers, his same age group friends—some of whom were self-employed, a few others were small businessmen and traders whereas quite a good number were also retirees. This would be *People and Social Engagement (PSE)* type of activity. Or, he might have dreamt of going on travels and tours from time to time; otherwise, when he was not on long distance trips he would have loved to go for long walks in nearby areas (*Physical Engagement* or *PE*).

On the day next to his retirement, he woke up expecting that his long cherished dream will come true. But his spouse's vision of her partner's retired life was quite different. She had been expecting that he, after his retirement, will take care, during the first few months of his retired life, of all the household needs which had not been seriously attended to when he had not retired—household needs like first getting the pest control done, thereafter getting the repairs done to the electrical wiring, furniture, fittings and the old house. She had also expected that her husband will go to the local market every day for the fresh daily provisions and, occasionally, to the nearest main market for the fortnightly and monthly provisions. She had also her dreams suppressed and did not share them with the husband.

So when on the very first day after his retirement, in early morning she expressed her desire that he should go to the local market, he was furious. And, then the conflict started due to a gap in the expectations of the husband and the wife.

Factor Seven: Dominance of 'Greed'

Many of us are not guided only by what we 'need'; we tend to go for extras and thus we are governed by 'greed'.

Let us take for example the case of our daily calorie intake. When our energy expenditure requirement demanded by the activities in which we engage is not more than 2,000 Calories (that is, kilocalories), we consume 2,500—500 Calories extra simply out of greed. This propensity, what we are describing as 'greed', is genetic as there is a strong innate urge of building up a reserve for our rainy days when we may not get food due to some natural inclemency like drought, flood, earthquake or cyclone. It used to be a threat for our ancestors, the pre-historic men a few million years ago and, in course of evolution, the human species developed some special genes to help building up an energy reserve from our intake whenever we got some food to eat and some drinks and beverages to drink.

Extra energy from food, drinks and beverages means it will take the form of *sugar* (*glucose*) and *fat*—two primary sources of chemical energy in any living system, to be collected whenever those inputs were available and stored. While sugar takes care of the day-to-day and short-term needs, fat which is deposited in the body has the potential to take care of the future and long-term needs.

This *acquisition instinct* which applies to the collection and storage of biochemical energy is also relevant in the context of material acquisition and asset creation which includes 'money'.

We go for earning extra money than what minimum we need for our subsistence. When it is only for subsistence, we can describe it as just for a 'convenient living'. When we go for the extra income, the level beyond just 'convenient living' is 'comfortable living' and a further higher grade is 'luxurious living'. The higher we move from mere 'convenient living' our 'comfort zone' and 'tolerance zone' both become narrower and more restricted and our proneness to *stress* increases if there is any deviation from the comfort standards taking place more than two or three times.

The extra money is also needed for our future economic security—the rainy days, just like the build-up of fat reserve in the body. All super-annuation and retirement benefit schemes and long-term saving and investment schemes are based on this principle only. There also, it could be the bare minimum for 'convenient living' and a lot of wealth for 'comfortable' and, thereafter, a 'luxurious living'.

When we save and invest the extra money for our future, we also consider the 'Return on the Investment (ROI)' factor—at what rate the money saved and investment made will multiply over a specific period. So from this ROI point of view, there are various channels of investment, such as in: land and buildings which are 'fixed assets'—the values of which generally appreciate with time. The value of gold, silver, some other precious metals and commodities generally also appreciate with time. 'Movable assets' like machineries, gadgets, tools and accessories—the value of these generally depreciate with time depending on wear and tear that those items face with use. Their resale value will also depend on the demand-and-supply position. We also invest in secure schemes like bank and post office deposit and savings accounts and government bonds and certificates. There are also company deposits and non-banking financial companies' schemes where we do invest and these are generally more secure than investment in company shares unless you belong to share trading profession where it is your livelihood when you know the activities in and out and can minimise your chances of a low ROI or even loss.

In comparison to material and financial assets, by acquiring knowledge and experience and developing proficiency in skills and habits, you also build up intangible human capital assets which when practically applied will lead to reasonably good—even high ROI. Let us quote the words of

Professor Anil Gupta of IIM, Ahmedabad who says: "The Indian dream to become a knowledge society depends upon India's ability to make knowledge assets more valuable and precious than physical assets. The lack of possessing physical or financial assets would then determine to a much lesser extent the destiny of an individual or group than the possession of ideas, innovations, and other knowledge assets. We must sow the seeds of imagination and innovation early in life." (8) [(8) Anil Gupta's comments have been cited in: Gandhi Maneka, "Wisdom of the ancients," 8th Day, a supplement of *The Statesman, Kolkata,* 9 January 2011, p. 4.]

For the post-retirement phase of life and old age happiness, you should give up your *greed* and ought to be generally guided by your *needs.* Otherwise, if you're controlled by your greed, there are chances of your becoming unhappy time and again whenever you have a low level of ROI or incur a loss. And, as regards build-up of fat as a long-term saviour in modern times (it was a good strategy indeed in pre-historic days) is concerned, it becomes a liability unless you burn the extra fat regularly and may lead to diseases affecting your digestive system, endocrine system, cardio-respiratory system—even your nervous system. We have talked about effective *Energy Management* in the next chapter.

APPLICATION TIPS

- Have you gone through the 'Seven Critical Unhappiness Factors (SCUF)'? Go through (don't rush—take it easy) and try to digest each of them well.

- Which of the SCUF seem to affect you most?

- Plan out and implement strategies for getting read of those UF that would tend to act as barriers to your *greying gracefully* and *old age happiness.* Check the progress of your remedial actions periodically and, if necessary, get in touch with us.

Chapter 2

Practical Intelligence (PI):
Your Happiness Tool

"There's a little story about Henry Ford.......As you know, Ford was a multi-millionaire at a time when a million dollar was still a lot of money. Someone once asked him what he would do if he lost everything. Without a pause, he replied, 'I'd have it all back in less than five years.' How could he do that? He could do it, because he knew that his real wealth was what he had in between his ears: the intangible, the invisible, the knowledge he had about what money is really all about."

—Robert T. Kiyosaki,
In: *If you want to be rich & happy, don't go to school,*
Fairfield, Connecticut: Asian Publishing, 1993, p. 79

Do you remember *PI*? We had talked about *Practical Intelligence (PI)* in the 'Introduction' part of this book. You'll now see how it can become a handy happiness tool for you.

A SIMPLE REVERSAL STEP FOR BECOMING HAPPY AS YOU ADVANCE IN AGE

As you advance in age, your ROI expectations in family, social and work roles generally increase, as it is observed. So, just like we'll get into a practical discussion on *reversal of the biological aging* process shortly, we'll talk about another simple reversal step here. One main step for raising your HQ would be to give up your ROI expectations (even the simple *trading* mentality) for you to *grey gracefully* and have a long happy life irrespective of whether you retire from active working or not. A mention of this strategy has already been made in Chapter 1.

Let the beginning be made by you from your *Physical Energy Management (PEM)*. Your *PEM* involves your daily 'Energy Input' in terms of food, beverages, drinks and other such consumables and daily 'Energy Output' by way of energy expenditure (your basal metabolism to make your life's clock ticking plus activities for living and working). You should practice *calorie restriction* so that there is no energy surplus in your body. Your body should not feel indebted to you for the extra energy that you give it for getting deposited inside and increasing its net worth so that you don't suffer when energy is in short supply or not available at all. Nor should there be any deficit so that you feel indebted to your body and have the guilt feeling of a debtor.

Another kind of Physical Energy Management (PEM) or rather Physical Energy Acquisition (PEA), at a subtle level, starts with the *control drama* between the parent and the child when the parent tries to practice his command-control- coerce style of handling the little child and steals or kills the child's energy. This is the parent's selfish gene's one of the natural propensities: *desire to win* to gain power—repeat the pleasure of controlling others, and avoid the pain of being controlled by others. (1) [(1) Ganguli, Siddhartha, *Conscious Management: Managing and Leading Happily at the Workplace and at Home*, New Delhi: Allied Publishers, 2011].

The Brain-Body/Mind-Body/Psychosomatic Interface: Inside you and me and everyone else, there are two distinctly different personalities: the brain or the mind and the body—the *psyche* and the *soma* from which the adjective 'psychosomatic' is derived. These two personalities are placed in the 'internal supplier' and 'internal customer' relationship: what the body's requirements (essentially need-based for survival, growth and stability) and expectations (beyond the need-based ones, something based on the individual's likes and dislikes in terms of quantity, quality, taste, time and so on) are, must be met by the brain's supply system. Both the personalities are, nevertheless, guided totally by circuits controlled by living chips in the form of *genes*.

If the individual has a team of dominant emotionally hypersensitive overprotective benevolent genes which feels insecure and anxiety-prone

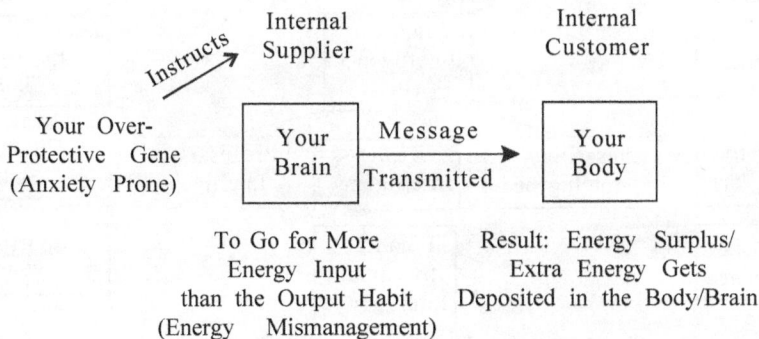

Fig. 1: Energy Mismanagement (Indebtedness of Your Body to the Brain)

about the future uncertainties regarding availability of suitable energy inputs, it sends a message to his brain (the *psyche*) to supply more energy input than the output demands or slows down the energy expenditure process by making the person lazy and less active (through automatic adjustment of the concerned neurotransmitter levels—mainly *serotonin* and *acetylcholine* so that there is energy surplus—a positive energy balance which gets deposited at certain specific sites as savings or reserve for the future. (See Fig. 1)

So, the brain goes beyond the 'need' and stimulates the 'greed'. This is a replica of the economic behaviour of man when he sets as his goal: maximisation of income and minimisation of expenditure so that

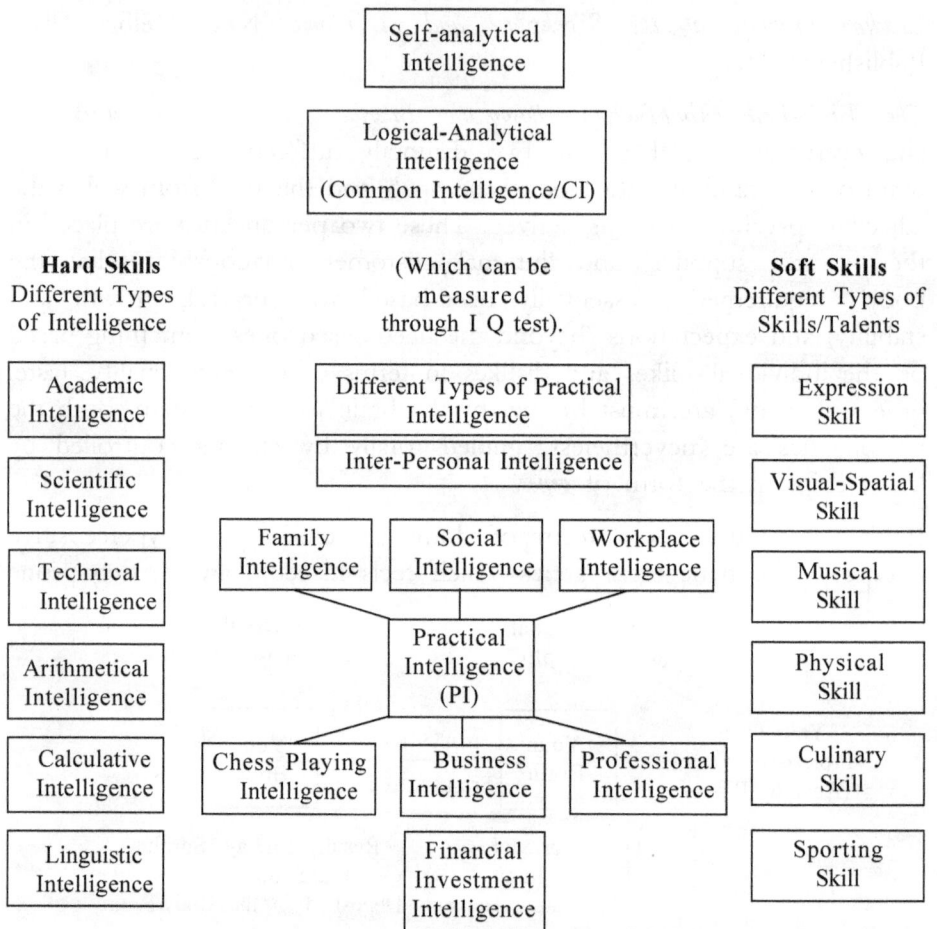

	Self-analytical Intelligence	

	Logical-Analytical Intelligence (Common Intelligence/CI)	

Hard Skills Different Types of Intelligence	(Which can be measured through I Q test).	**Soft Skills** Different Types of Skills/Talents
Academic Intelligence	Different Types of Practical Intelligence	Expression Skill
Scientific Intelligence	Inter-Personal Intelligence	Visual-Spatial Skill
Technical Intelligence	Family Intelligence / Social Intelligence / Workplace Intelligence	Musical Skill
Arithmetical Intelligence	Practical Intelligence (PI)	Physical Skill
Calculative Intelligence	Chess Playing Intelligence / Business Intelligence / Professional Intelligence	Culinary Skill
Linguistic Intelligence	Financial Investment Intelligence	Sporting Skill

Fig. 2: Different Types of Intelligence (Practical Intelligence or 'PI' in the Centre)

maximum surplus is generated. As regards PEM, it represents a neuro-economic behaviour. The body or *soma's* attitude may be either of the two following: It may develop indebtedness to the brain being the owner of extra energy reserve without having asked or asking for it; or, it may resist and not implement it if it is guided by some *practical intelligence (PI)* or consciousness. (See Fig. 2)

On the other hand, if there is a strong set of practically intelligent protective and preventive genes in the individual's biological repertoire then that will instruct the brain to practice *energy management* (see Fig. 3) by adopting either of the following alternative strategies:

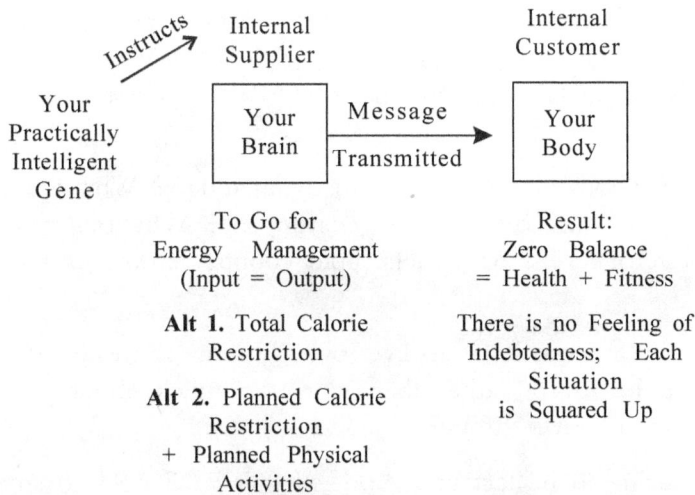

Instructs → Internal Supplier   Internal Customer

Your Practically Intelligent Gene   Your Brain | Message Transmitted →   Your Body

To Go for Energy Management (Input = Output)   Result: Zero Balance = Health + Fitness

Alt 1. Total Calorie Restriction

Alt 2. Planned Calorie Restriction + Planned Physical Activities

There is no Feeling of Indebtedness; Each Situation is Squared Up

Fig. 3: Energy Management (No Feeling of Indebtedness)

Alternative I—Go for Total (Full) Calorie Restriction: Energy input must balance the current energy output requirements.

Alternative II—Go for Planned (Partial) Calorie Restriction: Energy input partially reduced, energy output proportionately increased by incorporating planned physical fitness activities in the daily time schedule.

In either of the cases, the body does not suffer from the guilt of indebtedness to the brain and the brain also does not look down upon the body as a debtor. In fact, once it has had one need-based input, it gives a feedback to the brain that: "My stomach is three-quarter full and I'm going to stop taking any more input now. The game is over. I'm totally under control." The practically intelligent gene, which is responsible for such a balanced attitude, believes in prevention rather than cure and in need-based, self-controlled behaviour–free from any excess in anything.

As a matter of fact, there is no scope for so much roundabout discussion. The matter is most simple. It is the brain's primary duty to have a life-style so that all the potential powers of the body and the brain are properly maintained and positively and productively utilised as it used to be the case with our forest- and cave-dwelling hunter-gatherer ancestors. That would be what we may describe as real *human resource management (HRM)* at the 'personal' level.

You know of Dr Brian Weiss, don't you? The psychiatrist who, while having a few hypnotic psychotherapy sessions with a young lady suffering from some psychosomatic problem, had a chance discovery of a non-invasive treatment technique which he termed as *past life therapy?* He has done extensive studies on psychosomatic cases and has almost established the genuineness of the principle of *reincarnation.* Our HRM approach is not at tandem with that of Dr. Brian Weiss's thoughts when he says:

"Why is everybody so obsessed with living longer? Why squeeze a few more unhappy years out of the geriatric end? Why the preoccupation with cholesterol levels, bran diets, lipid counts, aerobic exercise, and so on?

Doesn't it make more sense to live joyously now, to make every day full, to love and be loved, rather than worry so much about your physical health in an unknown future?

I am not saying to neglect your body, that it is all right to smoke or to drink excessively or to abuse substances or to be grossly obese. These conditions cause pain, grief, and disability. Just don't worry so much about the future. Find your bliss today.

The irony is that, given this attitude and living happily in the present, you probably will live longer anyway." (2) [(2) Weiss, Brian, *Only Love Is Real: A Story of Soulmates Reunited*, New York: Warner Books, 2000, p. 57.]

Therefore, let us not get over-preoccupied and obsessed with the objective of increasing our longevity. Let us play it calm and cool, give up our ROI expectations, practice sharing and giving rather than making people feel indebted, modestly avoiding to get into any indebtedness in anything; but make it a point to implement real *Human Resource Management (HRM)* in your lifestyle as we will be discussing in detail.

APPLICATION TIPS

- For greying gracefully and happily, you'll have to start using your *Practical Intelligence (PI)* consciously if you have not been using it so far.

- The first step for you would be to give up your 'Return on Investment (ROI)' expectations on every physical or mental investment that you make from now on.

- It should start by adopting the 'Energy Management' strategy where you restrict your daily energy intake to 1,500 to 1,800 Calories to strike a balance with your energy output demands after retirement or stick to your present 2,000 Calories intake and burn 200 to 500 Calories by performing planned physical fitness activities which should include some household physical work and aerobic activities like brisk walking in the morning and evening and freehand stretching-bending exercises.

- This action on your part would not allow your body to suffer from indebtedness to your brain which would happen with 'Energy Mismanagement' where your input is much more than your output of energy and you generate an energy surplus which gets deposited in your body and some of the surplus energy particles may move through your bloodstream affecting your health and fitness.

Chapter 3

Start with Your Resourcefulness Audit

"What we are today comes from our thoughts of yesterday, and our present thoughts build our life of tomorrow: our life is the creation of our mind."
—The Dhammapada, the Buddhist sacred text

RESOURCE AND RESOURCEFULNESS

A brand new car or a computer is fresh and powerful. It is a pack of energy and has the potential to operate at maximum efficiency. Nevertheless, as it gets on age and is being used more and more, its powers, energy and speed—all slow down and its resourcefulness diminishes due to wear and tear.

In economic terms also, any equipment's money value *depreciates*. Its resale price would be much less than what you had paid for at the time of purchase of the original equipment unlike it happens in the case of a land, a building or a factory shed. If any of these fixed assets is at a prime location, the value *appreciates* very fast at a high rate. Even for other than prime locations, the value of such properties would go up but slower and at a lower rate.

Anything which has a value—economic or even otherwise in terms of its utility, is considered a *resource* and its value can be described by the term *resourcefulness.*

HUMAN RESOURCE (HR): ITS RESOURCEFULNESS

A human being is a natural resource unlike the car, the computer, the building or the factory shed that we have talked about. These are all man-made resources.

Any member of the human species would be described as a *human resource (HR)* because of his resourcefulness in terms of his body and brain powers. However, unlike a brand new car or computer, a newborn human child becomes ready for efficient operational performance and has maximum resourcefulness only when it attains youth and maturity at around 25 years. Up to that stage of its life, it is like a piece of equipment under development and construction.

From 25 to 35 years is the decade of one's life when the individual is geared for peak performance—physically and intellectually. 35 to 45 years is the middle age period. Our way of looking at old age is in terms of three phases: young old (45 to 55 years), middle old or mid-old (55 plus to 70 years) and old old (70 years and beyond).

Today, man produces what he consumes unlike his forest and cave-dwelling ancestors who used to live on natural products like objects of prey and wild fruits, berries, roots and tubers. The processes of evolution and natural selection had endowed the primitive man with certain remarkable powers of the body and brain for working, for living on natural products and for saving himself and his folks from any danger including sudden attack by ferocious creatures.

TODAY'S HUMAN PERFORMER: HAPPY OR UNHAPPY

As we said, today man produces what he consumes and in order to produce he has to *perform*. So every individual is a *performer* in that sense. 'Performance' in any modern business and industry means performing: with material inputs, some of which are hazardous; with machines including computers and its associated accessories many of which are not designed keeping the human user in view; using methods which are alien to the human brain; utilising money the presence and touch, even the very thought of which makes many of us greedy; and, finally, men, many of whom are negative in attitude and cannot be handled in a simple and straightforward manner to perform and deliver the desired results. Such circumstances may cause *stress* in many of us leading to *unhappiness*.

Potential Assets (PAs) and Non-Performing Assets (NPAs): A newborn child is a package of *Potential Assets (PAs)* in terms of dormant body and brain powers, for performance of different types of activities—physical as well as mental. These are the gifts of millions of years of evolution, based on the practices and habits of our primitive ancestors. These powers are waiting to blossom as the child grows. (See Fig. 4)

Thrust on Material Assets Creation: As the child grows up, there is a natural genetic urge in him (we are using the male gender for brevity's sake only—we have no gender bias) to use and utilise those PAs, but he does not have to (his modern lifestyle is such); moreover, his physical as well as family and social environments do not allow him to use those. So those PAs become *Non-Performing Assets (NPAs)*. From the family and social circles, the main thrust laid on the growing child is for preparation for entry into a secure and satisfying economic career for material assets

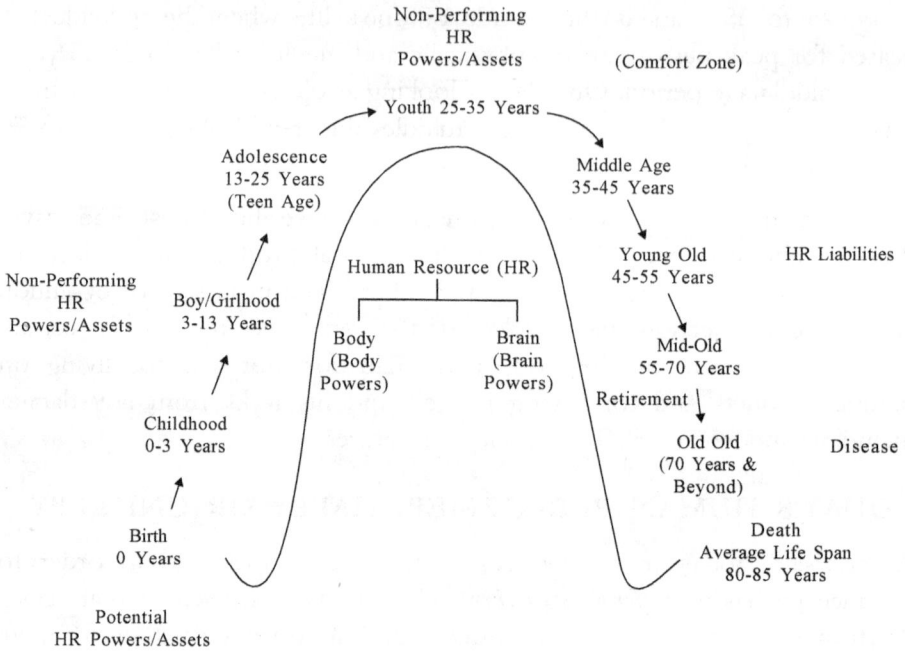

Fig. 4: Biological Life Cycle (Birth to Death) (Today's youth aspire to get more and more into 'comfort zones' both for living and working and the 'comfort zone' gets more and more restricted/limited as people grow in age restricting the use of their natural powers)

creation rather than on proper utilisation of the *PAs* for healthy and fit biological assets creation.

From Non-Performing Assets (NPAs) to Liabilities (Ls): Biologically, the 'youth' phase of one's life is from 25 to 35 years on an average. The child who has now become a young man or lady takes up an economic career with those *NPAs.* As the young person crosses the youth phase of life, the conditions of those *NPAs* begin to deteriorate further. Beyond 35, the *NPAs* start getting affected further due to non-performance as all living body and brain cells follow the inevitable 'use it or lose it' principle of biology and with the aging process setting in with full vigour, many of those *NPAs* may turn into *Liabilities (Ls)* and, eventually, the individual may develop some disease or even more than one or multiple diseases.

Gap between Capabilities and Realities: On top of this, as we have already said, the 5-m's, 1-i and 1-t (materials, machines, methods, money, men, information and time) that he has to deal with in his household as well as at the workplace, are not necessarily tailored to the powers available to him as the latter had developed through millions and millions years of evolution when he had faced situations and circumstances of totally different kinds. There is a gap between his capabilities (what he is capable of doing and handling) and the realities (what all he faces in real life).

Outcome: Unhappiness: The natural outcome, therefore, is 'unhappiness' leading to frustration giving rise to anger or fear. So we find in people engaged in economic pursuits like employment and entrepreneurship, umpteen signs and symptoms of *stress* and unhappiness in the form of: socially acceptable addictions, work avoidance; citing silly excuses for low performance or non-performance (including putting the blame on others in an unjustified manner); absenteeism; non-cooperation; inter-personal/inter-departmental conflicts; seeking a change, transfer, voluntary retirement; and, in extreme cases, resignation from the organisation or occupation to get freedom from the environment that has been causing unhappiness to him.

HUMAN LIFE: DAY BEFORE YESTERDAY, YESTERDAY AND TODAY

Day before yesterday, meaning in 'pre-historic' times, our primitive ancestors, the cave-dwelling bush men, never retired; on the contrary they died at a young age. 42 to 45 years was their average lifespan. This, of course, is nothing but a wild guess as they did not know how to count and calculate; nor did they have any method or tool for record-keeping

The wide variety of diseases that dominate the healthcare scenario today were also not known to them as they suffered and died from insect bites, water–borne diseases, food poisoning, strange high fevers, and wounds resulting from animal attacks which developed into dangerous gangrenes.

Yesterday, meaning in 'ancient' times, when the kings and lords ruled the lands, our old-fashioned ancestors also never retired but they became old like the pre-historic people but may be their lifespan was a little longer than their predecessors'.

In metros, towns and well-developed villages, modern man's lifespan has increased to 75 to 80 or even, in some cases, 85 years. The reasons are many, including the following:

• families have become smaller so there are not many mouths to feed in each family unit—each member in every family is thus getting adequate diet of nutritive value;

- lifestyle of a typical middleclass household has also become reasonably comfortable;
- those who can afford have access to the basic healthcare and medical facilities;
- the earning members of the family need not work until the last day of their life; they have the option to retire from their working career.

Retirement becomes justified mainly because of two reasons: firstly, the earning member's need to earn has ceased to exist as his next generation members have started earning; secondly, the children have taken up their own careers, got married and settled elsewhere so the requirement of funds every month has reduced only to sustain the elderly couple.

As the veteran cardiologist Dr Tarun Praharaj who, at the time of writing, heads the B M Birla Heart Research Centre (cardiac catheterization laboratory), Kolkata, said: "Nobody is so old that they would not like to live for a few more years". (1) [(1) Mukherjee, Writankar, "Hearty news for elderly patients", *The Economic Times, Kolkata*, 20 June 2008, p.24].

Organisations operating in the organised sector all have schemes for retirement. Normal retirement age is 58 (in some cases 60 and in academic assignments 65 and, in a few special cases, even 70) years. Many organisations have gone for Voluntary Retirement Schemes (VRS) a few years ago in order to implement their downsizing policy which became necessary for computerisation, automation, mechanisation and such other system-dependent rather than worker intensive (both manual and knowledge) steps that they have taken.

Moreover, many high-tech organisations have started believing in and practicing lean management and lean organisation principles. We observed that during the period 1985-2005, in India, many people in their early or mid-forties had applied for VRS, got approval, and they happily retired. Some of them took up other economic assignments, some went for social work, some set up their own businesses, and some totally retired from their work roles to pursue activities that they loved passionately and enjoyed immensely but could not devote any time to as they had to earn their livelihood by engaging themselves in some other activities which they never liked from the core of their heart.

Retiring at 62 instead of 60 became law in France only recently. It has been a victory for President Nicolas Sarkozy's conservative government and a defeat for the unions that waged massive strikes and street protests to try to stop the austerity measure. French union workers and others were angry over having to work an extra two years. The French government emphasised that the entire pension system would have been jeopardised without the change because French people are living longer— an average of nearly 85 years for women and 78 for men.

DIFFERENT PEOPLE: DIFFERENT ATTITUDES TOWARDS RETIREMENT

Not all people look at retirement from the same angle. Different people have different outlooks and attitude.

There are some individuals who had never enjoyed their working life; so they desperately look forward to their retirement as that would give them respite from the drudgery of their career and make them feel relaxed. They are the *comfort-seekers*.

Then there are just the opposite of these comfort-seekers—the *compulsive retirees* who never wanted to retire and, for them, retirement would come as a compulsion.

We also have the *carry-on* types for whom post-retirement will not make any difference from their pre-retirement days.

There are also a few who have already thought of taking up some challenging activities like setting up a business enterprise or a NGO for which there was no time while they were working. They are the *challenge-seekers*.

There are still a few who have creative talents which did not find much scope for self-expression while they were engaged in a work role. They propose to pursue and devote themselves to creative pursuits once they retire. They may be described as the *creative retirees*.

However, as we will discuss now, preparedness for change is the first mental condition or attitude to develop while planning for happy retirement.

PREPAREDNESS FOR CHANGE: THE FIRST STEP FOR PLANNING FOR HAPPY RETIREMENT

When any change comes suddenly—almost unexpectedly, very few us can accept it positively, as a welcome one. Some of us try to resist it as 'resistance or reluctance to change' is an automatic reflex move arising from the limbic system located in the inner or lower portion of our brain, which we have inherited from our animal ancestors as a biological 'fight-or-flight' switch to cope with any stressful situation. 'Resistance' represents the 'fight' strategy. Some others amongst us may accept the change unwillingly as they feel there is no better way for them than accepting it. 'Unwilling acceptance' represents the 'flight' strategy.

There may be a few of us who welcome the change and accept it willingly. 'Willing acceptance' of change, if it is to get relief from a stressful situation, then it is another form of the 'flight' strategy; whereas if it is guided by a positive motive to get a different and fresh exposure, then it is the handiwork of our outer and upper brain which constitutes our 'mind' providing us with the thinking as well as feeling powers. We may describe the latter category of people as positive 'change-seekers'. This category of people is thus prepared for change.

There may be a few amongst the positive 'change-seekers' who are going to be 'change-makers'—who are going to bring about some change in their environment; may be in the family circle, or in the neighbourhood to which they belong, or in the society at large in a significant way.

The essence of this discussion is that one must be prepared for change. 'Preparedness for change' is the first step for change management and it is very much applicable in the case of planning for retirement. There are a few changes that are involved here and an aged person must be prepared for them. First is the biological change due to aging which should not be taken as unexpected. Then there is the occupational change due to retirement as from an occupational fullness the retiree is entering into a vacuum; this is going to affect his time structuring over which he will have little control initially unless he is ready with a plan in advance. And, of course, there is also a social change involved as a big chunk of his social circle—the people with him he had close daily working relationships and cohesive social bonding due to many years of working together; they fade away from the retiree's daily life. Most important of all, there is an economic change; before retirement, the individual had economic security—now he has to make sure that money flows regularly from all his channels and adds up to a figure that enables him to meet at least his expenses.

Can you analyse, while we are on this topic, what has been your general attitude towards any significant change in your life so far? Take a stock as to:

• how many times have you resisted changes and what kinds of changes were those;

- how many times have you accepted changes unwillingly and of what type were those;
- how many times have you accepted what type of changes willingly;
- have you ever sought any change on your own initiative and, if so, under what circumstances;
- have you ever served as a change-agent and brought about some change—if you have, what kind of changes were involved;
- now that you are an experienced person and approaching the twilight zone, would you be accepting any change (like getting old) gracefully?

AUDIT YOUR PERSONAL RESOURCEFULNESS

Others may feel that you are much resourceful if you are economically well-off and have acquired fixed assets. Or, people may envy you because of your wide contacts—the social resources which you have acquired over the years as you had always been interested in people. However, the most important of all these resources, particularly in your old age, are your personal resources—your body and brain powers, which make you healthy and fit—physically, emotionally and mentally. You will be in a position to enjoy your economic and social resources which you have built up, only if you are reasonably resourceful biologically—in your body and brain.

There has recently been a pooling of data from 33 studies by British scientists at the Medical Research Council of UK, according to which elderly people who could still give a firm handshake and walk at a brisk pace were likely to outlive their slower peers. They found simple measures of physical capability like shaking hands, walking, getting up from a chair and balancing on one leg were related to life span, even after accounting for age, sex and body size. (2) [(2) "Want to live longer? Get a grip!" *The Economic Times, Kolkata*, 16 September 2010, p.1]

While you prepare yourself for the ensuing changes in your life's journey (getting old, facing retirement and so on), first assess your *personal resourcefulness*, as to what extent you can still get advantage from the powers of your body and brain during your post-retirement years and in old age. You have to, like the accountants do, conduct a *personal resourcefulness audit* on yourself which people normally miss out. They take a stock of their economic and social resourcefulness and the like.

In order to carry out a *personal resourcefulness audit*, you have to use the three charts given in Annexures I, II and III.

Use the 'Height–Weight Chart' given in Annexure I, to find out your present weight corresponding to your height. For the elderly, plus or minus 10 per cent of the range of weight that is applicable to your height is allowable. If you have satisfied this criterion, then you have satisfied twenty-five per cent of the *resourcefulness* requirements for post-retirement life phase. Mind you, improving your mood to remain happy might be the link to your maintaining a balanced body weight, suggests a research study conducted at the Group Health Research Institute in Seattle. According to the lead scientist of the study Gregory Simon: "Increased physical activity leads to improvement in depression and improvement in depression leads to increased physical activity." (2) ["Want to lose weight? First, drive the blues away." *The Times of India, Kolkata,* 13 December 2010, p. 16.]

Use Annexure II, 'The 10 Powers of Your Body' for self-scoring. For the elderly, for any power factor, a score of 75 to 80 per cent is considered to be 'highly satisfactory'. If you have attained such a level of score on an average, then you have satisfied another thirty-five per cent of the *resourcefulness* requirements.

Now take Annexure III, 'The 10 Powers of Your Brain'. Again, like in the case of the ten powers of body, you have scored an average 75 to 80 per cent on the brain front too, then you have satisfied the remaining forty per cent of the *resourcefulness* requirements for old age.

You are now prepared to face the consequences of retirement most happily. However, if you fall short of the standards that we have just laid down, don't lose heart and hope. We are going to provide a roadmap for you to follow to reach the end of your life's journey with minimum hassles.

Wish you a *bon voyage*!

Read the confession of a retired person who is still reasonably resourceful:

> "I got out of bed
> on two strong legs.
> It might have been otherwise.
> I ate cereal, sweet milk,
> ripe, flawless peach.
> It might have been otherwise.

I took the dog uphill
to the birch wood
All morning I did
the work I love.

At noon I lay down
with my mate.
It might have been otherwise.

We ate dinner together
at a table with silver
candlesticks.
It might have been otherwise.

I slept in a bed
in a room with paintings on the walls,
and planned another day
just like this day.
But one day, I know,
it will be otherwise."

—**Jane Kenyon**
(*Otherwise: New and selected poems*,
St. Paul, MN: Graywolf Press, 1996.)

APPLICATION TIPS

- You are a package of resources—body and brain powers which are entirely your own but many of which have become *Non-Performing Assets (NPAs)* and may be some of them have even turned into *Liabilities (L)* due to lack of attention and utilisation or wrong use as your thrust might had been on materials assets creation like all other people. Try to develop a proper perception of yourself from this angle.

- You will also evaluate yourself as to what kind of attitude you have towards retirement; whether you belong to the group of 'comfort-seekers', 'compulsive retirees', 'carry-on types', 'challenge-seekers' or 'creative retirees'.

- You will need to ascertain the state of your preparedness for the change from active working life to retirement, if you're still working and have not retired.

- And, finally, you'll do your *'Personal Resourcefulness Audit'* (PRA) using the three charts given in Annexures I, II and III in addition to an audit of your fixed assets and social contacts.

Chapter 4

Audit Your Post-Retirement Vision

What Now?

Retired.
Off the treadmill.
Out of the rat race.
Affairs in order.
Paper read.
Bills paid.
Laundry washed and folded.
It'll only take a minute to put it away.
Enough time for everything.
Then some.
Too much of a good thing.
Too many crossword puzzles.
Too many naps.
Errands I used to do on the way from point A to point B
have become major events.
Is this what it's supposed to be like?
I retired on insufficient data.
Now I'm expected to live another 25 years.
Almost 10,000 days.
A slow death.
Travel?
Romantic involvement?
Don't think so.
Need to do something productive,
Significant,
Meaningful,
Gratifying.
Like re-invent myself.
Start all over.

—**Bob Burdett**
(From *Aging in America*, Edited by Olivia J. Smith,
New York: The H.W. Wilson Company, 2000)

DO PEOPLE PLAN FOR RETIREMENT AND OLD
AGE HAPPINESS

The Global Story: A global study (reported in *Hindustan Times, Kolkata,* 30 June 2008, p.12) has revealed that respectively over 81, 58, 46 and 31 per cent of Mexican, Australian, US and UK-based employees had not taken any steps to determine the post-retirement income need or any sort of retirement planning, especially financial planning, at the time of the study.

UK—The Most Prepared: According to the study, 71 per cent of UK workers had taken steps to determine their households' retirement needs; 69 per cent had started actual planning; and 34 per cent were concerned about outliving the funds to be obtained on retirement.

Mexico—Worries vs. Planning: Mexico featured as the worst case as regards the gap between retirement worries and actions taken to mitigate them. 74 per cent of the employees were concerned about the fact that they had no choice but to work full- or part-time to live comfortably during the retirement years; and 67 per cent were concerned about outliving their retirement money.

The Indian Scenario: Over 80 per cent of Indian employees do not plan for retirement independent of any government plans, a MetLife survey had found (reported in the news cited above). While 35 per cent employees were observed to have taken steps to determine their financial needs for sustenance after retirement, only 20 per cent had gone into some detail to chalk out a concrete plan. Unfortunately, 71 per cent Indians were concerned about outliving the funds that they were expected to get on retirement. Interestingly 33 per cent of the people surveyed expected not to retire ever.

All the above studies have highlighted the concern of the people surveyed for their post-retirement economic subsistence and security. There is only one study that we came across which came up with some interesting observations other than merely the financial or economic implications of retirement. We are providing a summary below.

Kaufman's Study—Ageless People: Kaufman (1) [(1) Kaufman, S.R., *The Ageless Self: Sources of meaning in late life,* Madison: University of Wisconsin Press, 1986; referred by Ikels, Charlotte and Cynthia M. Beall, "Age, Aging and Anthropology" in *Handbook of Aging and the Social Sciences,* edited by Robert H. Binstock and Linda K. George, New York:

Academic Press, 2001, pp. 125-140] has obtained unexpectedly interesting findings from his study on a group of San Francisco elderly citizens. His informants had refused to conform to the image of old age created by gerontologists. Instead of accepting identities as old people, a category other than "adults", they saw their later years as continuations of the lives they have been living all along. Age did affect their energy levels and their options for activities of daily living and working, but it was not an intrinsic aspect of their identity; they saw themselves as "ageless".

YOUR LIFE'S GOAL

When you were young or even when you had crossed forty and were approaching your middle age, coming almost close to the end of the first innings of your life, had you set your life's goal—where would you like to be, where would you like to see yourself at the end of your life's journey? Perhaps, in the hurry-burry of enjoying your youthful days and also with the burden of increased family responsibility of your early forties, this important task of your life's planning did not receive the priority that it deserved or had just escaped your notice.

People with a high 'Practical Intelligence Quotient (PIQ)' wouldn't do that. They would have their perception of a successful life—set not only with one but at least three alternative visions of their future based on a thorough analysis of their own 'Strengths (S)' and 'Weaknesses (W)' *vis-à-vis* the foreseeable 'Opportunities (O)' and 'Threats (T)' that they were likely to face in the ever-changing environment. (2) [(2) For details of life's goal-setting and personal success planning, consult: Ganguli, Siddhartha, *SUCCESS: Can be Planned and Earned,* New Delhi: Allied Publishers, 2010.] They would sieve out the 'constraints (insurmountable weaknesses)' from the list of 'weaknesses'—leaving out only the relevant 'deficiencies (surmountable)' to work on for remediation.

By reading all this, you shouldn't give up in despair if you had not even been contemplating on the skeleton of a plan so far. Just a year or two before you plan to retire from your employment, self-employment or business career, try to visualise what you are going to do—how you are going to spend your time, energy, body and brain powers and, of course, money meaningfully after your retirement. We'll call it your *post-retirement vision*. You may not have just a single vision; you may have more than one. It's good to have multiple, at least three or four, visions so that if one does not work you can easily switch to another.

THE POST-RETIREMENT VISION

Many elderly persons nurture a vision about the post-retirement days—not very formally though—not in a planned and systematic manner. However, the question that every elderly individual should ask himself is: "Will I be happy to retire?" Should you be at the threshold of retirement at the time of reading this book, you should also address the same question to yourself.

If someone's answer to the question is 'yes', then it possibly indicates that he is suffering from *stress* in his work role and would like to be relieved of it by retiring. If someone's answer is 'no', that would indicate that he is enjoying his work role immensely and would suffer from *stress* when he retires. Both are wrong signals.

Should You Like to Live Long: If you have a desire to live fairly long, hale and hearty, after a stressful worklife, pack up and shift yourself lock stock and barrel to Montacute, near Yeovil, Somerset, England where people in their late eighties and nineties, have been having a habit of eating an onion or two a day and plenty of fresh local vegetables grown without using any chemicals. They also never miss drinking spring water from a nearby hill.

Henry Allingham is currently the Western world's oldest man being 113 years' and 14 days' old on June 19th 2009. Allingham took over from John Evans, a Welsh former coal miner who died in 1990 aged 112 years and 295 days. In the East, a Japanese retired civil engineer, Tomoji Tanabe, wore the mantel of being the oldest surviving person on this planet. He died on 18th June 2009 in his sleep, aged 113 years and 274 days leaving behind 50 great grandchildren.

Allingham has seen three different centuries, six monarchs, two world wars and 18 world cup matches. His dynasty includes 6 grandchildren, 12 great grandchildren, 14 great-great grandchildren and 1 great-great-great grandchild. Unlike Allingham, Tanabe had never consumed alcohol or smoked cigarettes.

You must plan your life and manage your lifestyle in such a way that you should be happy in your work role, you must find your work activities enjoyable; and, you should also be happy outside your work-life; you ought to be able to live happily and strike an excellent work-life balance; and, you should not suffer badly even when you retire from your working career. (2) (3) (4) [(2) Ganguli, Siddhartha, *SUCCESS: Can be Planned and Earned, loc. cit.*; (3) Ganguli, Siddhartha, *Live Happily, Work*

Happily, New Delhi: Allied Publishers, 2009; (4) Ganguli, Siddhartha, *Conscious Management: Managing and Leading Happily at the Workplace and at Home*, New Delhi: Allied Publishers, 2011]

WILL YOU BE HAPPY TO RETIRE

Will you be happy to retire? If your answer is 'yes', then when asked 'why', the possible answers could be: (a) I have not been keeping good health; (b) Of late, I was not enjoying my work; (c) Towards the end of my career I have been a victim of gross injustice and prejudice; (d) I had an estranged relationship with my 'boss'; (e) I had a terrible time handling some of my most negative subordinates/colleagues (from own department/other departments.); (f) My spouse has been seriously ill and I have to be the care-giver as there is nobody else to play that crucial role now; (g) I'll have plenty of time to do what I always wanted to do but never could manage myself to do; (h) Any other reason. Many of these thoughts represent a kink of unhappiness and diffidence in your mind and disturb your sustained mental peace.

If your answer is 'no', then the possible answers could be: (a) I'll miss the company of people with whom I have been so close for so many years; (b) I cannot stay without any work responsibility—everything becomes vacant and meaningless; (c) My daily busy schedule will suddenly become vacant; (d) I don't enjoy being at home all the time; (e) I feel my importance to people (in the family, neighbourhood, my marketplace, my relative and friend circles) will reduce; (f) Although it may not be true in real life, I may subconsciously feel dependent on others for something or the other; (g) any other reason.

In this group also, most of the points represent an unhappy and diffident stand as far as your post-retirement days are concerned.

THE WELCOME RETIREE

If you're a confident individual, you will welcome retirement from your employment happily as you'll accept this change in your life's journey as a normal and most natural event in tune with your organisation's policy and rules. And, you will plan your retirement days in such a way that you'll still feel useful and your time will be spent in a worthwhile manner, as purposefully and meaningfully as possible. You'll behave like a wise elderly man who accepts the reality.

Those who have been able to accept their elderly disposition and retirement positively and graciously, they have been observed to live in a healthy physical and mental state a few years longer than those who have not.

HIGH PIQ PERSONS ARE HAPPIER

Detailed studies have shown that taking up regular physical fitness activities (including exercises), giving up smoking, maintaining a standard body weight, practising *pranayam* (deep breathing exercises) and other lifestyle measures can keep a retired person not only happy but also physically and mentally resourceful. One who will adopt a lifestyle incorporating all such measures, no doubt, would have an above average PIQ (practical intelligence quotient). An individual with a higher PIQ will be happier if his blood pressure is under control and the level of harmful or bad cholesterol in his blood is low. However, happiest is that retired person who thinks positively, is optimistic, and indulges in some meaningful, purposeful activities which he enjoys. Such a person when asked how he is doing would say: "I'm doing fine—just like when I was active in my career as a young person 25 to 30 years ago".

ADVANCE PLANNING FOR HAPPY RETIREMENT AND OLD AGE

It is observed as well as expected that those who do their advance planning for retirement and old age well in advance are happier than who do not plan as much.

The boundary of human life today, on an average, can be put at seventy-five years. These seventy-five years have twenty seven thousand two hundred and seventy five days. By the time you'll retire, you would be fifty-eight or sixty years of age. That would mean you'd have spent twenty-one thousand one hundred and seventy or twenty-one thousand nine hundred days already. It is quite natural that, of all those days not one would have brought you anything exactly same as another.

The same principle would apply to the days that you have left until you breathe your last. There will be bright days and dark days......white days and black days.......sunny days and rainy days. Just like you have sailed smoothly in the past through the waves of your life, riding their crests and coping with the troughs or valleys, you have to cope with the same rhythms after your retirement. You have to plan your days in such a way that the dark patches (outcome of: loneliness, depression, lack of proper time-structuring, taking up activities that you don't enjoy and so on) are kept to the minimum, having more of bright patches (outcome of: devoting your time to pursuits and activities that you can afford and enjoy) to fill your daily schedule.

One anxiety that usually haunts people going to retire and getting into old age is related to the economic issue: whether there would be a sudden drop in the monthly income after retirement or with the cessation of some regular earning from some other source. This thought makes people feel insecure. You may also not be an exception to this emotional turmoil.

However, you can get relief from such emotional *stress* by taking steps well in advance—a few months before your final date of retirement. If you calculate and find out that you need to earn some money on top of the income that is going to come from the investment of your savings every month, you should explore a few possible avenues/channels wherefrom such income may come.

Should you need to earn even after retirement and not depend on your children or brother or sister, or you want to keep yourself busy and, at the same time, have some income, you can take up a full-time or part-time job or some special consultancy assignment if you're qualified and experienced to do so. However, before you take up any employment or assignment after retirement, please find out from more than one authentic source about your target organisation from which you might have an offer for employment or some kind of an association—its financial status, its policies, its work culture and other features that may have an impact on you. Generating income through self-employment may take you some time unless you have already lined up some such assignments just before you retire.

If you have some earned or privilege leave due as you had not availed of your entitlement fully and had accumulated some days/weeks/months, try to take leave before you retire to explore all kinds of possibilities of generating income after retirement from: (i) investment of the provident fund/gratuity/leave encashment/other money that you are going to get on retirement; (ii) funds already invested by you in different channels (bank term deposits/company deposits/govt. bonds/ mutual funds/ post office term deposits/ company shares etc.) ; (iii) investment of any amount due from insurance; (iv) repayment of any loan(s) that you had given to friendly borrowers; (v) any employment/self-employment/ becoming a trader-businessman-small industry owner; (vi) your spouse's income (in case she has any source of income like employment/ investments etc); (vii) income from rent from property in your/your spouse's name; (viii) sale of property/commodities etc. and investing the income in liquid yet secure investments like bank deposits etc. (also see Chapter 18: The Old Age Financial Plan).

If you are not dominated by an economic need nor do you want to be in a work environment again, you can pursue some hobbies or mission which you could not cultivate while in active employment as it did not offer you any economic return as such. You can, if you like, take up some social work which is close to your heart.

Your body might have undergone depreciation with the aging process setting into your life. But, like land and buildings which don't depreciate; rather they appreciate in value, many of your brainpowers also have the potential for appreciation in value provided you have been taking good care of them.

Find out some such brainpower application area where you have been and still are ahead of others and, as such, others come to you for service and suggestions. Keep it as sharp as the razor's edge to sustain your motivation and interest in life, to make you feel confident in the presence of others who may be better-off compared to you in some other respects. This will give a meaningful old age existence; otherwise you'll feel useless and suffer from depression.

It is worthwhile mentioning here the case study of an elderly woman who was mentally totally down and out until she could rediscover a talent that she owned and which placed her on a much higher pedestal than all others in her environment. She suddenly remembered that she could write very well when she was young. She rediscovered her writing talent, sharpened it through regular practice for two months, which helped her to regain her confidence and made her happy even when she had retired from active life as all her children were well settled in life. She did not have to do much to run her household which made her feel useless especially when her husband was not only pursuing his career but was at its peak for quite some time.

SOCIAL IMAGE OF THE RETIRED AND THE OLD

Immediately, it comes to our mind that there are two opposite views nurtured in the society to which we belong regarding the retired and the old.

To those who are more materialistic and commercial-minded, a retired and an old person is regarded as an economically unproductive elderly. And others who are more family-oriented, although they do not look at the old and the retired from the same angle but some of them do nurture a selfish motive. For them, an aged member of the family is considered useful for taking care of the home and the kids. Some of these people may also take advantage of the situation and expect the retired, elderly male member to carry out many family chores such as going to the market and the drugstore, reaching the kids to school or to the school bus stop, going to the bank or to pay the electricity and telephone bills; and the retired, aged female member to baby-sit and mind the kids, tutor them and take care of their studies and, at times, attend to the kitchen duties, and so on. However, if the retired, old family member himself or herself offers such service, then there is, of course, no question of any exploitation.

There is also a third group whose members maintain a safe distance and do not like to antagonise the retired elders as they may be worth a handsome fortune because of their land and building properties and accumulated wealth invested in various financial schemes. Very few property owners hand over the reins of their properties—their immovable and movable assets to their heirs unless they have reached a stage when they get disabled and cannot manage anything.

Nevertheless, this scenario prevails mostly in the case of people who retired from some employment career. It is not usually so with business persons who would like to involve their younger generation (both children as well as blood relations) in their business operations by the time they reach their late teens. And, these business people hardly retire. From this angle, their nature is similar to farmers and cultivators who go on pursuing their farming occupation until they reach their ripe old age when they may not be able to carry on any longer. In the farming community, just like it happens in a traditional business community, the young farmers always prefer and desire to have more male children to stand by their side when the fathers grow old and the sons reach their adolescence.

Because of their perceived image as 'useless' and 'good-for-nothing' in the society, many technically and professionally qualified and experienced people want to remain engaged meaningfully even after retirement. Some of then seek employment, some others seek opportunities for self-employment, whereas a few others plan to set up something which will keep them occupied meaningfully and also bring some economic return.

Some of the retired yet active people start giving voluntary service through some NGOs and local clubs and libraries where the younger employees who join such organisations are mostly transient unless they are totally dedicated to social work. For retired people who want to remain occupied, getting engaged in some NGO is a wise proposition also for the organisation.

When skills are in short supply, some professionals can easily remain in work (full or part-time) for many years after the usual retirement age.

There is an interesting and useful way of utilising the knowledge, skills and talents of retirees that we have recently read about. Procter & Gamble, USA uses an approach of connecting with an altogether different pool of technology experts from an underused demographic: P & G retirees and retirees from other companies. These people worked for many years in their respective specialties and were not expected to lose their brainpowers post-retirement. P & G set up a separate company, *Your Encore.com* to utilise the expertise of retired technical specialists. Apart from the founder company P & G, many other companies have started utilising the services of *Your Encore*. (5) [(5) Lafley, A. G. and Ram Charan, *The Game-Changer*, New York: Crown Business, 2008, First edition, pp 137-138.]

In another interesting article, three ardent researchers, based on their yearlong project, have offered "recommendations for gaining the loyalty of older workers and creating a more flexible approach to retirement that allows people to continue contributing well into their sixties and seventies." They have strongly felt that "companies can no longer afford to think of retirement as a onetime event, permanently dividing work life from leisure." (6). [(6) Dychtwald, Ken, Tamara J. Erickson and Robert Morison, "It's Time to Retire Retirement", In: *Harvard Business Review on Talent Management*, Boston, Mass: Harvard Business Press, 2008.]

APPLICATION TIPS

- Have you had a plan for your retirement and old age happiness? 'Yes' or 'No'.

- If your answer is 'Yes' then is it only a post-retirement financial plan? Have you not planned for some solid chunk of time to be devoted to some really meaningful activities apart from what you would enjoy (like painting, reading, writing on light or serious topics, gardening, taking music lessons, learning a language or going back to university)—something through which you can contribute to the society which has given you so much over all these years and has brought you to the level to which you belong today? (In fact, you can achieve both—your own enjoyment and fun and contributing to your society, through a common pursuit. Think about it and I'm sure you'll find something. Read the poem with which this chapter began and try to get the message.)

- If you had set a life's goal when you embarked upon your career and you had been re-inventing and changing it from time to time as you moved along your life's journey, to what extent your current post-retirement dreams tally with what you had in your life's corporate plan?

- If your answer to the first question is 'No', why don't you sit down and plan something right now before moving on to the next chapter as the topic covered there (that is *Aging*) may depress you?

Chapter 5

Aging and how to Keep it at Bay: A few *Magic Mantras*

"If the first 25 years of a person's life are spent in learning, the next 25 years in earning and the rest of the 25 years are spent on returning, India would be a different country."

—**Deepak Parekh, Chairman, HDFC**
(In: "50 is the new 25", *The Times of India,*
Kolkata, 10 January 2010, p. 18)

AGING AND ITS NATURAL FEATURES

Aging Starts Unbelievably Early

If you draw up a balance sheet of aging, on the credit side, you don't have to clip your finger and toenails so often as they are growing slower; and you have less body odour to worry about as your sweat glands are waning.

The debit side starts around the age of 25, when the ability to detect odours begins to go. The power of your lungs and brain size reach their peak around this age in the lifecycle and thereafter start incurring depreciation. General shrinkage sets in around 35, after which your height diminishes and inflexible muscle degeneration begins. After 40, the skin begins losing its youthful properties. Pinch the back of your hand at 45 and it smoothes out in 2 seconds; by 65, it generally takes ten times more—20 seconds.

Slowing Down of the Body

While we may remain young at heart, as we age our body slows down. Many body functions eventually decline, and we start losing lean muscle while amassing more fat in our bodies. We will not need so much energy from high-calorie and high-fat foods, we should instead choose foods that are richer in fibre and important nutrients, compared to their calorie contents. We lose more fluids but may feel less thirsty—thus increasing our requirement of water consumption.

After 50, our tissues start drying out. This is one major reason why our weight may start dropping after 55. Erotic daydreams, closely linked to sexual activity, dwindle and typically fade out around 65. The nose and ears elongate. Different organs and different physical and physiological functions start their downtrend at different times for an individual and, that too, vary from one individual to another.

Thus you cannot really pinpoint on a few standard biomarkers of aging.

Aging: Simply Explained

Aging is the result of a very natural process inside *genes*, the building blocks that make your body. As long as you were far away from retirement, in your childhood, boyhood/girlhood, adolescence, and youth, you get one old, heavily worked cell replaced by a new one— absolutely fresh, as active as the previous one that you lost. At those stages of your life, if any deviation from this natural process took place, that might have been due to some distress, some malfunction inside your system. When you crossed forty (in some cases forty-five), you got replacement of a lost cell but the new one would generally not be as young and healthy and as bulky as the one which you would get during your adolescence and youth. The replacement will have the same features and properties as the aging cell that you just lost. Consequently, as you advance in age, the size of your liver, spleen and other parts shrink, which cannot be brought back to their original conditions. **As per Nature's law, there is no method available for reversing this process of aging**.

The impact of aging becomes visible externally in symptoms, such as you look aged, you lose your hair or your hair turns grey, your skin becomes loose and may develop wrinkles, your muscles become slackened. Apart from these external manifestations which others can see but you cannot see so clearly just like the outside façade of your dwelling house, there are several other signs which others cannot see unless they are very observant and specially looking for your discomfort and distress signals, but you can feel as they take place mostly internally. These include: reduction in your muscle power (you can't stand or walk for long as you would have done a few years ago, your gait is affected), body's many internal parts and processes becoming weak, a drop in the secretion of your hormones which are essential for happy living and working.

Can you do something to decelerate such negative consequences of aging? Let us see.

Genetics and Aging

With the advent of *genetics*, now it seems that the phenomenon of aging is emerging as a science. A study of 1,055 centenarians and 1,267 controls has identified 150 genetic variants that can predict extreme longevity with 77 per cent accuracy. There is no single gene that would guarantee 100-plus years of life. The centenarians carried different combinations of the longevity genes. Surprisingly, the centenarians had as many disease-associated variants as the controls. But the longevity gene variants they inherited protected them against the disease-associated factors. They tend to get many of the age-related diseases only in the mid 90s. Environmental and other lifestyle factors like diet, smoking and physical activity play an important role in determining longevity. (1) [(1) "Key to longevity", *The Week-Health,* September 19, 2010, p. 10].

There has also been a research investigation where scientists have discovered the "Methuselah" genes whose lucky carriers (possibly only one person in 10,000) have a much improved chance of living to 100 even if they indulged in an unbalanced lifestyle. This pool of genes named after the biblical patriarch who lived to 969, appears to protect people against the effects of smoking and bad diet and can delay the onset of age-related health problems up to three decades. The owners of such genes metabolise fats and glucose differently, their skin ages more slowly and they have lower prevalence of heart disease, diabetes and hypertension. Although the human 'genome' (or gene collection) contains about 28,000 genes, they are controlled by a tiny number of regulator genes like those categorised as "Methuselah". (2) [(2) "'Methuselah' genes key to living till 100", *The Times of India, Kolkata,* 17 May 2010, p.6]

However, genetics is pointing towards the possibility of lengthening human lifespan by the relatively simple manipulation of a small number of genes. Such a possibility has its obvious pitfalls. One of them will be that our planet will be too much overcrowded leading to crisis in every respect. Another will be that several generations would have to co-exist with their typical generation gaps. However, adopting the genetic route for coping with the problems of aging is still conceivably beyond the reach of common man and, therefore, we can only highlight the possibility in principle. We have to discuss and come up with some down-to-earth practical approaches.

DEALING WITH AGING: THE *MAGIC MANTRA* OF CALORIE RESTRICTION

Each living creature possesses a kind of lifespan rheostat (a resistor for regulation of energy expenditure) embedded in its genes. This genetic rheostat probably evolved, over millions of years, so that animals, including humans, could adjust to their circumstances by applying the body's inner resources either to reproducing fast or to guarding their cells against the ravages of time. Peak reproductive years are 25 to 35. Soon after this period, genes that protect us from aging start losing their beneficial force. Then things get random, and our bodies wear out as insults such as 'free radicals' (a discussion will soon follow), the notorious chemical cousins of oxygen that can invade our genes, attack the DNAs and other cellular molecules mercilessly to weaken their strengths.

Certain stimuli, such as *calorie restriction*, can twist the rheostat to cell-maintaining 'hibernation mode'—it pays to hunker down and put reproduction on hold when food is scarce. The message that gets transmitted to the cells, while on the 'calorie restriction' lifestyle is: "Food is scarce and, therefore, go into the cell-maintaining 'hibernation mode'." Several recent studies suggest that a small number of genes, perhaps fewer than ten, govern the rheostat in mammals.

This theory of aging was first suggested by immunologist Peter Brian Medawar. British researcher Thomas B.L. Kirkwood subsequently came up with the 'disposable soma' hypothesis. According to Kirkwood, the more energy we invest in reproduction the less we can spend on metabolic systems that slow aging. One such metabolic system includes antioxidant enzymes that mop up the free radicals our cells churn out as they burn sugar to produce energy. Individuals, who grow fast and reach puberty early, enabling speedy reproduction, may be genetically geared to put fewer inner resources into making antioxidants; hence they age faster than those who are not built for reproductive speed.

Thus postponing the act of reproduction (which is totally controlled by your *selfish genes*) to a later stage of life can prompt a person to live longer. This decision has to be implemented in practice by enforcing *calorie restriction*. (See also in the 'Introduction' part). Now, although procreation is limited to physical reproduction, procreative urge can be satisfied through creative pursuits. So, if you retire with the idea that all your work is over and all that you wanted to do in your life you've already done, then there is no further productive goal. You'll have to set a fresh goal considering that your work, your service to the society is not complete as yet. You have got many more things to do for the society, for others. (See also Chapter 4 where this point has been highlighted).

This kind of goal combined with *calorie restriction* will help you to *grey gracefully*. And, in pursuing such goal, you'll have to operate from the higher brain plane, beyond the call of your *selfish genes* with the spirit of altruism and giving—not expecting any *Return on Investment (ROI)*. You should not live longer only to see that your grandchildren are growing up, getting settled and married, and setting up their families—and spreading your selfish genes.

CR (calorie restriction) also provides us with the power to protect ourselves against heat and other kinds of stress.

Calorie Restriction (CR): A Chance Finding in the 1930s

The concept of *Calorie Restriction (CR)* was first considered in the 1930s when Clive McCay of Cornell University found, through a classic set of experiments, that cutting rats' usual dietary calories by about a third (just enough to fulfil their nutritional needs but not adequate to maintain their usual weight) extended their average life spans by 20 to 40% and, in some rare cases, even up to 75% than rats raised on a normal amount of food to which they had been habituated. Some of the experimental rats lived even twice as long. The underlying principles are simple and smart and the results are astonishingly magical.

- The more food and other dietary inputs you take, the more energy goes to your digestive system. The energy cost turns out to be high and it attracts more blood for its activities under such circumstances; you feel cold when your stomach is full as other areas of your body has less supply of blood.

- The more is your food and other intakes, the longer time it takes for your digestive system to process the stuff and the higher is the load on your *metabolic process*—the *metabolic cost* of the activity is much more than when the intake is less and of restricted quantity (settle on a 1,500 to 1,750 kcal per day diet once you've crossed sixty) as well as planned and compatible with the individual's digestive system and process (that is, the person who likes vegetarian food is provided with a vegetarian diet whereas one who loves fish is served some fish as the non-vegetarian item). The best result is obtained when what you'll eat and drink is totally under your own control or decided upon in close consultation with you. However, certain basic standards must be maintained (such as, less oily, fatty and spicy food is a must as our digestive system which we have inherited from our forest-dwelling ancestors is not designed for such rich stuff). As a result, the genes responsible for boosting longevity are activated.

- If the input is more than the output (energy expenditure) demands then you generate a surplus energy (or, positive balance) which is not burnt due to any physical activity nor is it removed by any other means. It tantamounts to *energy mismanagement*. The extra energy gets deposited in your body leading to weight gain (if you have a natural tendency for obesity) or atherosclerosis (deposits inside blood vessels if you have a fibrous, athletic body) or amyloid deposit (development of wax-like substances which are found in the brains of patients suffering from Alzheimer's disease) in the brain tissue if you have a lean and thin, skinny, bony constitution. [In the prehistoric days, the more you became a victim of *energy mismanagement*, the greater were the chances that you would be predated by ferocious animals or by members of enemy tribes; and, in modern times, by stressors or life-threatening diseases.]

- Due to *CR*, since you do not have enough chemical savings to be passed on for reproduction, you are trading fertility for longevity.

- You are so conscious about your body that you refrain from reproduction in the true sense of the term although you do not refrain from sex.

- There are some key metabolic changes that drive its life-extending effect come about with *CR* practice.

- *CR* activates genes that make 'heat-shock proteins'—cellular guardian angels that help protect tissues from damage caused by heat and other kinds of stress and develop resistance to various insults such as toxins, radiation and heat and generate anti-oxidant enzymes.

THE INVASION OF *FREE RADICALS* AND ITS IMPACT ON AGING: THE *MAGIC MANTRA* OF *ANTI-OXIDANTS*

A little more than hundred years ago from today, biologists proposed the 'rate of living' hypothesis to explain differences between species as far as 'maximum life span' is concerned. (3) [(3) Whalley, Lawrence. *The Ageing Brain*, London: Phoenix, 2001, p.12]. They had come to the conclusion that animals with the highest metabolic rates were most likely to have the shortest life spans.

Metabolism directs and conducts the life-giving process of your entire biological system including your brain. It constitutes the chemical processes in living things that change the inputs like food, beverages and drinks into energy and elements for growth (such as new cells) and waste products for elimination. Metabolism ensures that the body and brain tissues are broken down by wear and tear *(catabolism)* and rebuilt *(anabolism)* continuously. *Basal metabolism* is the energy used by a body at complete rest being the minimum necessary to maintain life. (4) [(4) Roper Nancy, *Pocket Medical Dictionary*, Edinburgh and London: The English Language Book Society and E & S Livingstone Ltd., 1966, p. 304.]

For running this process, you need adequate quantities of oxygen. Oxygen is the life-giver for organisms. After its entry into your body, it passes through several phases in its own style and before it reaches the last stage, a few chemicals are generated in course of its long journey through the pipelines and crevices. One group of chemicals, amongst these, are known as *free radicals*. *Free radicals* are small groups of atoms, each of which carries an unpaired or singular electron. Just because it has no equivalent in the living system, it has tremendous dormant power and is extremely reactive and thus potentially destructive to body tissue—including proteins, fats and genetic material.

In 1956, Harman suggested that *free radicals* generated during aerobic respiration cause the cumulative damage of aging. (5) [(5) Harman, D.A., 'Theory based on free radical and radiation chemistry', *Journal of Gerontology, Vol. II*, 1956, pp. 298-300].

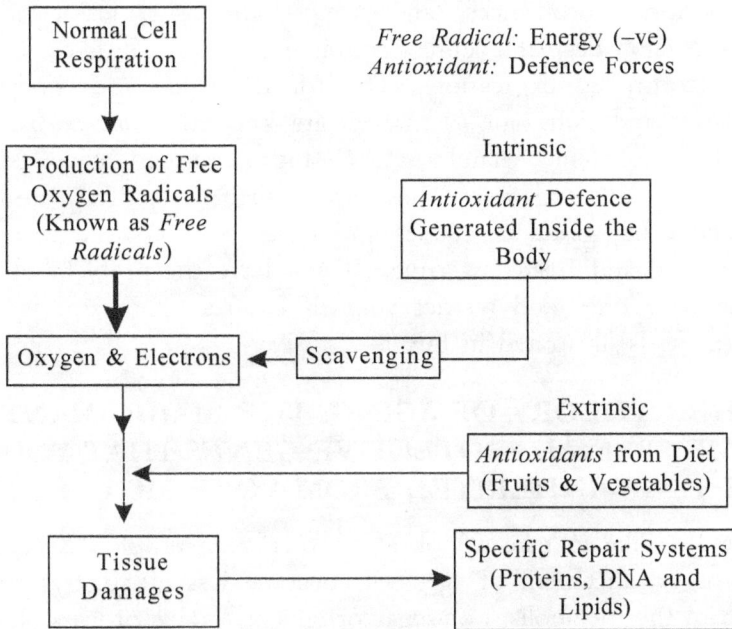

Normal Cell Respiration

Free Radical: Energy (−ve)
Antioxidant: Defence Forces

Production of Free Oxygen Radicals (Known as *Free Radicals*)

Intrinsic

Antioxidant Defence Generated Inside the Body

Oxygen & Electrons ← Scavenging

Extrinsic

Antioxidants from Diet (Fruits & Vegetables)

Tissue Damages

Specific Repair Systems (Proteins, DNA and Lipids)

Fig. 5: How Free Radicals are Generated

One *free radical* is equivalent to two in its strength. Its chemical process is indeed most forceful. The process has a positive as well as a negative side. The positive side is that it destroys any harmful virus or germ very quickly. And, its negative side is that it damages the *DNA*s inside any cell which results in the death of living cellular constituents of your living structures and systems.

There are certain *free radical*-friendly elements inside the living body which help the *free radicals* in their destructive activities. These are: arsenic, cadmium, lead and nickel which are solid metals and a liquid chemical like mercury.

Free radicals get manufactured not only inside the body; they also get carried into the system from outside through ultraviolet solar rays, carbon monoxide emitted owing to combustion of petrol or diesel, smoke caused by cigarette, bidi, cigar or tobacco smoking, pesticides, and elements like chromium, nickel, cadmium, lead, and mercury. *Free radicals* production inside the body is increased, while you're exposed to x-ray or any other nuclear radiation—directly or indirectly or work with poisonous chemicals.

In addition, something which is beyond your imagination also generates *free radicals*. That includes: negative thoughts, unnecessary worrying habit, emotional turbulences (anger, rage, animosity, jealousy, hatred, intolerance, ego, despair, depression, anxiety and the like) and their sudden uncontrolled expressions. The friends inside your body which can confront and fight out *free radicals* are known as *anti-oxidants* which include: beta carotene, vitamins A, C and E, amino acids, selenium, copper, zinc and manganese. These are available plentifully from fresh fibrous and other green vegetables and fruits. So you need to consume plenty of salad and fresh raw fruits. If you have the problem of acidity, avoid the sour ones and restrict yourself to fruits that are sweet. The whole process is illustrated in Fig. 5.

ANOTHER THEORY OF AGING: THE *MAGIC MANTRA* OF SOME SPECIAL PROTECTIVE *GENES* THAT YOU MIGHT HAVE INHERITED FROM YOUR MOTHER

You may also like to take a look at another *theory of aging*. According to it, with the advancement of age, cells become less efficient at acquiring energy from the metabolism of sugar or 'glucose'. This process, known as 'cellular respiration', takes place in the mitochondria of your cell, which are specialised structures. These structures contain some *DNA* derived from the mother and constitute an important site of *free radical* production. Therefore, if you are lucky enough to inherit a robust set of mitochondrial genes from your mother which do not allow the *free radicals* produced to devastate your *DNA*s because of their having adequate repair enzymes for offering local protection, then you may enjoy a healthy retired life up to a ripe old age.

Britain's oldest female smoker who puffed more than 170,000 cigarettes for over 95 years and died a month short of her 103rd birthday in August 2010 was perhaps an example of this genetic theory of aging. The great-great grandmother, Winnie Langley, who loved a good party and always enjoyed a smoke and a drink, had beaten cancer in her 90s and outlived not only her husband and son but also all of her 10 stepchildren.

THE *MAGIC MANTRA* OF YOUR *BRAINPOWER* APPLICATION TO DELAY THE AGING PROCESS

On top of it, if you have been proving yourself to be more intelligent than others, by having an intensely questioning and probing mind, you would obviously continue to exercise your high intelligence even after retirement, as a consequence of which you will not age as fast as others who are not as intelligent as you or, even being equally intelligent, would have stopped using their intelligence after retiring from their working careers.

That brainy people (is it who possess a high *PIQ* or 'practical intelligence quotient'?), are likely to live around fifteen years longer than others, due to the presence of the *SSADH gene* (which makes them very sharp and clever), has been one of the main findings of a recent study at Calabria University in Italy. (6) [(6) 'Brainy people outlive others by 15 years', *The Times of India, Kolkata*, 14 June 2008, p. 17].

Lower IQ in children is a possible risk factor for vascular dementia (as observed in the elderly Alzheimer's patients) later in life as the intelligent upper brain is deprived of supply of enough quantity of blood. (7) [(7) "Low IQ linked to dementia", *The Economic Times, Kolkata*, 27 June 2008, p. 24].

It is a well-known fact now that individual human *genomes* (that is, the complete set of *genes* in a human cell) change throughout a person's life influenced by environmental or nutritional factors and self-induced habits. This may explain why illnesses such as cancer come with age due to smoking, tobacco abuse and other lifestyle- related causes. But why do the *genomes* change? Certain important properties of a person's *DNA* modify over the course of his life as a result of dietary and other environmental exposures; and the extent of such changes is similar among family members due to inherited common propensities.

Let us take the case of the bad habit of smoking. People having a high PIQ will never go for smoking or, even if they had been addicted to smoking at some stage of their life will give up with the dawning of PI. Many smokers reach for a cigarette to ease their anxiety during stressful periods. But recent research studies have shown that quitting smoking makes people happier, and the effect lasts as long as they manage to kick the habit. (8) [(8) "Quitting smoking improves your mood", *The Times of India, Kolkata*, 7 December 2010, p.16]

THE *MAGIC MANTRA* OF *OMEGA-3* FATTY ACIDS

You've heard or read about the beneficial power of the *Omega-3* fatty acids. Isn't it?

Omega-3 fatty acids from fish oil preserve the genetic 'fuse' that determines the lifespan of cells.

Omega-3 has a direct effect on biological aging by slowing down the rate at which protective caps on the ends of chromosomes shorten. The caps, called *telomeres*, are made from copied strands of DNA and prevent the ends of chromosomes—the 'packages' of DNA in the cell nucleus—from becoming damaged and keep the DNA organised and contained.

Each time a cell divides, its telomeres get shorter until a critical point is reached. DNA then becomes damaged and the cell stops dividing, and may die. In this way, the telomere acts like a biological fuse.

The rate at which the fuse 'burns' can vary both between individual people and individual cells. This is believed to have an impact on age-related diseases.

THE *MAGIC MANTRA* OF CO-OPERATION WITH NATURE

If you want to remain young as your chronological age advances, you must co-operate with Nature and this must begin well before your retirement.

By co-operation with Nature, we mean that:

• You'll not eat unless you're hungry.

- And, when you eat, you must be guided only by your need and never fall a prey to the demon of your greed. This will certainly help you to regulate the rhythms of your hunger and you should be able to follow, with ease, regular meal timings.

- You should honour your thirst every time you feel thirsty, the only exception being avoiding drinking water during the 30 to 45 minute period prior to and immediately after a main meal. You should go for plain water or fresh fruit juice and avoid alcoholic and carbonated drinks and too many cups of tea or coffee.

- You must not suppress the pressure to excrete unless it is absolutely impossible.

- You'll satisfy your body and brain cells' hunger for recreation—particularly play.

DEALING WITH AGING BY CONSIDERING IT AS A DISEASE

Chronological aging is unstoppable but there is an emerging school of thought which calls for a fresh look at the biological process and tries to sell the idea that aging is nothing but a disease. A logic that they are using to justify their claim is that the ability of humans to live longer is being demonstrated in abundance across the world. Another logic is that the human life span has been increasing over the years—particularly in modern times. Average life expectancies extended as much as 30 years in developed countries during the 20th century and experts expect the same to happen in this century.

However, we doubt whether this point of view will stand the test of time as with greater lifespan come a heavier burden of age-related diseases. The advocates of the disease school continue to stick to their stand. Their current endeavour is to find out ways and means of delaying the onset of such diseases and they are pretty hopeful that something would be found out soon.

DOES LIFE REALLY BEGIN AT FORTY

The adage that "Life begins at forty" is no longer a myth, a new study conducted by an insurance firm has revealed. (9) (10) [(9) "Life does begin at 40", *The Economic Times*, Kolkata, 26 June 2008, p.22; (10) Vijay Dutt & Agencies, "Fact: Life does begin at 40", *Hindustan Times*, Kolkata, 26 June 2008, p.14]. Besides, a most recent investigation at the University College, London has claimed that the human brain does not stop developing until people are in their 30s or 40s—meaning that many still have something of the teenager about them long after they have become adults. The region that goes through the most protracted development is the *pre-frontal cortex* at the front of the brain, which is involved in decision-making, planning and inhibiting inappropriate social behaviour and also things like social awareness and understanding other people and empathy. (11) [(11) "Blame it on the brain", *The Statesman, Kolkata,* 17 December 2010, p.5.]

40 to 45: The Magic Prime Period of One's Life

Another justifying logic is that most people usually achieve what they want by the time they have reached the 40's decade of their life. 40 to 45 years represents the period of an individual's chronological age, which has been found to be the *magic* prime period when a large number of people would have accumulated the most belongings they would not want to lose.

Although a person can continue to develop and learn new skills after this middle age phase of life, the basic structural changes driven by genes and biology rather than by what they are seeing or doing will tend to have been completed.

If this is true, then climbing up the age ladder is not much of an energy-costly experience for people who are moving towards retirement and looking at the post-retirement years with depression in their minds. As a matter of fact, pre- and post-retirement years, for those who have already reached their peak in their mid-forties, is a time for enjoying the fruits of their hard labour that they had put in before they attained the fourth decade of their life.

SEX AND OLD AGE

Men with a low level of male sex hormone *testosterone* (can be ascertained through 'blood test') are likely to die early due to several fatal diseases including cardio-arterial problems and cancer. This is normal to happen in old age. Such people are generally more obese, and have a greater prevalence of *diabetes* and high *blood pressure* compared to men of the same age who had higher levels of the same hormone.

The precautionary measures for such men are to have: a healthier lifestyle (as lifestyle and *stress* management possibly determine the levels of *testosterone*), including weight control, regular exercise and a healthy diet.

(12) [(12) "Low levels of testosterone can kill early", *The Times of India, Kolkata*, 19 June 2008, p.15].

The Japanese society has an interesting picture to offer. A WHO report released in March 2008 observed that one in four married couples in Japan had not made love in the previous year while 38 per cent of couples in their 50s no longer have sex at all. These figures attributed to the stresses of Japanese working life. Yet, at the same time, the old age (post-seventy) porn industry in Japan is booming. (13) [(13) "Sex after seventy: Japan's new porn craze", *The Sunday Times of India, Kolkata*, 22 June 2008, p. 18].

The *Magic Mantra* of *Spermidine*

While we have taken a look at the relationship between the male sex hormone and longevity, there is a special magic in the male sperm. *Spermidine*, a substance released during sexual intercourse can extend your lifespan. In the absence of a compatible partner, the male can go for self-sex or porn-sex for spermidine secretion. If that also becomes difficult you as you have turned cold due to your age, you can obtain it from soybeans as well as grapefruit where it is abundantly available.

The *Magic Mantra* of Nurturing the Sex Hormones

The male sex hormones *testosterone* and *androgen* represent masculine activities which represent risk-taking, initiative and enterprise. Aged males can nurture their sex hormones by initiating some new ventures which may be purely voluntary. But it has to be a venture, an enterprise; joining a voluntary or social welfare organisation or offering free service to a religious body will not stimulate the sex glands.

The levels of the female sex hormone *oestrogen* and the compassion chemical o*xytocin* which is secreted while breastfeeding the infant, can be raised by spending more time with members of the third generation—the grandchildren and children of their age group and not only taking care of them but also seriously parenting them.

GREYING GRACEFULLY

Okinawa, a southern prefecture in Japan, has the highest percentage of centenarians in the world, as well as the longest disability-free life expectancy in the world.

Just how do the people of Okinawa do it? Is it something in the air, the water or the food in Japan? Or does the secret lie in their spiritual and active lifestyles?

The answer is yes, to all of the above. Eating right, exercising regularly, and keeping mentally active and positive are important factors for active aging. According to Aubrey de Grey, a young biomedical gerontologist and chief scientist of a foundation dedicated to longevity research, aging is the outcome of lifelong accumulation of various types of molecular and cellular damage throughout the body and the brain—which is very much in tune with our concept of *greying gracefully*. (14)[(14) 'First person who will live till 150 already born.' *The Times of India, Kolkata*, 7 July 2011, p.11.]

APPLICATION TIPS

- To delay or slow down your aging:
  - (*i*) Practice *Energy Management* by following *Calorie Restriction (CR)* strictly.
  - (*ii*) Have enough *anti-oxidants* (fresh fruits and vegetables) to fight the *free radicals* generated inside your body as a result of the metabolic process.
  - (*iii*) Although you might not have inherited some special genes from your mother to protect you from fast aging, you are fully equipped to use your *brainpower*—your *Practical Intelligence (PI)* in everything non-routine (decision-making/problem-solving) that you do in your old age instead of being guided by simple emotions or impulse.
  - (*iv*) If you're a non-vegetarian, adopt a fish-rich diet and go for bony fishes and sea fishes which contain *Omega-3 fatty acids*—good for your brain.
  - (*v*) Co-operate with Nature's laws to delay aging and prevent age-related diseases (for example, don't eat when you're not hungry; go for a nap when you feel sleepy and so on.)
  - (*vi*) Maintain a balanced *testosterone* (male sex hormone) level by being physically very active.
  - (*vii*) Get engaged with life's natural flowing process.

Chapter 6

Happiness *versus* Unhappiness

"...if a man has lived his whole life making every moment and every phase of it a beauty, a love, a joy, naturally his death is going to be the ultimate peak of his whole life's endeavour. His death is not going to be ugly as it ordinarily happens everyday to everyone. If death is ugly, that means your whole life has been a waste."

—**Osho**

In: "Saying Goodbye with Grace",
The Times of India, Kolkata, 1st December, 2010, p. 18

HAPPINESS-UNHAPPINESS: ARE THEY JUST WINDFALLS

Happiness or *unhappiness* is not just a windfall. The black box, your brain [or shall we call it the 'Central Processing Unit (CPU)' in computer language] has a switch hidden in it for your happiness or unhappiness. That switch gets triggered on automatically as a response to any 'external' or 'internal' stimulus.

The fine structure of your brain, a masterpiece of engineering, is partly genetically determined and partly the product of your experiences. If you have inherited a brain which remains positive even under negative circumstances, then you have a strong possibility of having *happiness* as your steady companion; and, you would experience this in your real life.

On the contrary, if you have not been so fortunate and your brain turns negative even with slightest provocations from the external environment or you have frequent negative self-talk and untoward emotions invading your mind, then you would have experienced *unhappiness* from time to time in your life's journey so far.

TRAIN YOUR PLASTIC BRAIN FOR *HAPPINESS*

However, you should not, in utter despair, give up the possibility of enjoying *happiness* as brain can be trained. It has tremendous learning capacity and is plastic by nature.

Your brain cells are like little children—always ready to explore, investigate, experiment and learn. And, there are around 10,000 million of such cell-kids inside your brain.

Contrary to a computer, the construction of which is permanent (and its hardware is quite separate and different in nature from the software), in your brain the networks of brain cells can organise and reorganise themselves to do specific tasks. They can, in response to demands, change their patterns of connections (in number and shape) in tune with newer and newer experiences and learning. They can replace redundant connections and construct totally new sets of circuitry corresponding to new tasks. The conditioning stimulus and exposure has got to be repetitive, nevertheless.

All living organisms are electro-chemically activated biological systems. Each individual member of the trillions and trillions of cells that we are made of has both electrical vibrations and chemical secretions going on inside all the time and it is the cell's inherent electro-chemical activities that represent the life force.

Happiness is the outcome when we enjoy the activity in which we are engaged, when we succeed, when we the get the result that we had expected. It immediately leads to the discharge of positive *'feel good'* chemicals (*endorphin, dopamine, melatonin, serotonin* and *oxytocin* are a few amongst them) inside our brain and *beta-positive* brain waves (14 to 24 cycles per second) get generated. (In women, *oxytocin* is released during labour and breastfeeding. In men, a closely related brain chemical called *vasopressin* is released when they become proud fathers.)

Unhappiness is the consequence of lack of enjoyment, frustration or failure. We become unhappy when we miss to reach our goal or are compelled to do something which we don't like. This state of mind leads to the discharge of a negative *'feel bad'* chemical (either *adrenalin* or *cortisol*) inside the brain and *beta-negative* brain waves (25 to 32 cycles per second) come into play.

Unhappiness could be physical (due a bodily discomfort or a disease) in the form of pain; mental (your decision was not found to be correct or the solution to a problem that you had suggested did not work out) in the shape of frustration; or emotional (you got emotionally hurt due to some unexpected incident or you were forced to do something which you did not like) agony.

However, people vary one from the other as regards their 'comfort zones' (what give them comfort or pleasure or satisfaction beyond the limits of which discomfort starts) and 'tolerance zones and limits' (how much they can tolerate without immediate recourse to the in-built, instinctive 'fight-or-flight' strategy). This explains why when one individual suffers badly or becomes badly upset due to some 'stressor' (or stress-generating factor), the same stressful stimulus can be easily tolerated by another individual and he does not feel bad at all. He may start feeling bad with a higher intensity stressor.

IS HAPPINESS AGE-RELATED

There is a small group of scientists at the Stony Brook University, New York who have observed, through their most revealing research studies on over 340,000 American men and women between 18 and 85 that despite advanced age and increased risk of debilitating diseases people in their fifties worry less and nurture a positive state of mind. 50 seem to be the landmark age when mental worries happen to fade gradually and feelings of happiness happen to surge. Perhaps by that age and stage of life, most people who have been trying to succeed in life get settled, would have attained satisfaction due to the fulfilment of their general needs including reaching a certain level in their career, and have developed a mutually understanding family environment and a set of good friends and an intimate social circle. Interestingly, the investigation found that variables such as having young children being unemployed, or being single did not affect the age-related patterns of well-being. While these findings are striking, everyone in their fifties may not be so fortunate to taste happiness in the fifth decade of life. (1) (2) [(1) "Happiness begins at 50", *The Times of India, Kolkata,* 19 May 2010, p. 16; (2) "Happiness begins at 50", *The Statesman, Kolkata,* 19 May 2010, p. 6.]

We have an example here! Corporate guru and author Gurcharan Das took up writing as his principal occupation in his 50's. "Since the human life span has been increasing one can plan for two lives and have two careers." says Das, who took early retirement at 50 to devote all his time to writing. "People are afraid of experimenting and they get into a rut. One must consider the whole life as a work of art," he says. (3) [Sinha, Seema, "Late Bloomers1" *Times Life!,* a *Sunday Times of India* supplement, 23 May 2010, p. 1]

WORK-LIFE BALANCE

Attaining a reasonably high level of happiness by the time you're 50 years of age is possible. Why not? Nevertheless, amongst the conditions that are to be fulfilled, one is of vital importance and, that is, achieving a *work-life balance.*

By the time you are close to 50, if you consciously try for achievement of work-life balance, only then it is possible. Otherwise, in reality, the situation is just the opposite. The more you advance in your chronological age, the stronger is your ambition and the more impatient you become to grow in your career. You work very hard and, to work hard, you devote more time to your work role irrespective of whether you are an employee, a self-employed person or an entrepreneur. Your family and social roles suffer and, in spite of your personal career growth, you have some unhappiness and you make your family members and friends unhappy as well.

There are various ways of achieving a balance between your work role and family and social roles and certainly not at the cost of your career progress. Some of the better strategies are: grooming your subordinates to attain a certain level of proficiency and when you feel they are ready to take on some of your responsibilities, you empower them and may be, in the long run, giving them some share of your authorities too— particularly for planning, decision-making and problem-solving; honing your own brain skills so that your response time and action time are much reduced—you become a much faster cerebral person; developing yourself into an effective prioritiser and time manager; keeping yourself healthy and fit so that physically also you're prompt and active and you can take on more; and spending quality time with your family and friends and having fun and games with them to keep them in excellent humour (even just humorous communication will keep them happy and hearty).

USE THE *MAGIC MANTRA* OF REMEMBERING WHAT TYPE OF ACTIVITIES MADE YOU HAPPY

Film-making and not the money that Sanjay Leela Bhansali (director of *Devdas, Hum Dil De Chuke Sanam, Black, Saawariyan*, and *Guzaarish*) makes gives him happiness. In his own words: "My work is not inspired by money.....I don't know how much money Guru Dutt had, I only know the films he made. I also make films. Not money. Not for myself and not for anyone who comes to me to make them." (4) [(4) "Sanjay's Guzaarish", *Calcutta Times*, a supplement of *The Times of India*, 1 December 2010, p.1]

One can get maximum happiness from what he enjoys doing—what kind of activities he likes to spend his time on. When you get involved in such activities and there is no pressure on you to change over to something else that you do not like, happiness chemicals start getting secreted inside your brain. When you plan to get started on any such activity of your own choice, *dopamine* gets produced and once you get actively engaged and things start happening in your favour, you get a flow of *endorphin*. Your brain also gets poised and peaceful with the electrical waves inside the brain settling down at *beta-positive*—14 to 25 cycles per second.

Dopamine also serves as your brain's reward chemical. When you accomplish something—run a race and win—your brain triggers its release. Though exhausted physically after the race, you get a surge of energy—supplied primarily by your mind. It gives you happiness and confidence and makes you raise your hands in unconscious excitement having become the winner. The losers, on the other hand, become unhappy and depressed and thus get no such dopamine surge. They immediately run out of energy, collapse at the finishing line, and feel awful about themselves. By hijacking our *dopamine system*, addictive substances give us pleasure without having to work for it.

However, the activities that one enjoys could be classified into two categories. The first group of activities are those that are related to *physical pleasure* or *creaturely comfort* such us eating good food, going for an addictive pursuit (like smoking, drinking alcohol, or taking narcotic drugs), or indulging in sex. These are purely selfishly personal and, although each of these have some economic significance (like sale of food, drinks, addictive substances, contraceptives, condoms and so on), none of them add any value or contribute to social, technical or economic development and progress. Activities which lead to any such value-addition or contribution bring *happiness* into the performer's mind. These represent satisfaction of a much higher order. (5) [(5) Ganguli, Siddhartha, *Live Happily, Work Happily*, New Delhi: Allied Publishers, 2009]

Whenever you need a little physical as well as mental refreshment, remember the days you have now left behind when you used to engage yourself in activities which you not only enjoyed to the brim but those were also of some social, technical or economic significance—which made you play the role of a *value-addition agent (VAA)*.

USE THE *MAGIC MANTRA* OF YOUR PAST ACHIEVEMENTS VISUALISATION TO CHEER UP

Learn the *magic mantra* to cheer up and make your mind feel *happy* which we, the ardent students of the science of happiness, have come to understand through painstaking studies on people.

Now that you have attained old age, you would have already lived the first five, six, even seven decades of your life reasonably successfully with a few major achievements to your credit, which are really the milestones of your life's journey so far.

You can flood your brain with *'feel good'* chemicals *dopamine* and *endorphin* and bring in *beta-positive* brain waves by practicing your past achievements visualisation. Try to relive, in your memory, with some of your remarkable past achievements which really make you proud and raise your self-esteem, one at a time, and you will bring back those happy moments in your mind, the positive impact of which will spread all over your body and your senses. (6) [(6) Doidge, Norman, *The Brain That Changes Itself*, New York: Penguin Books, 2007, p. 108]

MANAGEMENT OF UNHAPPINESS: CAN THE IN-BUILT 'QUICK-FIX' TRIGGER HELP US TODAY

In our pre-historic forest-based ancestors, any 'threat' (like non-availability of food due to bushfire, flood, famine or monopolisation of the limited quantity of food available by a rival tribe; or chasing by a predator) would result in two typical forms of ultimate outcome of unhappiness—anger or fear. We can, straight away, describe this type of unhappiness as *'stress'*.

For coping with such *'stress'*, they had readily available to them a tool or a technique—a product of billions of years of evolution. Located deep inside the inner and lower portion of the human brain (inherited from man's primate ancestors) there is a *'quick-fix'* device: a *'fight-or-flight'* trigger, which when clicked, would set in motion a few common physiological responses: the heart starting to beat faster creating a rush of blood from the heart directly to the limbs to help them 'fight' or 'flee';

the blood pressure naturally going up; a sudden rise in the *adrenalin* hormone level in the blood secreted from the *adrenalin gland* to make them all set to attack or escape; the breathing rate increases; and, the pace of the heart's rhythm becomes irregular and erratic. All these would happen to help the stress victim to confront attack and fight out the source or generator of *stress* or to flee and escape from the stressful situation.

This biological switch is still available with us, but its operational outcome *'fight-or-flight'* is socially not acceptable. Nobody, even somebody near and dear, would ever expect to face a person under *stress* to go out of his mind and becoming physically most aggressive and violent or trying to run away and go into a hiding. These things may happen even today but such incidents are extremely rare and most of such rare incidents would be considered abnormal out-of-the-box phenomena and, at the first available opportunity, would be referred to psychiatrists.

The list of 'stressors' was short and simple in the ancient past. Today, there are hundreds of stress-generating factors. One main reason is that you and I are in a society where there is an abundance of all kinds of consumer products and each category having a wide variety of choices. Our urge to own, consume or use such products has increased. We have, quite some time ago, come out of the circle of need-based consumption. Today, beyond need satisfaction, most of us are governed by greed.

Apart from this *greed factor*, we have already discussed about other factors like the 'Return on Investment (ROI)', Debtor-Creditor, Generation Gap, and Ego-attachment in Chapter 1. There could be a few other possible causes of old age *stress* leading to unhappiness as listed below.

OTHER POSSIBLE CAUSES OF OLD AGE 'STRESS' LEADING TO UNHAPPINESS

- Comparison with others: what they have which you don't have;
- Family expectations that could not be met by you;
- Negative deviations from the desired outcome—what you had wanted and what you've got, what you had deserved and what you were given;
- What you had expected your children to achieve and to be and what they have really achieved and what they really are;

- Non-fulfilment of requirements and expectations from your spouse;
- Immediately on retirement from an economic occupation, sudden fall from family and social prestige, from activity to inactivity;
- Sudden stoppage of inter-dependent working habits and starkly naked loneliness for a solid nine to ten hours every working day—lot of vacant space available with difficulty in time-structuring;
- Compromise in the standard of living as there may be a down trend in your economic standard despite inflation in the environment.

TYPICAL POST-RETIREMENT STRESSOR ANALYSIS

Let us take the post-retirement situation as a case for study and try to analyse a few typical stressors.

Case I

Are you going to be a 'burden' for your folks? By 'burden' we mean 'dependence' in a negative sense.

If your answer is 'yes', then is it: (i) from an economic standpoint; or (ii) in terms of the physical/mental disabilities that accompany the aging process; or (iii) both. In order to elaborate on point no. (ii), we can include: impaired sight, hearing, mobility or mental functions (cognitive abilities/memory/grasping power) and psychological feelings like a strong generation gap/technological handicap (for not being computer and such other gadget-savvy/information handicap (in this modern age of information explosion).

Case II

Do you already have a disease; or are there any signs and symptoms of ill-health visible in your case (such as: high blood pressure, high blood sugar, loss of memory or dementia)?

If your answer is 'yes', then what steps have you taken already to have your health problem properly attended, or in the case of a disease, cured; or, what steps are you going to take to ensure that the health disorder does not overcome you?

Case III

Have you become extra sentimental and emotional as you miss your children who are away from home—studying or working somewhere else within the country or abroad?

If your answer is 'yes', then read what follows. If you dream about your children doing well in their careers, you must get used to their absence considering the bright and positive side of the circumstance. Besides, there are so many ways available now—the Internet, web camera, cell phone and so on to keep regular touch with the absentee family member. And, instead of having a lot of vacuum space in your life every day, fill with old or new activities which you enjoy. Keeping a pet is an excellent solution.

APPLICATION TIPS

- Recent scientific studies have revealed to us that happiness or unhappiness is not just a windfall. There are typical bio-electro-chemical conditions associated with each of these two states of mind.

- You can train your *plastic brain* for happiness by trying to adopt the following strategies:

  (*i*) If you are in your late 40's or early 50's, by striking a work-life balance by the time you are 50.

  (*ii*) In case you are in the beyond-60 stage of life, regularly remember what type of activities had made you happy earlier and also vividly visualise your past achievements and talk about those to your children and grandchildren with pride.

- Identify the 'stressors' which are causing unhappiness to you—analyse them with clinical precision and try to reduce their impact on you or totally eradicate.

Chapter 7

In Search of Longevity

"It's good to be happy in your job because such people tend to live longer."
—Christopher Peterson, Professor of Psychology
and author of *A Primer in Positive Psychology*

LONGEVITY'S TIME LINE

It is recorded in the ancient Indian shastra, the *Bhagavad Puran*, that the *devas* (gods) and the *asuras* (demons) carried out the *samudra manthan* or churning of the ocean of milk. Their objective was to obtain *amrit*, the nectar of immortality.

During the *Vedic Age*, we find it had been documented in the *Mahabharata* that King *Yayati*, cursed with premature old age, borrowed years of youthfulness from his youngest son. *Aswathama*, *Samitinjaya*, *Vibhisana*, *Hanuman*, sage *Kripa* and sage *Vyasa* were cited as having eternal life with some noble purpose.

In 1000 B.C., in Greek myth, *Tithonus* was known to have eternal life, but not eternal youth. His wife had mistakenly asked the gods for eternal life for him instead of eternal youth.

In 400 B.C., a Chinese text recorded that King *Chu* had received anti-death potion.

In 1513 A.D., *Juan Ponce de Leon*, the then governor of Puerto Rico, had searched for the "Fountain of Youth" but failed to find it. He discovered Florida instead.

In the early 20th century, there was a race to isolate male and female hormones as anti-aging tonics.

In the 1930s, *Clive McCay* found that rats lived longer on a starvation diet. This finding led to the *calorie restriction (CR)* strategy for keeping healthy and fit in spite of forward movement of one's chronological age.

In 1986, *Cynthia Kenyon* and coworkers at the University of California, San Francisco made nematodes live longer by altering their genes.

In mid-1990s, *Leon* and *Guarente's* research group at the Massachusetts Institute of Technology (MIT) made yeast cells live longer and observed that reduced food intake was the key. (Once again the *calorie restriction* strategy's flag flew high!)

In 2002, British scientist *Sydney Brenner* of Cambridge shared the Nobel Prize in physiology or medicine for showing how genes dictate the development of organs and tell some cells when to die.

In November 2003, Boston University's School of Medicine group found out that centenarians were likely to have a gene related to fat processing.

November 2010: The Times of India, Kolkata of 18th November 2010 carried a path-breaking news item on page 10 which had as its lead line: "Software to help actors regain youth onscreen". Reported from the *Sunday Times*, London, the text of the report said that the 60-year old Oscar-winning actor Jeff Bridges was all set to play a younger version of him with the help of a new computer technology that will reverse his age by three decades on-screen. The new technology would hopefully make it possible to record the actor's facial movements in minute detail and then superimpose them onto a digital model of his younger self in 'TRON: Legacy', a 3D Walt Disney production to be released shortly. Bridges had starred in the original film 28 years ago and has now revived the role of video games developer Kevin Flynn, who gets trapped in a cyber universe for 20 years. The technology development has marked a new era in film-making. As well as allowing actors to play younger versions of themselves, the programme will also let them grow old gracefully. The technology was first used in "The Curious Case of Benjamin Button" starring Brad Pitt. (1) [(1) "Software to help actors regain youth onscreen", *The Times of India, Kolkata*, 18 November, 2010, p.10]

February 2011: The *Hindustan Times,* Kolkata edition of 11th February had a news flash on the front page about the country's longest-serving lawyer YG Krishna Murthy, who has been arguing cases in different courts for a staggering 75 years, wanting to call it a day very soon. Murthy turned 100 only last month and, during the same month, he appeared before the Andhra Pradesh high court to argue a case. Although most of Murthy's contemporaries are dead, he is still going strong without any perceivable health problems, which is indeed most remarkable. He still walks two miles a day and is a strict vegetarian. He reads a lot and has no age-related loss of sleep—going to bed at 10 pm and sleeping till 5 am. He was felicitated at the 17th Commonwealth Law Conference held in Hyderabad recently and he was honoured by

President Pratibha Patil in January 2011 for his contribution to the legal profession. There might be a few cases like Murthy in our country and elsewhere about whom we do not get to know because of their obscure existence. How many of them do get prominent media coverage?

By 2015 what is going to happen in the field of aging research? MIT's *Guarente* predicts that a pill is likely to be available to add 10 to 30 years to human life.

LONGEVITY: CAN IT BE INCREASED

Aging is a disease that can be cured, or at least postponed. In other words, longevity can be increased. You can add about 15 years to your life span by keeping a long distance from cancer, heart disease and other principal causes of death by maintaining a well-balanced lifestyle.

Fig. 6: An Aging Man

Evolution would not favour *genes* that extend an organism's life much beyond its reproductive years as that is the most fundamental purpose of life—to live behind your genetic imprints. **Therefore, apart from the 'balanced lifestyle' strategy, longevity can be boosted provided an individual has some meaningful purpose to live longer and, by meaningful purpose, we mean some contribution to the society without expecting any 'Return on the Investment (ROI)' which would be an ego-attached project. Living only for the sake of living would be purposeless.** Should it be something big? Certainly not. In order to clearly understand the dimension of the endeavour, we need to echo the voice of the noble doctor Albert Schweitzer to say: "Even if it's a little thing, do something for others—something for which you get no pay but the privilege of doing it." Lawyer YG Krishna Murthy about whom we have just mentioned is known not only for the love of his profession but also for his deep passion for it—which is certainly helping him to conquer the woes of the aging process and live on as a victor. His living till 100 certainly has a meaning. (2) [(2) '75 years of courtship looks set to end', *Hindustan Times, Kolkata,* 11 February 2011, p. 1]

In *The Gita, Krishna* clearly states that *ego* and *desire* are what lead to the end of one's mortal life. If one frees himself from the sense of 'I' and sees himself as a part of the supreme energy, considers others too as a part of the same omnipotent energy, and sincerely takes it up as a mission to add some value to that energy ocean, in a very small way though, he can strongly dispense with the need of bodily death at least for some time.

LONGEVITY: GENE-INFLUENCED OR LIFESTYLE-RELATED

However, the basic question still remains unanswered; and, that is, *longevity:* is it gene-influenced or lifestyle-related? Here, in this volume, we are laying stress on the *lifestyle management* principle even though some research study has led to the discovery of the *longevity genes.*

Professor Nir Barzilai, director of the Institute of Ageing at the Albert Einstein College of Medicine in New York has studied 500 Jewish people in the age group of 95 to 112 to arrive at the conclusion that one could go on to live for 100 years despite following a poor diet and even smoking, only if their genes were programmed for longevity. These genes insulated them from the effects of adverse environmental factors. (3) [(3) "Magic pill to make you live to 100", *Hindustan Times, Kolkata,* 12 May 2010, p. 13.]

There is another set of findings, published in the US journal *Proceedings of the National Academy of Sciences,* based on the analysis of biological samples of more than 8000 people in Hawaii. The study screened 213 of the long-lived participants' *DNA* and 402 of the average-lived focusing on five genes in the insulin pathway. (4) [(4) "Longevity gene discovered", *The Statesman, Kolkata,* 2 September 2008].

Nobel Laureate biologist Gunter Blobel had once shared his own perception about the truth of the concept of *aging* when he said: "The cell arose three and a half billion years ago. So as we sit here, we are really three-point-five billion years old! So for practical purposes, we can really speak of eternal life! And the Resurrection!"(5) [(5) In: Weiner, Jonathan, *His Brother's Keeper,* New York: ECCO (An Imprint of Harper Collins Publishers), 2004, First Edition, p. 327]

The Role of Genes in Aging and Longevity

To provide a simple overview of the role of genes in aging and longevity, one can say that the *DNA* of a person comprises four types of *base proteins* located at different parts of *chromosomes*. These are represented by four letters: *A (adenine)*; *C (cytosine)*; *G (guanine)* and *T (thymine)*. (6) [(6) Ridley, Matt, *Genome: The autobiography of a species in 23 chapters*, London: Fourth Estate, 1999, p.7].

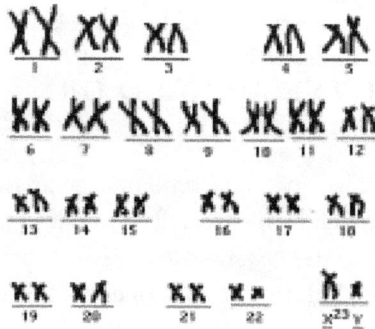

Fig. 7:   Chromosomes

Chromosomes are thread-like bodies into which the 'cell nucleus' divides during the cell division process *mitosis* and which split longitudinally in that process. The *chromosomes* carry hereditary factors (*genes*), the number being constant for each species—in man, 46 in each cell, except in the mature ovum and sperm where the number is halved as a result of reduction division. A set of 23 *chromosomes* is inherited from each parent.

The location of the *base proteins* is responsible for different traits in humans. The study cited above (4) calculated how the *DNA* bases found at three locations of each *gene* were correlated with health criteria including chronic diseases, disability and insulin levels.

People in the higher age group have the *base protein 'thymine'* substituted by *'guanine'* at a particular location of the chromosome. It was found that those having *guanine* in one *chromosome* were twice likely to reach between 98 to 106 years and those having on both *chromosomes* had thrice the chance of reaching that age group.

That was a top level scientist's insight. On the other hand, get another view from a recent media report which said: "Imagine living to a healthy 125 years. Well, your imagination might someday turn into reality, thanks to scientists who have made a genetic breakthrough that they claim can prolong human life and remove cancer threat. A team at the

Spanish National Cancer Research Centre in Madrid has based its conclusion on tests on rodents which made them live nearly 45% longer and also left them free from tumours. According to the scientists, if the experiments on mice can be replicated in people, human lifespan could also be extended." (7) [(7) 'Genetic study may prolong human life', *The Economic Times, Kolkata,* 1 September 2008, p. 18].

FAMOUS SEPTUA– AND OCTOGENARIANS STILL GOING STRONG

The US magazine *Businessweek* had compiled a list of world's top 50 septuagenarians in 2008. It included names like: Warren Buffett (78), the wizard investor; Rupert Murdoch (78), the media magnate; Hugh Hefner (82), *Playboy*'s editor-in-chief; George Soros (79), the billionaire investor; Alan Greenspan (80), former US Federal Reserve chairman; and Run Run Shaw (100 years), the Chinese TV tycoon. American jazz maestro Dave Brubeck, who has entered into his 90's decade, is still thinking of starring in Clint Eastwood's latest film. Pope Benedict XVI, who is 83 presently, has not shed his international tours and public appearances and broadcasts which are very much parts of his Pontiff role. Queen Elizabeth, the British queen, currently 84, has become a great grandmother for the first time when the Canadian wife Autumn of her grandson Peter Phillips has given birth to a baby girl.

Among the Indian ripe old business persons still going strong in 2008, those enlisted by *Businessweek* were: Basant Kumar Birla, the 87–year old head of the B K Birla group; Keshub Mahindra, the 84–year old chairman of the Mahindra and Mahindra group; Captain Krishnan Nair, the 89-year old Hotel Lila Venture chairman; and the 77–year old DLF group chairman K P Singh.

Businessweek had commented that 60 years was the new 40 and 80 years was the new 60.

All these Indian septua- and octogenarian business tycoons have their cutting edges. Mr B K Birla still maintains his 9–to–5 office routine and is still very much in at the helm of several companies which he runs from his base at Kolkata although plans for handing over the reins to his successors are in the final stages of formulation. Despite Mr Keshub Mahindra having opted out of day-to-day management of the Mahindra and Mahindra Group of companies long ago by delegating the task to his nephew Anand Mahindra; the latter refers to him as the hidden force and a competitive advantage for the multi-divisional organisation.

Captain Krishnan CPK Nair turned an hotelier and started the *Leela* group of hotels by setting up The Leela Kempinski in Mumbai at the age of 65 years after a successful army career. He oversees his business although the daily operations are managed by his son Vivek. Mr K P Singh of DLF transformed a New Delhi suburb into a call centre hub when he was close to 60 years of age. (8) (9) [(8) "70 & still going strong! Four India Inc Bosses Feature with 'Playboy' Editor", *The Economic Times, Kolkata*, 1 September 2008, p.6; (9) "Mahindra, BK Birla among world's top 50 septuagenarians", *Hindustan Times, Kolkata*, 1 September 2008, p.11].

Most of us in this part of the world think *Bata*—a household name for us even in the interiors of our small towns, as an Indian shoe company. In fact, it is originally a Czech entity, having been founded in 1894 in the town of Zlin by Tomas Bata, ninth generation descendent of a family of cobblers and shoemakers, and the father of Thomas Bata, who died in Toronto, Canada on 2nd September 2008 at the age of 94. It was Thomas who took over the company after his father's death at the age of 18. From Nazi-ruled Europe he arrived in undivided India in the mid-1930s, travelling from Karachi to Calcutta where he set up a big shoe-making base. Thomas, died at a ripe 'old old' age as he remained most active all through to oversee, from the *Bata* headquarters at Toronto, his international operations delegated to professional employees. (10) (11) [(10) Rajghatta, Chidanand, "Thomas Bata leaves behind indelible footprint in India", *The Times of India, Kolkata*, 3 September 2008, p. 15; (11) "Bata shoe mogul dead", *The Statesman, Kolkata*, 3 September 2008, p. 2].

If you move out of the Indian business world and get into the world of Indian art, culture, literature and politics, you'll meet, amongst several others, the 93-year old painter M.F. Hussain (who passed away in June 2011) and his friend and contemporary artist Syed Haider Raza (whose seminal work 'Saurashtra' sold for a staggering Rs. 16.42 crore at a Christie's auction on June 10, 2010), the writer and former editor Khushwant Singh who is 96 in body and half that age in mind, the respectively 92-year and 90-year old two former Chief Ministers of West Bengal, Siddhartha Shankar Ray and Jyoti Basu both of whom left this world recently, the thespians Dev Anand and Dilip Kumar, the music artistes Manna Dey, Lata Mangeshkar and Asha Bhonsle, sitar maestro Pandit Ravi Shankar, muscle-man Manohar Aich and the former President of India Dr APJ Abdul Kalam. Indian intellectuals and celebrities who died after crossing the 100-year threshold in recent years included Nirad Chandra Chaudhuri, Lila Majumder and Prabhu Dayal Himmatsingka and who had just missed their centenaries by only a few years were Swami Ranganathananda, Swami Bhuteshananda, Annada Shankar Ray, Professor Hiren Mukherjee and Paritosh Sen.

LIFE SPAN: PAST, PRESENT AND FUTURE

A recent discovery in Spain of ancient bones, including a prehistoric pelvis, claims that their owner lived around 500,000 years ago. Investigations reveal that these fossils belonged to the world's first known elderly human with clear signs of aging and impairment. We have no idea about the exact age of this ancient man. (12) [(12) "First disabled, elderly man?" *The Times of India, Kolkata,* 13 October 2010, p. 15.]

In general, from pre-historic times to the dawn of the Industrial Revolution, the average life span remained below 45; it went up to around 47 in 1900. Only 10 per cent of the general population used to make it to 65; only 4 per cent used to be more than that. In 1990, more than 12 per cent of the population was over 65. Today 80 per cent of the population lives at least that long. Looking into the future, 20 per cent of the population will be over 65 by the year 2020. A UN study says that over two billion people—or about 22 % of the world's population will be over 60 years of age by 2050. (13) [(13) Singhal, Rajrishi, "Ageism at workplace", *The Economic Times, Kolkata,* 2 July 2007, p. 5.]

MORTALITY RISK

According to Shoven, director of the Institute for Economic Policy Research at Stanford University, our concept of 'old' has itself become old-fashioned. He recommends using modern mortality risk measure-ments—or the chance a person has of dying within the next year—to measure age. The higher the mortality risk, the 'older' a person is. Today's 65-year-old man can expect to live another 17 to 20 years and has the same mortality risk a 59-year-old man did in 1970 or a 56-year-old man did in 1940. (14) [(14) Shoven, John B. "New Age Thinking", *Foreign Policy*, January-February 2008, pp. 82-83].

THE 'YOUNG OLD': HOW ARE THEY DOING

Moreover, both intellectual performance and health have significantly improved among older adults over the last four to five decades, which is particularly true for those frequently labelled as the 'young old'; that is, those roughly between 65 and 80 years of age. (15) [(15) G. Manton, Kenneth and Xiliang Gu, "Changes in Physical and Mental Functions of Older People: Looking Back and Looking Ahead"; In: *New Dynamics in Old Age: Individual, Environmental and Social Perspectives*, Edited by: Hans-Werner Wahl, Clemens Tesch-Romer and Andreas Hoff; Amityville, New York: Baywood Publishing Co. Inc., 2007, pp 25-42].

Among the non-celebrities, we have the glaring example of 85-year-old Sunil Kumar Mondal (date of birth: 28 February, 1922) who happens to be the oldest research student at Indira Gandhi National Open University (IGNOU), New Delhi. His subject of study is Netaji Subhas Chandra Bose and his activities in the Northeast. (16) [(16) Thakur, Joydeep, "Defying age for Netaji quest", *HT Live Kolkata,* 24 January 2008].

AGE AT THE WORKPLACE

However, 70-year-olds running the show is not the norm at all amongst employees in the government sector and public and private business and industry. In advanced countries of the first and second worlds, 65 years happen to be the normal cut-off age in the private sector. The corresponding retirement age in India is 58 years; however, in many cases it has now been extended to 60—even 62 years. A recent news report says: "The association of Health Service Doctors' demand for creating new posts in medical colleges and timely promotion may actually make the state health department increase the retirement age of the non-teaching staff to 62 years." (17) [(17) Sengupta, Sulagna, "State health dept. mulls retirement age hike", *The Statesman Kolkata Supplement 'Kolkata Plus'*, 1 September 2008, p. I]. The retirement age for college and university professors and the IIT directors are respectively 65 and 70 years currently.

AGE DISTRIBUTION IN INDIAN POPULATION

At the time of writing, every 12th Indian is an elderly person. 8 million Indians are over 80 years, 29 million over 70 and 77 million above 60. Experts predict that the proportion of people above 60 years in the Indian population is expected to rise from 7.4 percent in 2008 to 12.5 percent by 2025. 33.1 percent of the Indian elderly live without their spouses and only 30 percent are financially independent. (18) [(18) "Greying with grace", *Hindustan Times, Kolkata,* 6 January 2008, p. 4].

THREE WAYS OF 'AGE' CALCULATION

Your interpretation of how you are aging and what you think your current 'age' is, are critical to what happens to you over the next one or two decades. People don't grow old; when they stop growing, they become old. And, the visible signs of stoppage of natural healthy growth are: wrinkles, thinning body hair, sagging muscles and flagging libido.

Shankara, the greatest of Indian sages, had said: "People grow old and die because they see others grow old and die".

Most interestingly, there are three different ways of looking at your 'age':

Chronological Age (CA): Your calendar age.

Biological Age (BA): Your 'health' and 'fitness' status. You may be of 60 years of age by the calendar, but 'health & fitness'-wise you present the picture of a 75-year old. You have high blood pressure—your heart is behaving erratically—your lungs are not always co-operating—your digestive system frequently breaks down.

Psychological Age (PA): You may be 60 chronologically but you are very young at heart—almost equivalent to a teenager—you're playful, fun-and-game loving, humorous and jovial.

Amongst these three ways of looking at your 'age', only the first one, that is, *chronological age*, is fixed by the almanac and thus unchangeable; although it is the most unreliable one. The reason is very simple. Your calendar age may be 65 years, but the age of your body and mind may not be in tune; it may be equivalent to 75 years as physically you have an ill health and affected fitness and psychologically also you allow all kinds of negative thoughts and worries to overpower your mind.

In the age range of 20 to 25 years, all young men and women attain a certain *anatomical/physiological standard* barring those afflicted by some disease or deformity. However, as the young man or woman advances in age and crosses the boundary of youth at around 35–36 years, the biological and psychological ages start varying according to the body- and mind-styles followed by them.

Amongst the last two—the biological and psychological ages, the former moves slowly, when normal health and fitness are maintained, as most critical organs can function satisfactorily at only around 30 per cent of their respective peak capacities. Thus the impact of aging on your biology is slow. But the influence of social and psychological factors, your lifestyle and how often you suffer from stress, what kind of sensitivity and tolerance limits you have, determine how your standard biological conditions would tend to get affected.

Calorie restriction, regular physical fitness activities, periods of relaxation, rest and sound sleep can help you maintain your *biological standards* such as properties of your blood (including blood pressure and blood sugar level), heart rate, quality of breathing and respiratory rate, body weight, joint mobility, and physical stamina. If you can adopt a more active (at the same time, balanced in every respect) lifestyle compared to what is generally observed in the case of senior citizens (who reduce their physical activities to enter more and more into the 'comfort zone' by being sedentary, entertaining themselves through TV-watching, radio/music listening and net-surfing rather than playing with grandchildren or pets), you can improve your life expectancy by ten years, on an average.

If you can enjoy, keep your mind cheerful (instead of becoming too finicky, irritable and worrying too much unnecessarily) and be prepared to face all the realities of life (such as some illness or bereavement in the family, laggardness or failure of your kith and kin) and keep your desires under control, your psychological well-being will co-operate with you and help you to reverse the aging process.

This generates an interesting exercise for you. Can you stop reading the chapter for a while and analyse your *CA, BA* and *PA* with a cool, undisturbed mind and note your assessment down on today's date. Before we close the book, we'll give you tips as to how to use the data.

WHAT CONTROLS THE LONGEVITY AND AGING PROCESS: THE *INSULIN* EFFECT

Different creatures have different life spans. Consider a mouse, a dog, a canary, a parrot and a bat. The mouse lives for two years whereas a healthy dog's life is limited to twelve to fourteen years. The bat can live up to fifty years and the canary lives for about fifteen or so years—a parrot up to twenty or twenty-two. They are all small animals and warm-blooded. And, they're not that different really in such a fundamental way from each other. A fairly small number of genes may control the creatures' differing life spans.

Researches in world-class laboratories have already scientifically proven that the aging process and longevity can be controlled. There are two observations available to us.

According to the first one, longevity and the aging process has a close link with the *insulin*-regulating/signalling neural pathways which spur the breakdown of *sugar*. Thus, one way to prolong life is to decrease sensitivity to *insulin* at the cellular level. *Insulin* comes in the way of prolonged lifespan. Too much *insulin*—a hormone that tells our cells to use sugar from the bloodstream, thus helping us to avoid metabolic complications that lead to diseases such as *diabetes*—in the brain may not be a good sign. The signalling pathway of *insulin* governs growth and metabolic processes in cells throughout the body.

Therefore, most would find it difficult to accept the idea that *insulin* can reduce lifespan.

As a matter of fact, a *low-tech* life extension strategy would be to adopt the habit of starvation diet. Total starvation diet being an impossibility, one could safely go for *calorie restriction (CR)*, as has already been pointed out and discussed, which can be reckoned as the only proven strategy for life extension other than *genetic engineering*. A professor emeritus of pathology at the University of California, Los Angeles, and a member of the 1991-93 *Biosphere2* experiment, Ray Walford undertook a much publicized experiment on himself. For years, he ate a nutrient-rich diet of just 1,600 Calories a day in the hope of extending his life. He died in 2004, but hundreds of Walford disciples are restricting themselves to as far as 1,500 Calories a day in hopes of living longer.(19) [(19) Hall, Stephen S., "Kenyon's Ageless Quest", *Span*, May-June 2005, p. 23-27].

As a matter of fact, *calorie restriction (CR)* without malnutrition is supposed to be very effective in improving health and life span. It would also reduce concentrations of *free radicals* (an atom or group of atoms with one or more unpaired electrons). These highly reactive molecules degrade biological compounds present in cells.

The *gene* responsible for *insulin* signalling is called *Irs2*. When both the copies of this gene were knocked off in the brain but retained in cells in other organs, it led to an increase in the lifespan. Diet, physical activity, and lower weight keep one's peripheral tissues sensitive to *insulin*. This reduces the amount and duration of *insulin* secretion required to keep glucose under control when one eats. This way, the brain is exposed to less *insulin*. And, since *insulin* turns on *Irs2*, the lower the *insulin*, the lower would be the *Irs2* activity. The body is programmed to metabolise, say, one tonne of sugar over a lifetime. In how much time one does it is entirely up to that person. (20) [(20) Jayan, T.V. "Slowing Down Life's Clock", *The Telegraph, Kolkata*, 6 August 2007, p. 9].

Although it is scientifically possible in principle, implementation in practice is still out of bounds and there are most likely to be some unwelcome side-effects including stunted growth and reproductive malfunction.

FRAILTY

One of the persistent mysteries of aging is why would one person remain hale and hearty while another, who had seemed just as healthy, start to weaken and slow down, sometimes as early as his 70s? The question is why some age well and others do not often heading along a path that ends up in a medical condition known as *frailty*. *Frailty* involves exhaustion, weakness, weight loss, and a loss of muscle mass and strength. In many cases, a single factor—undetected cardio-vascular disease—is often a major reason people become *frail*.

YOU'RE ONLY AS OLD AS YOU THINK YOU ARE

The second finding is most interesting and important—you're only as old as you think you are. Studies now show that seeing or hearing about what it is like to be old can make people feel and become old. (21) [(21) "You can be as old as you think you are", *Hindustan Times, Kolkata*, 7 October 2006, p. 14]

HANDIEST: CALORIE RESTRICTION (CR)

The handiest practical way of aging control and longevity increase is *dietary restriction*. If you give an animal 70 percent of its normal intake, it will live 20 to 30 percent longer. For us, human beings, that adds up to an extra 15 to 20 years of life. A restricted diet is not the same as near starvation and must consist of a balanced mix of nutrients to be effective, as has been discussed elsewhere in this volume.

The scientific background of this strategy is worth discussing. *Mitochondria* are little energy packs inside our cells. These are very important for staying healthy and youthful and, as we age, we lose them and they get less efficient. There is a family of *enzymes*, '*sirtuins*' controlled by *genes* called SIRT1, SIRT2, SIRT3, and SIRT4. The *enzymes* controlled by these *genes* help preserve the *mitochondria*, the little organs inside the cells that provide their energy. SIRT3 and SIRT4 make proteins that go into *mitochondria*. For a cell, even if the rest of it is destroyed—the nucleus and the other parts, it can still function if the *mitochondria* are alive. **Fasting** raises the levels of another *protein* called

NAD. This, in turn, activates SIRT3 and SIRT4 in the *mitochondria* of the cell and these help keep the *mitochondria* youthful.

THE SUPERGENE

We are told that there is a *supergene* that helps people to live to age 90 and beyond. It may also ward off *Alzheimer's*. People with the *supergene* have a much higher chance of living to the century mark without developing *dementia*—the confused thinking and memory loss that so often plagues the oldest of the old. The *supergene* is called *CETPVV*. It helps people age slowly and resists life-shortening ailments such as heart disease. (22) [(22) Fackelmann, Kathleen, "Gene tied to long life wards off Alzheimer's: Study", *Hindustan Times, Kolkata,* 27 December 2006, p. 14].

APPLICATION TIPS

- Despite the fact that the *genetic factor* has the primary role to play, you can certainly increase your lifespan to a reasonable extent by maintaining a well-balanced lifestyle, with a thrust on *Calorie Restriction (CR)*.

- Apart from the 'balanced lifestyle' strategy, you can boost your longevity by having a meaningful yet unselfish purpose to live longer—to make some contribution to the society. Now, it is your turn to give back something to your society for what all it has done for you in your life so far by throwing up opportunities which you have availed (you could not have come up in life where you're today unless your society had offered you opportunities) instead of expecting any 'Return on Investment (ROI)'.

Chapter 8

Impact of Aging on the Powers of Your Body

"The secret is to view life as a painting you're creating. Then, you'll never grow old because you think with fresh eyes and a young heart."
—**Dev Anand, 87-year-old legendary actor**
(In: Ahmed, Afsana, "Forever Young",
TimesLife! A Sunday Times of India supplement, 9 January 2011, p. 3)

BODY IMAGE OBSESSION

Some aged women and, in a few cases, aged men also are obsessed with their body image. Many of them are concerned about how they look and what others are thinking about their appearance—are they being considered as beautiful and handsome or ugly.

One aspect they attach importance to is symmetry—particularly related to face, as symmetry makes faces more attractive. Another thing they look for is averageness—do they represent familiar looks to others or somewhat different—a deviation, which may not be acceptable so easily.

A face can convey a person's health too. If the skin texture and colour appear fresh, bright and reddish (representing good blood circulation), then it is a sign of good health; whereas if it is dull and yellowish, then it stands for something different—may be some liver problem or the result of too much of plant-based diet.

Fig. 8: A Couple: Aging but Looking Happy

It is the people who are obsessed with their body image that go for artificial beauty boosters and devote a lot of time to dressing before going out anywhere. They also try to dress up well to greet visitors at their homes.

There are three categories of people in this group. The first category people attach importance only to outside appearance, outfits and accessories. The second category people give priority to health and fitness. They are conscious about their diet—in quantity and quality and take regular exercises or go for walking or jogging or participate in some games or sports on a regular basis. Some of them are so obsessed on this front that when some essential vitamins are not available in their natural form from food, they go for vitamin supplements. In the second category, there are a few who are not indifferent about clothes and other outfits but as they cannot afford to take care of that aspect, have to remain happy only with good health and fitness. There are still others who, despite their affordability, do not attach much value to clothes and accessories; their only thrust is on the physical body—its shape, size and quality. The third category of people attaches importance to both—the artificial and the natural.

We will talk here about the physical body powers.

HOW AGING AFFECTS YOUR BODY POWERS

There are quite a few powers of your body that get affected as you advance on age. The major ones are discussed here.

Strength: This health and fitness factor is the first to be affected by the aging process after retirement especially if you reduce your physical activities. By the age of 65, the level of strength can be less than 70 per cent of what it was at the age of 30.

Endurance: This health and fitness factor is represented by the capacity to utilise oxygen, measured as "VO_2 max", can decline as much as by 20 percent with the aging process. In order to maintain an endurance level of even 80 per cent, you will have to pursue *aerobic* exercises, brisk walking, stair climbing and stationary jogging activities on a regular basis.

Flexibility: This is also a very vital health and fitness factor. The connective tissues, tendons and ligaments thicken during normal growth; so flexibility could be considered to start declining from birth. With appropriate stretching, these stiffening effects can be greatly minimised and unlike strength, speed and endurance, improvement in flexibility can be continued well into old age. On the other hand, if not cultured or trained, loss of flexibility can be one of the most dramatic effects of aging.

Capacity for Tissue Repair. This is connected with your health and fitness. In older men and women, the body tissues are less elastic and resilient. They are thus more vulnerable to injury, and injuries take much longer to heal.

Body Fat. As regards this critical health and factor, you ought to know that accumulation of *body fat* is not directly proportionate with age. The common increase in body fat with age is simply due to lack of diet adjustment, decrease in levels of physical activity and in rates of *body metabolism.* As *body metabolism* becomes less efficient after retirement due to aging and various decelerating factors, less energy is available for the metabolic process. Therefore, dietary intake has to be controlled, regular brisk walking and stretching and bending exercises and endurance activities are to be performed.

Oxygen Consumption. Aged people use oxygen less efficiently when they exercise. They use about a fifth more oxygen than young people while walking or exercising. As hearts slow with age, they deliver less blood and oxygen to the body. However, the situation can be reversed with exercise.

AGE-ACCELERATING AND DECELERATING FACTORS

The *most common age-accelerating negative factors* include:

Most Damaging and Harmful

Depression; suppression of negative emotions (like anger, unhappiness, anxiety and fear); lack of regular routine (a systematic way of structuring time); lack of meaningful occupation (under-load: the impact of sitting idle).

Damaging and Harmful

Inability to express emotions (like love, affection, need for care etc.); loneliness (including a self-created state despite being in the midst of other family members); inability to adjust with the impact of retirement; excessive worrying habit (regarding matters like financial burden, unsettled children etc.); frequent remembrance of sacrifices made in the past or an unsuccessful career; low self-esteem (due to a feeling of loss of importance).

The West and the East: The Twain Meet

In this context, there is a most relevant and recent research study to be quoted. This "research is the largest to date to investigate how '*ikigai*', or 'joy and a sense of well-being from being alive', affects mortality risk, and only the second to examine death from specific causes, according to Toshimasa Sone and colleagues from the Tohoku University Graduate School of Medicine in Sendai, Japan." (1) [(1) "Lack of joy in life ups early death risk", *The Times of India, Kolkata,* 3 September 2008, p.17].

The investigators looked at nearly 44,000 men and women 40 to 80 years of age, living in the Ohsaki region of Japan. All of them were followed up to a period of seven years, during which time 3,048 died. All were asked, "Do you have *ikigai* in your life?" In answer, 59 per cent said 'yes', 36.4 per cent said they weren't sure, and 4.6 per cent said 'no'. The researchers observed that people with no sense of *ikigai* were 50 per cent more likely to die from any cause during follow-up compared to those who did have a sense that life was worth living even after retirement. They had a 60 per cent greater risk of death from cardiovascular disease, most commonly *stroke*, and were 90 per cent more likely to die of 'external' causes. Of the 186 deaths due to external causes among study participants, 90 were suicides.

In another study by the Dutch professors of Rotterdam's Erasmus University, released in August 2008 by Ruut Veenhoven (cited in the same press report as quoted above), observed that *happiness* could increase a person's life span by 7.5 to 9 years. The study revealed that the effects of *happiness* on longevity were "comparable to that of smoking or not".

The *most common age-decelerating positive factors* include:

Most Rejuvenating

Happy married life and partnership; feeling of personal happiness; well-structured daily schedule; a history of successful career; physically active life; good rest and sound sleep.

Rejuvenating

Ability to express, enjoy and laugh freely; satisfactory sex life; ability to make and keep close friends; control over own time and personal life; satisfying hobbies and pastime; economic balance leading to feeling of financial security; living in the present.

APPLICATION TIPS

- Going for regular physical activities including exercises and brisk walking is recommended to slow down the degeneration of the powers of the body which tend to deteriorate with age.

- Try to ensure that you do not have any age-accelerating negative factors affecting your body and its powers—especially health and fitness. Instead, you try to bring into your life the positive impact of the age-decelerating factors.

Chapter 9

Health and Fitness in Old Age

"The spirit indeed is willing but the flesh is weak".
—**The Bible (Mathew: 26, 41)**

COMMON OLD AGE PHYSICAL DISORDERS

There are several lifestyle-related factors which lead to speedy depreciation of your body-brain system when you get old if you're not taking its proper care. These generally include: consumption of junk food; lack of proper balanced nutrition; side effects of pharmaceutical drugs which you have been taking from your mid-forties; smoking; alcohol abuse; dehydration; depression; sexual frigidity; and inactivity.

The World Health Organisation (WHO) estimates that about 75 per cent of deaths in people over the age of 65 in industrialised countries are from heart disease, cancer and cerebro-vascular disease (such as stroke). Another major cause of disability and, sometimes death too, is osteo-porosis and associated bone fractures, which affects many women due to post-menopausal bone loss.

Fatigue

Fatigue is a common problem experienced by many in old age, particularly after retirement. For anxiety-prone serious people who get tensed while carrying out duties and responsibilities, it may be due to many months, weeks and days of working very hard before retirement, leading to a bottled-up weariness which could not be released while in active service. Or, it could just be a psychological tiredness due to a sudden change from a most active to a totally inactive life, as you had not done any retirement planning well in advance. Otherwise, it could be due to a variety of reasons like: chronic infection, heart problem, onset of cancer or respiratory disorders, affected bone and joints due to disuse, insomnia, frequent irritability and loss of temper, anxiety, repression of emotions, or withdrawal symptom on abruptly giving up some addictive habits. Planned diet, planned physical fitness activities, planned sound sleep, periodic deep breathing and meditation, and pursuit of enjoyable activities are expected to provide relief.

Gastro-Intestinal Disorders

The nature of your mind, whether strong or weak, practical or sentimental, hard or soft, can get reflected in the condition of your *digestive system*. Lack of mental strength and confidence to cope with the unexpected events of unplanned retirement and old age, over-sentimentality and helplessness will show up in the form of mild *gastro-intestinal* disorders such as indigestion, acidity, gas, wind, gastritis, flatulence, loss of appetite, constipation and loose motion. Under extreme conditions, you may even develop ulcers and various types of colitis (or inflamed colon). Now-a-days, many retirees do suffer from most stressful *Irritable Bowels Syndrome (IBS)* which involves lower abdominal pain with alternating constipation and diarrhoea. Bland diets containing milk and antacids will give you temporary respite from the sufferings, but the symptoms will never disappear altogether; instead those will appear and reappear again and again.

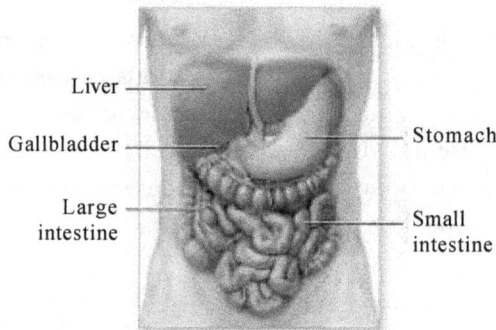

Fig. 9: The Digestive System

Planned diet, planned physical fitness activities, planned sound sleep, planned time and stress management measures would certainly go a long way to give you a better lasting relief from these problems.

'Hypertension' or High Blood Pressure

It is a very common problem faced by the elderly as the *Blood Pressure (BP)* increases with age. *BP*, simply speaking, is the pressure applied by the blood to the blood vessels or blood carrying pipelines as it circulates through them. *BP* is recorded by *sphygmomanometer*, in mm of mercury using the blood pressure cuff that inflates around the upper arm to create the pressure. *Systolic pressure* is the pressure recorded when the heart is 'contracting' (normal range: 120 to 140 mm) and *diastolic pressure* is the same when the heart is 'relaxing' (normal range: 70 to 90 mm). Whenever

BP exceeds 140/90, the condition is called *hypertension*. It is simple to realise that *high BP* causes damage to the vital organs since it represents an abnormal condition. If not timely tackled, it may lead to heart failure, stroke, or kidney failure.

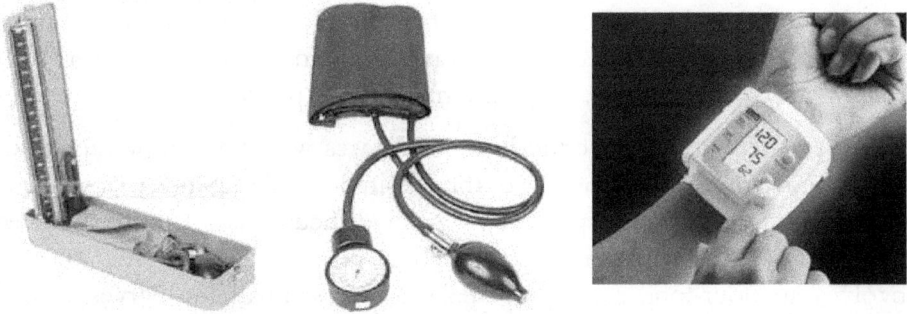

Fig. 10: Different Types of Blood Pressure Measuring Instruments

High BP, or hypertension, seems to result from excessive constriction of the smallest blood vessels, the heart then having to work harder to force blood around the system. In response to these extra demands, it becomes enlarged, and later may fail completely. Similarly, the kidneys are unable to cope with the increased pressure, and as they fail, may make the hypertension worse. With increasing age, the walls of arteries lose their resilience, and if the blood pressure is sufficiently high, arteries supplying the brain may rupture, causing a cerebral stroke, with bleeding and damage which can be followed by paralysis of parts of the body or death.

A few major attributable factors include: genetic propensity (a history of *hypertension* in the family), chronic stress, high intake of salt, hormonal imbalance, frequent emotional outbursts (anxiety, fear, anger, depression) and mood swings leading to chemical changes in the brain. Therefore, to keep *BP* under control, you have to take stress management measures (like regular physical fitness and deep breathing exercises, meditation practice, laughter-pet-or-music therapy), reduce your salt consumption and make it a point to stay with positive feelings such as love, compassion, peace, courage, confidence, motivation, faith and hope, living in the present and not in the unhappy past or the uncertain future.

Some fresh finding revealed by a recent research conducted at the College of Nursing at Seattle University has been most heartening for senior citizens suffering from high *BP* problems. The study has shown that the soothing sound of ocean waves along with a calming voice guiding to relax can significantly lower blood pressure in elderly people. In the experiment, twenty older adults were asked to listen to a 12-minute audio-guided relaxation-training program (ATP) with background sounds of ocean waves and a calming voice for three times a week for four months. It showed blood pressure to drop from 141/73 to 132/70 mm of mercury (mmHg). (1) [(1) "Ocean waves, calming voice can lower BP", *The Times of India, Kolkata,* 19 September 2008, p. 19].

However, there are a few critical high BP cases where all known methods of BP control do not produce the desired results. Studies are being conducted currently to explore how such difficult cases can be handled and there is an invasive therapy which is being tried out. This therapy involves an hour-long surgery to make a few sympathetic nerves related to the raising of blood pressure dysfunctional and the surgeons claim that they are observing a post-surgery 20% reduction in BP.

Heart Disease and Heart Attacks

Our heart beats, tirelessly, about 75 times each minute. At times of stress it can speed up enormously, to as much as 250 beats per minute, but then would quickly return to its normal rate. The sole purpose of the heart is to circulate blood around the body, against the resistance of the smallest blood vessels.

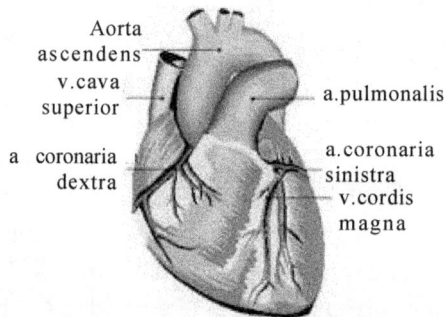

Fig. 11: The Human Heart

Coronary Artery Disease (CAD), which is a common 'heart disease', involves hardening of the coronary arteries—the blood vessels that carry not only blood but oxygen to the heart. When these blood vessels become blocked by hardened deposits of plaque, the heart muscle is deprived of oxygen, and it results in the death of heart muscle leading to 'heart attack'.

The common risk factors include: genetic propensity, obesity, high blood pressure, psychological stress (typical in case of *Type A* personality indicating dominant features like aggressiveness, impatience, tension-proneness, hard-driving nature, inability to relax, and always being in a hurry), high levels of cholesterol (a fatty chemical or lipid) in the blood (directly related to cholesterol-rich diet such as eggs and red meat), smoking, lack of any physical exercise habit, uncontrolled diabetes, and old age.

Most of these risk factors are under your control and you can prevent such disease possibilities provided you have the will to adopt and follow a plain, simple, controlled lifestyle. Regularly eating vegetables from the 'broccoli' family, namely, cabbage, Brussels sprouts, cauliflower and lettuce, which contain a compound called *sulforaphane*, boosts the production of enzymes which protect our blood vessels from the damage caused by high blood sugar. Some British studies claim that adding some amount of wholegrain food like porridge to the daily diet can slash rates of heart disease by 15% and strokes by 25%. It can also cut down high blood pressure. (2) [(2) "Eat porridge to protect heart", *The Times of India, Kolkata,* 11 December 2010, p.16.]

So many cardiac patients above 80 years of age, now-a-days, want to maintain a normal lifestyle. Cardiac procedures like *angioplasty* offer the best treatment option in such cases. The risks are no doubt high, but recent success of such procedures has made them acceptable as alternative treatment strategies. However, one has to remember that *stent angioplasty* of coronary arteries for patients above 80 years of age have more acute cardiac and non-cardiac complications like renal failure, bleeding and in-hospital mortality, especially for any one above 90 years.

Stroke

Hardening and deterioration in the natural properties of blood vessels that causes heart attacks also causes *strokes* but, in this case, the brain gets affected instead of heart. *Stroke* takes place when one of the blood vessels carrying the supply of blood to the brain is blocked or ruptured. A poor diet and lack of exercise contribute to the chances of suffering a stroke.

Mild *strokes* may result in muscle weakness, blurred vision, unclear speech, and other sensory defects. Severe *strokes* can lead to paralysis or

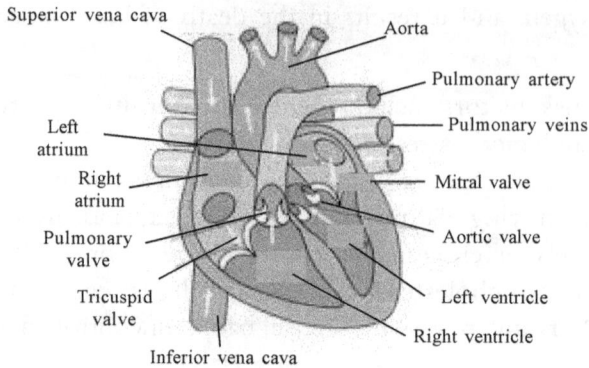

Fig. 12: The Inside of the Human Heart

death. The preventive measures discussed for heart disease are equally applicable in the case of *strokes* too. Elderly people who ate baked or broiled fish high in *Omega-3* fatty acids are likely to be more susceptible to *strokes* due to "silent" brain lesions according to a Finnish research study. (3) [(3) "Fatty fish may prevent memory loss" *The Times of India, Kolkata,* 7 August 2008, p. 17]. *Omega-3* fatty acids, which are good for the brain and the primary source of which are bony and sea fishes, would tend to make a positive contribution provided the fish is boiled or lightly cooked and not baked or broiled.

Lung Diseases

At rest, we breathe in about half a litre of air with each breath, and exhale the same quantity but containing less oxygen and more carbon dioxide than what we had inhaled. The lungs bring the inhaled air into near contact with blood, allowing the red blood cells to take in oxygen. At the same time, carbon dioxide, a waste product, passes out of the blood and is exhaled.

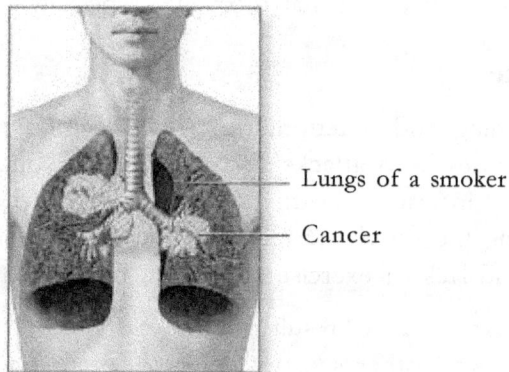

Fig. 13: The Lungs of a Smoker Afflicted by Cancer

Air enters the lungs through the nose and mouth, and passes down the trachea, an armoured flexible tube. This then subdivides into bronchi (the site of bronchitis) and smaller bronchioles, terminating in tiny bladders called alveoli. The alveoli are well supplied with blood vessels, and oxygen and carbon dioxide pass freely through their walls.

We inhale and exhale by two mechanisms. In the first mechanism, the rib cage can be expanded by muscles attached to the ribs and spine. This reduces the pressure in the lungs, causing air to enter. As the muscles relax, the rib cage contracts, forcing air out.

In the second mechanism, known as diaphragmic breathing, contraction of the diaphragm (which is a sheet of muscle separating the lungs and heart from the organs in the abdomen) leads to an increase in the volume of the rib cage, causing inhalation, followed by exhalation as it relaxes.

The delicate tissues lining the lungs are particularly prone to infection, and also to mechanical damage. The airways are lined with tiny beating hairs or cilia which cause a steady current of mucus to carry inhaled dust and other unwanted material out of the lungs and back to the throat, when it is periodically swallowed.

Cigarette smoke causes immediate damage to a person's lungs and their DNA even in small amounts, including from second-hand smoke. Smoking paralyses the cilia, and allows mucus and the tar from cigarettes to accumulate in the lungs, causing "smoker's cough". Prolonged contact with these substances can give rise to lung cancer. Other substances can also evade the lung's defences, such as coal dust, asbestos fibres, and several types of mineral dust, all capable of causing particular types of serious lung disease if inhaled over long periods.

A new study conducted by University of Exeter and Peninsula College of Medicine and Dentistry researchers has revealed that drinking beetroot juice can help the elderly and those suffering from heart and lung-related ailments engage in physical exercises. Beetroot juice can reduce the amount of oxygen required to perform even low-intensity exercises. In principle, this effect could help people do things they would not otherwise be able to do. When consumed, beetroot juice has two marked physiological effects. Firstly, it widens blood vessels, reducing blood pressure and allowing more blood flow. Secondly, it affects muscle tissue, reducing the amount of oxygen needed by muscles during physical activity. (3) [(3) "Say cheers to beetroot juice!" *Calcutta Times, a Supplement of The Times of India*, 1 January 2011, p. 7].

The Liver

Our heaviest organ, it weighs about one and a half kg., and is located in the upper abdomen, overlying the bulk of the intestines. Its primary function is as an energy store. Glucose, one of the main products of digestion, passes straight to the liver and is stored as glycogen until needed. When we undertake strenuous activity demanding more energy than normal and glucose is needed by the muscles, liver converts glycogen back to glucose, under the influence of a hormone produced by the pancreas.

The liver contains the gall bladder, which empties the bile (a greenish-yellowish fluid which helps prepare fats for digestion and is derived from red blood cells broken down by the liver) into the duodenum through the bile duct.

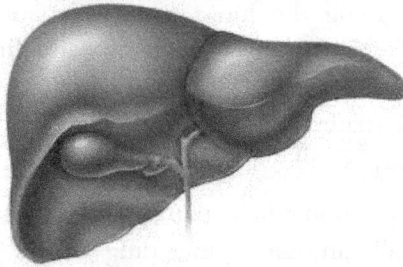

Fig. 14: The Liver

Liver also acts to remove from blood toxic substances, such as alcohol. Thus it becomes vulnerable to damage in case of drug overdoses or continuous abuse in alcoholism. It has remarkable powers of self-repair, but when severely damaged, jaundice results.

The Kidneys and the Bladder

The function of the kidneys is to maintain a stable external as well as internal aquatic environment for our cells (as they are bathed in plasma from the blood and even their contents are largely liquid). They achieve it by acting as biological filters in order to remove waste materials and to ensure that the proportions of the many chemicals in the blood remain constant.

Blood entering the kidneys passes through a network of small blood vessels, where many of its constituents diffuse through the walls of the vessels into kidney tubules. Here, most of the water is reabsorbed, together with the nutrients, leaving concentrated liquid waste, or urine.

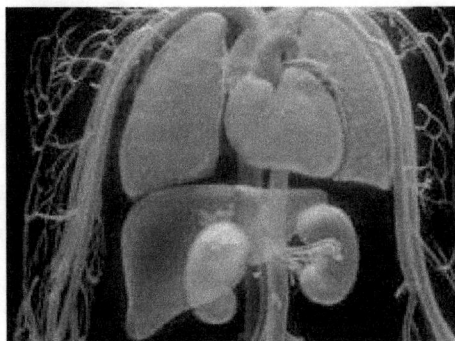

Fig. 15: The Kidneys

Urine passes from the kidneys to the bladder, via a pair of tubes called ureters. In the bladder, urine is stored until increasing pressure warns us that the accumulated liquid must be voided, when it is passed out along the urethra. In old age, our control to hold urine of a medium to large volume in the bladder for a reasonable period of time becomes weakened so an elderly person is compelled to pass urine more frequently than a younger or middle-aged person and with a moderate degree of weakness, seepage of urine occurs. It is a normal phenomenon in old age so there is nothing to worry that there may be some infection in the urinary system.

Gall Bladder

Gallstones are found in a seven to eight centimetre-long pear-shaped organ called the *gall bladder*, which is situated under the liver on the right side of the abdomen. It contains bile, an aid to digestion, secreted by the liver. It contracts and discharges the bile into the intestines periodically after food is eaten.

Stones are formed if the bile contains too much cholesterol (90 per cent of gallstones are cholesterol stones) or pigment (from the breakdown of red blood cells), or if the gall bladder does not empty properly. The propensity to form stones may be genetic. Women are more likely to develop stones because of the effect of the female hormones on the composition of the bile and the gall bladder. Stones are more likely with obesity, frequent fasting, rapid weight loss (crash diets), lack of physical activity, diabetes, alcohol abuse and certain medications. Most of these risk factors are preventable as they are the result of an unhealthy lifestyle. An ultrasound of the abdomen can usually detect gallstones. Endoscopic procedures can detect stones in the duct and remove them at the same time. All gallstones do not require treatment.

Erectile Dysfunction

Erectile dysfunction is a feature of normal aging in men, while urinary or bowel function doesn't necessarily decline with age. However, this disorder may not be a significant feature in men below 70 years of age.

There are a number of medicines developed for older men with erectile problems related to aging and blocked blood vessels in the penis. The term erectile dysfunction implies that these men have a problem in their penises, but in many cases, the problem is in their heads, in their sexual brain maps. The penis works fine when they use pornography or when they take the help of sexual imagery or resort to voyeurism.

The problem usually starts from the middle age as it happened to Sudhakar Rao whom we had met when he was just 47 years old. He had been married for twelve years yet his wife could not conceive. Both the husband and the wife had got them tested and nothing was wrong with the wife. Rao's sperm count was also normal; but he was suffering from erectile dysfunction. The root cause of the problem was in his mind.

Many middle-aged people—both men and women, develop tolerance to the sexual act as it has turned out to be a routine activity due to its regular avail. They need higher and higher levels of stimulation for satisfaction and experience withdrawal if they can't consummate the novel, non-routine addictive act like homosexuality or lesbianism or pornographic activities.

Thyroid Deficiency

An aging person may get affected by *thyroid deficiency (hypothyroidism)*, which is a state in which thyroid hormones (which regulate functions of many organs of the body) produced by the *thyroid gland* located in the lower part of the neck, are below normal levels.

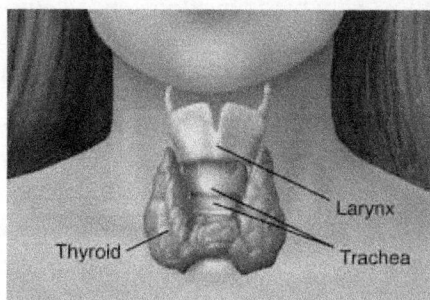

Fig. 16:   The Thyroid Gland

A common disorder, this mainly occurs in women.

It causes an abnormal decrease in metabolism, making its victims slow and dull, their hairs grey and skin wrinkled. There may also be weight gain, excessive lethargy, sleepiness and weakness, falling, coarseness or thinning of hair, dry skin, puffy face, and swelling in arms, hands, legs and feet, and hoarseness in voice. This untimely physical disposition disappears once normal levels of the missing hormone, *thyroxin* are supplied. Along with the characteristic symptoms, additional tests are required to confirm the diagnosis of *hypothyroidism*. However, an accurate indicator is an increased level of *TSH (thyroid stimulating hormone)*. Other tests like thyroid auto-antibodies and thyroid scan may be done if medically advised.

Cancer

It is a condition typically represented by an abnormal growth of cells in the body. These cells invade normal tissue and spread to other organs affecting their normal functions adversely. The main causes of *cancer* have been identified as: certain viruses, drug use, weak immune system, and poor nutrition.

Fig.17: Cancer (Symbolised)

A number of *carcinogens* or cancer-causing agents have been traced which include tobacco smoke and nicotine (responsible for lung, mouth, bronchial and bladder cancers); asbestos and uranium (responsible for lung cancer); vinyl chloride (responsible for liver cancer); meat-preserving nitrates and nitrites (responsible for stomach and intestinal cancers); arsenic, coal tars, dry cleaning fluid (responsible for skin, lung and stomach cancers); and, chronic stress (for throat, lung, pancreatic, liver and stomach cancers).

How *stress* is related to *cancer* is not exactly known. *Stress* triggers the release of hormones from the pituitary gland inside the brain, such as *ACTH*, which then causes the release of another hormone, *cortisol* from the adrenal glands. *Cortisol* is known to decrease the body's immunity to disease because it inhibits the production of antibodies and *'killer'* *T-cells*—cells produced by the thymus gland and responsible for protection from invasion by any disease. *Stress* is known to be higher in single people—a bachelor or a spinster elderly, a divorcee, a widow or a widower.

The current options for the treatment of cancer are: surgery, radiation, or chemotherapy, as appropriate, or a combination of two or all the techniques. For cancer-preventing diet, you should opt more for: whole-grain cereals, fresh fruits and vegetables specially roughages and high-fibre stuff. Another interesting reminder: your diet should not contain the same foods again and again—a variation in diet is recommended to prevent the intake of too much of any single *carcinogen* as we are not able to track which dietary ingredient contains how much of it.

Survival rates of four major cancers (breast, ovarian, colorectal and lung) diagnosed between 1995 and 2007 are higher in Australia, Canada and Sweden than in the UK and Denmark according to a study. The difference in survival rates are largely due to tumours being detected later in the last two countries, which makes the cancers more difficult to be treated. (5) [(5) "Cancer survival rates lower in UK", *The Times of India, Kolkata,* 23 December 2010, p.14.]

Some researchers have recently announced the first proof that regular consumption of aspirin can cut the risk of a range of cancers by up to 50 per cent. The benefit derived may not improve with higher doses of aspirin but increased the longer it was taken. The impact is also being found greater in older people because of the higher incidence of cancer. Over a period of 20 years, the reduction in risk ranged from 10 per cent for prostate cancer to 60 per cent for oesophageal cancer. (6) [(6) Laurance, Jeremy, "Aspirin Cuts Risk of Cancers" *The Statesman, Kolkata,* 8 December 2010, p.6.]   However, if you have not been taking aspirin all these years and plan to start now after hearing the good news, it is extremely doubtful whether you'll be lucky enough to get any benefit.

British scientists claim to have developed a new treatment for cancer, which renders malignant tumours 'dormant' thus stopping them from spreading around the body and so threatening life. The principle on which their cancer management strategy is based is most interesting. Ordinarily cell division is controlled by specific genes that kill or mend rogue or damaged cells. But cancers occur when these go wrong— especially if tumour suppressor genes are for some reason turned off. These cancer suppressor genes have to be switched back and reactivated to make the cancer cells 'dormant' by using proteins from salamanders that have been shown in the past to be able to switch on and off human genes. (6) [(6) "UK scientists make tumours 'dormant'", *The Times of India, Kolkata,* 14 January 2011, p.16.]

Diabetes

India survived several famines, and in the process we evolved genetically and developed a 'thrifty' gene. Its function is to conserve calories and convert food into fat which is then deposited in various parts of the body. This is why Indians, even thin individuals, tend to have a fat deposit in the abdominal region. The first place we put on weight is around the middle. Such propensities are genetic.

Risk for diabetes can be determined by recording certain biometric criteria, such as: elevated fasting blood sugar levels of more than 125 mg/dL or a random sugar value of more than 200 mg/dL; impaired glucose tolerance test; deranged lipid profile with triglycerides greater than 150 mg/dL; HDL cholesterol less than 40 mg/dL in men and 50 mg/dL in women; a blood pressure higher than 135/85. Those who exhibit these abnormalities are said to suffer from 'metabolic syndrome' or 'syndrome X'.

You can also evaluate risk factors on your own by using a weighing scale and a measuring tape. Risk factors are a BMI (body mass index = weight in kg divided by height in metre squared) of more than 30 and a waist-to-hip ratio (the narrowest part of your waist divided by the widest part of your hips) greater than 1 in men and 0.8 in women, and a waist measurement greater than 102cm in men and 88cm in women.

If three or more of these criteria are present, the person suffers from metabolic syndrome.

To prevent syndrome X and later its progression to diabetes in your old age, achieve and maintain the ideal body weight or a BMI of 23. Go for aerobic activities like walking as little as 30 minutes every day at a brisk pace (4 km/hr) to reduce insulin resistance which causes diabetes. An hour of walking, combined with calorie restriction (1,500 Calories/day) is ideal. No exercises other than aerobic activities (like fast walking, cycling, swimming, aerobics, climbing stairs up-and-down for 20 minutes etc.) will help in preventing diabetes. For calorie restriction, reduce the amount eaten during each meal by 25 per cent. Do not go for reading, watching television and other mind-diverting activities during meal times which increase calorie intake. Fill up on fruits and vegetables and avoid snacking.

One of the most popular weight-loss diets is the grapefruit diet as the fruit contains fat-burning enzymes. And it prevents sugar and starch accumulation. This diet involves drinking at least three glasses of grapefruit juice everyday, as it helps prevent weight gain and burning calories. Extremely rich in vitamin C, although grapefruit is sour and acidic in taste, it produces an alkaline reaction after digestion and is beneficial for treating acidity. One of its plus points is maintenance of elasticity and strengthening of arteries. It is highly beneficial for diabetics as it helps in bringing down blood sugar levels in the body.

Bone and Joint Diseases

Your skeleton supports your body, and allows movement—slow, medium, or rapid when necessary. All this becomes possible because of the bones constituting the structural framework, the muscles laid out along the bones and going over and across the joints. At the same time, the most vulnerable parts of your body continue to be well protected.

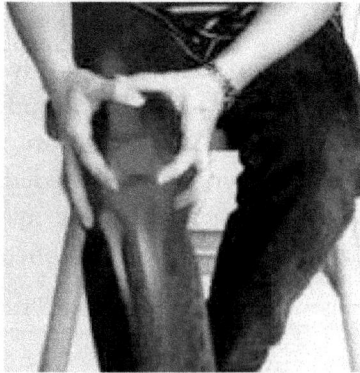

Fig. 18: Problem in the Knee Joint

Joints are necessary wherever bones tend to touch each other. Sometimes, these joints are fixed rigidly, as in the bones of the skull, but more often they form hinges to allow movements. In some cases, like the spine, the joints which allow movement also impart rigidity to the structure by limiting the amount of movement possible.

Bones, muscles, joints, tendons and ligaments remain in good health and fitness if they are used regularly and properly. For sedentary people, with advancing age, the muscular-skeletal system deteriorates in quality leading to common disorders like osteoporosis, joint inflammation, rheumatoid arthritis, spondylosis, and spondilitis. In old age, some bone and joint problem is quite common. In order to keep such problems to the minimum, one has to start taking care of the body right from the middle age. In case you have not been so conscious and have neglected yourself on the fitness aspects, you can always make a beginning even at an advanced age. Start with taking long walks regularly and, if possible, combine it with some freehand exercises.

STEM CELL THERAPY

I don't expect that you'll require this kind of treatment ever because, I feel whatever diseases you may suffer from in your old age would be manageable with conventional allopathic or some form of alternative medicine. But, still, so that you remain familiar with some ultra-modern terms and are not fooled around to go for something you do not understand, I thought I'll devote some space to stem cell therapy which is gradually emerging as a much used term in the field of health care and medical services.

What are Stem Cells

In a living human, most of the cells are highly specialised and differen-tiated from each other (such as heart muscle cells, liver cells, nerve cells and so on) and thus not inter-changeable. Moreover, once damaged, even a set of cells belonging to a particular organ or system and performing a specialised function, cannot easily be regenerated; one has to live with that cellular handicap.

However, *stem cells* are of a special variety that has the ability to grow into other kinds of cells. These serve as an internal repair system. There are essentially two kinds of stem cells: 'embryonic' and 'adult'. 'Embryonic' stem cells, derived from 3-to-5-day-old embryos are the most malleable as they can easily turn into almost any kind of specialised cell under the right conditions. 'Adult' stem cells, derived from adult organs or tissues (such as brain, bone marrow, blood vessels, skin, teeth, heart, gut and liver), although in general are relatively less versatile, some of them known as *mesenchymal adult stem cells* (available in the bone marrow), can also give rise to a variety of cells: bone cells, cartilage cells, fat cells, and the like.

What is Stem Cell Therapy

It is a strategy which can be adopted to cure diseases that are considered incurable. One example is that of a heart attack which has damaged some heart muscles. The damaged heart muscles cannot be regenerated by any known method of medical treatment. But, at least theoretically, stem cells can be used to regenerate new heart muscles that will replace the damaged ones. Similarly, stem cells offer hope to patients who have damaged their nervous system, liver, and so on.

The only problem is that stem cell research is still at a very early stage across the world today. No one knows what your chosen stem cells will do inside the recipient's body and what kind of cells they will turn into. Today, most of the therapy is focused on the use of mesenchymal stem cells which are adequately versatile and relatively less dangerous because they are less likely to lead to development of cysts. However, stem cell research has the potential to treat patients suffering from irreversible diseases and conditions such as Alzheimer's, Parkinson's, spinal cord injury, stroke, burns, heart disease, diabetes, arthritis—both osteo and rheumatoid.

Current Status of Stem Cell Therapy

In developed countries like the US and Europe, the stem cell concept and technique are still restricted very much to research which, again, is tightly regulated and monitored. No stem cell treatment has been approved for commercial use. In India, there is no such regulation as yet restricting the technique's application on patients for treatment. The Drugs and Cosmetics Act of the country, as it stands today, implemented by the Drug Controller General of India (DGCI) does not cover stem treatment. There are only some guidelines set and introduced by the Indian Council of Medical Research (ICMR). Therefore, it is a lucrative business for those who are knowledgeable on the subject both in the organised and unorganised health care sectors; and the charges in smaller clinics are very high as the big brands are still not fully in the game and there is no price control.

THE ROAD FOR YOU TO TRAVEL AFTER RETIREMENT

"Several decades ago, Franklin D. Roosevelt created the old-age retirement system in the United states. The magic age he set was sixty five. It was a safe bet that most people would never collect their pensions because the average life expectancy back then was sixty-two. Thus people approaching retirement didn't spend much time trying to decide what they were going to do once their careers were over." (7) [(7) Zelinski, Ernie J., *How to Retire Happy, Wild, and Free*, New Delhi: Macmillan, Indian Reprint, 2008, p.15].

Nevertheless, retirement for you now-a-days does not mean that you have reached a point of no return. On the one hand, retirement age in general has reduced to make room for the younger generations with fresher bodies and minds; and, on the other hand, the average life span has increased. But there are other problems. Let us read what 'leisure specialist' Zelinski says in his other best-selling book *The Joy of Not Working*:

"Most of us will spend the greater part of our adult lives working. Taking into account getting ready for work, commuting to work, talking about our jobs, and worrying about getting laid off, we will have spent more time during our working lives thinking about work than thinking about all our other concerns in life.

Many of us also spend a great amount of time thinking about how great life will be when we don't have to work any more. Indeed, many dream about how much better life will be with much more leisure time. When I worked as an engineer, I was amazed (and dejected) at how much time engineers and technicians in their twenties spent talking about the potential size of their pensions and all the activities they could pursue in retirement. Although I was in my twenties, I had more interesting subjects to discuss with others.....

As a matter of course, society leads us to believe that retirement and happiness are one and the same. Retirement is supposed to be the great escape from the stresses inherent in most jobs, a time to experience a fulfilling life derived from many enjoyable and rewarding activities. Unfortunately, this is not the case for everyone who retires." (8) [(8) Zelinski, Ernie J., *The Joy of Not Working: A book for the retired, unemployed, and overworked*, Berkeley, California: Ten Speed Press, 21st century edition, 2008, pp.4-5]

For most retirees, it is a sudden fall from the grace of their proximal societies, from the great heights of a meaningful existence with a busy schedule to a life of shed *roles*. Let us see how and why.

When you are active in employment or pursuing a professional or a business career, you are involved in three different roles: *family roles*, *social roles*, and *work roles*. Once you retire, your *work roles* automatically disappear. You're no longer a boss, a subordinate, a peer or a colleague, a senior or a junior to people around you in your world of work.

Your *family roles* also might have shrunk having lost your parents (and with that your 'son' or 'daughter' role being a thing of the past), with your sons having been married and having their own happy family existence—some with a career, some without one. Your brothers and sisters—some are there nearby, some may be far away abroad. Today, your family portrait has only two characters—your life partner and you. Just the two of you; the she and the he-pigeon, or the tigress and the tiger; choose whichever of these pairs you want to perceive yourselves as. Should you like to imagine your partnership as that of the tigress and the tiger than the romantic pigeon couple, the mighty pair is now powerless, feeling old and obsolete physically in the twenty-first century era of the Internet and fuel-efficient vehicles.

You have the *social roles* to tamper with. However, unfortunately, having lost touch with most of your friends and social acquaintances owing to your high-pressured career and many of them having left the shores of life, you may be left with only one or two of them and it may not be unlikely that you may even find them ailing and indisposed. So, in order to expand your social networking, you might have to make a few new friends; which you may not like at your advanced age with your salt-and-pepper hair. The latest development in the US is that the fastest adoptions of social networks like Facebook is found to take place with people 74 years of age or older, with use quadrupling in two years to 16% of the group. Older Internet users were also taking increasingly to getting news online. (9) [(9) "Net gain: Old catch up with young in cyberworld", *The Times of India, Kolkata*, 18 December 2010, p. 16.]

Problems aggravate as with the shedding of your *roles,* the responsibilities that used to be associated with those *roles* would also have been gone giving you the greatest hurt of your life. Along with your responsibilities and authorities having gone on the day everybody bade you farewell at the place of your work, your importance in your society would have also had a sudden drop as you could feel from the non-verbal and verbal expressions of your ex-boss, former colleagues, juniors and subordinates; and, more so from your family members. Where you would deserve their empathy to soothe your agony, they increase your mental pains by being indifferent to you and sometimes even ignoring you.

Look at the situation in which you are placed today from another angle. The only way you can come out this glut is to feel that your glass is 'half-full' and not 'half-empty'. Consider that today you'll be free to a large extent; and, you'll be placed precisely in a situation that you had been longing for when you had viewed the responsibilities that you had to shoulder as 'burdens'. **Will you or will you not enjoy this freedom?** Search your soul. Since you had been dreaming to reach this goal when you were burnt out due to the pressure of your *work roles*, learn to welcome and enjoy the change which will be beneficial for your health and fitness. You ought to keep serious diseases at a distance and learn to face trivial problems which are companions of aging. Your *retirement* from many *roles*, *responsibilities* and *authorities* is a phase of your life which you may really cherish. Be *active* in other ways. There are so many activity choices available to you as I'll discuss.

GENDER VIS-À-VIS THE IMPACT OF POST-RETIREMENT AGING

The number of men aged sixty-five living up to the age of eighty and remaining non-disabled in the year before death is around one in four. In the case of women, the number is one in six. This type of successful post-retirement aging in Western countries is found in those who maintain an active lifestyle, eat a healthy balanced diet, drink little alcohol, do not smoke, and continue social involvement.

Women generally live longer than do men (life expectancy for men: around 74 to 75 years, for women: 79 to 80 years). It is also found that women are stronger than men and they can handle old age pressures better than men. They have higher inner strengths like patience, tolerance, fine-tuning with family, friends, relatives and other people than elderly men, possibly because of their having been at the helm of their household and family management. Because of their direct home-making involvement, they have a more active aging than men.

There is no data available still on the impact of aging on working women in our country after they have retired from their career. Therefore, if your spouse is also working and about to retire soon, you should do your retirement planning together. That would be a safer proposition than the both of you making your plans independently.

APPLICATION TIPS

- Try to get introduced to some of the most common old age physical disorders. See if you are already affected by one or more than one of them. Follow the *lifestyle therapy* route first for a few months unless it is so serious that you have to go for medical help.

- Prepare yourself to adjust with the 'changed roles' situation in your family and social fronts and the 'shed roles' situation in your work front. Try to look at the 'zero work role' circumstances as a freedom which you can enjoy—it's entirely up to you how you'd like to enjoy it. Design some new roles in your life pursuit of which you should be proud of.

Chapter 10

Body Care in Old Age

"To continue activity as long as possible, contemporaneously keeps one young in thought, in contact with youth and its interests in contrast with the contagiousness of senility." **—Abraham Adolphe, The Human Machine,**
Harmondsworth: Penguin, 1956, p. 67

YOUR BODY MATTERS

In ancient times, the great Indian sage Patanjali had reminded us about the primary importance of our body which could be, if we wished, much within our conscious control. He had listed the eight stages (*ashtanga*) dealing with the postures (*asana*) and breath regulation (*pranayama*) before the other stages involving more of the mind—concentration, meditation and so on. He had also laid down the rules and procedures for *hathayoga*—the bodily discipline—more easily accessible to the ordinary, as the first step towards the higher developmental stages of *rajayoga* and *jnanayoga*. He and his school of thought wanted to emphasise that body is the route to all mental refinement.

WHAT YOUR BODY CAN DO EVEN IN OLD AGE

Let us first look at your body and what physical activities it can undertake even in old age and derive a lease of confidence from the endocrinologist, turned into a lifestyle guru, Deepak Chopra who says:

"For the past twenty years, gerontologists have performed experiments to prove that remaining active throughout life, even up to one's late seventies, would halt the loss of muscle and skeletal tissue. The news spreads among retired people that they should continue to walk, jog, swim and keep up their housework; under the slogan 'Use it or lose it', millions of people now expect to remain strong in old age. With this new belief in place, something once impossible happened.

Daring gerontologists at Tufts University visited a nursing home, selected a group of frailest residents and put them on a weight-training regimen. One might fear that a sudden introduction to exercise would exhaust or kill these fragile people, but in fact they thrived. Within eight weeks, wasted muscles had come back by 300 per cent, co-ordination and balance improved and overall a sense of active life returned. Some of the subjects who had not been able to walk unaided could now get up and go to the bathroom in the middle of the night by themselves, an act of reclaimed dignity that is by no means trivial. What makes this accomplishment truly wondrous, however, is that the youngest subject in the group was 87 and the oldest 96.

These results were always possible; nothing new was added here to the capacity of the human body. All that happened was that a belief changed, and when that happened, aging changed." (1) [(1) Chopra, Deepak, *Ageless Body, Timeless Mind: A Practical Alternative to Growing Old*, London: Rider—an imprint of Ebury Press, Random House, 1993, pp. 57–58].

Isn't it reassuring for us?

MAKE YOUR METABOLISM MORE EFFICIENT

Metabolism constitutes the chemical processes in living things that change the inputs like food, beverages and drinks into energy and elements for growth (such as new cells) and waste products.

In order to take control of your metabolism and make it run with maximum efficiency even at your advanced age:

• Avoid main meals that are too low in Calories as that may eventually lead to binging. A low-calorie diet at a time slows your metabolism as your body goes into 'survival mode' to conserve calories. It will lead to very little loss of fat. The diet has to be compatible with the processes so that there is minimum stress on the process infrastructure.

Fig.19: Put Thrust on Walking

- Don't skip meals. Eat nutritious but light snacks between meals. Breakfast is the most important meal of the day as it gives you energy and helps prevent heavy snacking closer to the mid-day meal.

- Take frequent walking breaks. The more you move around during the day, the more calories you burn. If possible, take a 5-minute walking break around your working or operational area (inside or out) every hour. Take the longest route when walking anywhere you go.

- Take the stairs by avoiding elevator and escalator rides. Climbing the stairs is an excellent aerobic exercise and it also builds strong legs. Limit TV watching at a stretch. Get up and move around during the commercials.

POSITIVE MIND CREATES POSITIVE BODY

You would have realised, by now, that your mind serves as one of the vital root causes of most of your old age physical health problems.

To give you a few concrete examples, we may say that blunt, straightforward, reactive, irritable people are ulcer-prone or allergic; so are those who, by nature, are over-anxious. Control-oriented, obsessive people, becoming victims of loneliness after retirement, may tend to suffer from painful gastro-intestinal disorders like ulcerative colitis and irritable bowels syndrome. Absent-minded, unalert persons meet with sudden accidents. People who are obese and cannot get over their greedy habits attract cardio-respiratory diseases.

Those who suffer from any negative thoughts related to anger, hostility, anxiety, fear or depression have their physiological activities and brain chemistry changed which also alters their physiology further. By the process of brain chemistry we mean the hormone secretion from various sites (like the *hypothalamus* and the *pituitary*) throughout the brain. These hormones then carry messages, to be followed, to distant departments and the departmental organs in the body. To cite some instances of physiological changes, one can mention of the development of rapid heartbeat, rise in blood pressure, blood rushing to the entire facial region during bouts of anger and hostility; tremor in hands, cold sweat and knotted stomach in case of acute anxiety and so on.

Both 'fear' and 'anger' involve whole body hormonal responses including those generated in the *adrenal glands* (steroids such as *cortisol* and *adrenalin*). These hormones interact directly with the brain. The neurons or brain cells in the region of *hippocampus* in the lower structures of the brain are packed with receptors able to interact with the steroid hormones to help cognition. *Adrenalin* interacts with the brain via *amygdala,* triggering neuronal pathways which also activate the *hippocampus.* The *hypothalamus* regulates the release of hormones from the *pituitary* whose major function is the regulation of the release of other hormones from the *adrenal glands, testes* and *ovaries.*

Incidentally, to highlight the extent of powerful influence that the negative brain and body chemicals has, we can say that severe maternal stress alters hormone balance, notably steroid hormones and elevated levels of *cortisol* change the pattern of development of the foetus.

On the contrary, a happy state of mind, thoughts representing warmth, compassion, empathy and understanding, responsive behaviour (as opposed to negative 'reactivity') introduces a flux of positive chemicals in the brain and helps to develop a positive physiology.

Therefore, just by practicing positive thinking and a happy feeling, one can create a positive ambience in our body and brain, equivalent to the 'placebo effect' so common in the field of medicine where a sugar-coated bland pill prescribed by the physician, consumed by the patient with trust and faith, leads to miraculous relief due to the production of positive brain chemicals.

YOUR PHYSICAL HEALTH MANAGEMENT

Have you been maintaining a good general physical health and nutrition to allow your brain to handle its most complex functions and compensate for the wear and tear of everyday life (which can be described as 'good housekeeping)?

Most probably, you have not been. Because, there is a general tendency in most of us and you might not have been an exception to it. That is, after we cross our youth and move into our mid-life, we endeavour to enter into the 'comfort zone' in every respect. We rely less and less on our physical powers and start depending more and more on engineered powers like two-wheelers, four-wheelers, washing machines, vacuum cleaners, microwave ovens, grinder-mixers, air-conditioners, elevators, escalators, and so on.

As a consequence, we don't utilise the powers available with us; at the same time, we don't reduce our energy intake by way of consumption of food, beverages, drinks and so on; on the contrary, we go for rich, oily, spicy food of a quantity which is much more than what our reduced energy output demands. You may be a victim of this common phenomenon.

As a very simple instance, we can cite the case of the use of hand tools like the knife, scissors, screw driver, spanner, hammer, shovel, axe, jack and so on instead of the same purposes being served by our palms and fingers engaged in different gestures which our forest-dwelling ancestors used to do; if we depend more on man-made tools for such day-to-day activities, the brain maps allocated for those functions will reduce in space creating problems for us as we grow old, based on the simple 'use it or lose it' biological law.

Thus, in order to manage your health and fitness in your post-retirement days, you have to take three firm steps: namely, planned diet, planned physical fitness activities (including planned movement of limbs, body parts, and fittings and fixtures like fingers and toes the activities of which have been replaced by man-made tools and gadgets) and planned sound sleep.

HOW CAN YOU DO A SELF-CHECKING OF YOUR PHYSICAL STATE

Ask yourself questions like:

- Is my gait regular and balanced, and not jerky and staggered?

or,

- Do I feel better that my gait is regular, balanced and better controlled by myself if I walk at a slow/slow to moderate/moderate/moderate to fast/fast speed?

- Do I have to look down when I climb up or down a flight of stairs or do I look up or straight like a healthy, fit, young person?

- Have my fingers and toes, palms of both my hands and arches of both my feet lost their flexibility and freedoms of movement and I feel stiffness in the joints and also pain when I try to move them occasionally; or, the problem with them is really not that much noticeable?

- However, do I feel much better after I deliberately move them in different ways for a few days or, may be a few weeks?

If you feel there are problems that you face in these areas of daily living and working, it could be due to one or a combination of the following reasons:

- Your body weight support system, while you stand or walk, is not functioning properly. There may be degenerative process already set in your bones. You might not have been taking any physical exercise to maintain your bones, muscles, ligaments, tendons and joints.

- You might have been over-dependent on artificial gadgets, man-made devices and tools which has led to lack of use of your own limbs, body parts, fittings and fixtures allowing you to move into and remain in a narrow and highly restricted 'comfort zone'.

- Your body's centre of gravity must have come up making you un-wieldy due to lean lower extremities compared to the upper half of your body.

- There may be muscular-skeletal pains either in the neck region or in the lower back or waist region or somewhere along the spine.

- There may be something wrong with your vestibular apparatus—the sensory organ for the balance system. It consists of three semi-circular canals in the inner ear that tells us when we are upright and how gravity is affecting our bodies by detecting motion in three-dimensional space.

- There is decrease in sensory feedback from your feet due to constant use of footwear.

- It may be a post-accident or post-stroke phenomenon.

- Your brain tissue might have suffered shrinkage thus increasing/reducing the pressure of the cerebrospinal/cranial fluid.

- There may be an early onset of *Parkinson's disease* due to *dopamine* deficiency in the inner and lower structures of your brain. *Dopamine*, as we already know, is your brain's natural balancer and reward chemical.

Any problem with your posture or gait, can give you mental fatigue as well, from being on constant high alert. It costs you a lot of brainpower to maintain an upright position—brain power that is taken away from such mental functions as memory and the ability to calculate and reason.

A 'stable' body image gives you a sense of well-being. The feeling of being firmly rooted on the ground and having your balance maintained gives the feeling of control over yourself. On the contrary, with loss of physical control over yourself, even a little physical weakness due to fever, stomach ache, diarrohea or acute headache or body ache instantaneously makes you feel unhealthy and unfit.

This aspect of our body language gets reflected in our words also when we express ourselves as 'settled' or 'unsettled', 'balanced' or 'unbalanced', 'steady' or 'unsteady', 'regular' or 'irregular', 'rooted' or 'rootless', 'grounded' or 'ungrounded'.

Old people are more frightened of falling than of being pushed or mugged. A third of the elderly fall and because they are falling, they stay at home, don't use their limbs, and become more physically frail. One main problem is that the vestibular sense—just like hearing, taste, eyesight, and our other senses—starts to weaken with age.

COPE WITH NEGATIVE BEHAVIOURAL STIMULUS TO PROTECT YOUR BODY

All the time, in the environment external to us, stimuli of different types are generated which are received at the various receiving stations—our sensory organs before they are transmitted to the brain through nerves. Mind is also considered as a sensory organ which serves as the receptor organ for others' behaviour.

Excessive demands, serious worries and nagging behaviour from others close to you—generally your family members, particularly your life partner may become important risk factors for development of *angina*. *Angina* is a pain or discomfort in the chest and is usually caused by coronary heart disease. Some might experience focused pain only in arm, neck, stomach or jaw. While many describe the feeling as severe tightness, others say it more resembles a dull ache.

Incorporation of planned diet, planned physical fitness activities, planned rest and sound sleep, and planned mental relaxation through any type of effective meditation including the one described in this book, into your lifestyle will increase your tolerance thresholds and enhance your comfort zone. Instead of 'reacting' to any such nagging or demanding behaviour, you ought to practice active listening with patience without interrupting the communicator followed by a tactful proactive response without any unwilling commitment.

APPLICATION TIPS

- Remaining active even up to your late seventies would halt the loss of your muscles and skeletal tissues.

- By controlling and making your metabolism more efficient what you can achieve is unthinkable. Follow the tips provided in this chapter.

- Maintain a positive state of mind to get a positive physical state in return.

- Regularly check up your physical state by following the checklists provided.

- Make it a point to cope with the negative stimuli invading you from your   environment.

Chapter 11

Diet Plan for Old Age

"A man who eats once a day is a *yogi* (sage)
A man who eats twice a day is a *bhogi* (worldly man)
A man who eats thrice a day is a *rogi* (sick man)
A man who eats four times a day has his one foot already in the grave".

—**Anon**

PLANNING YOUR DIET FOR OLD AGE

Your diet must be nutritive and balanced. About forty nutrients are available in a well-balanced diet. The three main calorie-yielding components are: carbohydrates, fats and proteins. You very much need the essential and non-essential amino acids that are found in proteins. Fourth are the minerals and fifth are the vitamins. We must not forget about water as our body and brain—both have very high water content.

BALANCING YOUR DIET

For an elderly person, the balanced diet composition should be a mix of different types of food having different types of utility and value for the aging body and brain. The combination recommended is: 50 percent fruits; vegetables 20 percent; whole grains 20 percent; and protein 10 percent. However, avoid eating a lot of these different types of foods at one meal.

A nutritious, well-balanced diet makes important contributions to general health, quality of life and mental function. The general dietary advice is for you to have a regular intake of adequate (though in restricted quantities as you'll see a little later) calories, plenty of fresh fruits and vegetables.

CALORIE RESTRICTION

Planned diet would primarily mean a 'calorie restricted' quantity: consuming what is needed and not being guided by any greed—not filling your stomach to the brim; on the contrary, always leaving some empty space, around 15 to 20 per cent. This, if followed, would reduce the chances of putting on weight, or any gastro-enterological, orthopaedic, circulatory, or respiratory disease due to overworked digestive system, heart, lungs and muscular-skeletal departments, and limiting the invasion of the free radicals which have the destructive tendency of damaging your normal cell structure and behaviour.

How do you know that you have succeeded in your attempt for 'calorie restriction'? Your stomach must never get inflated after a meal; rather if you press into your middle abdomen, you can feel that it is not full. However, if it is difficult for you to reduce your intake abruptly, you can do it in a few phases—slowly and gradually.

GENERAL DIETARY COMPOSITION

Intake of carbohydrates should be reduced from the usual Indian standards; emphasis should be on vegetable rather than non-vegetable proteins; fat and oil intake should be minimal—restricted to the extent of its use in cooking; sugar intake should also be very low; thrust should be on the consumption of fresh green vegetables, fibres (like foliages, cabbage, cauliflower, spinach, lettuce and broccoli) and fresh fruits which contain anti-oxidants needed to fight out your free radicals.

NON-VEGETABLE PROTEINS

Meat not an Ideal Input: Meat is nutritionally an unbalanced input for our system as it contains excess protein (we don't need that much) but virtually no complex carbohydrates, fibre or calcium and very few vitamins. Besides, since animals and birds also consume grains and vegetables like we do, why shouldn't we go for the benefits by consuming those directly?

Animals and birds may carry undiagnosed diseases which can be passed on to us when we consume them. And, even if they are not carriers of diseases, they are unhealthy as they are kept in captivity and are not allowed to move freely for health and fitness maintenance which is not the case with fish.

Thrust on Fish: Amongst non-vegetable proteins, major thrust should be on fish. Fish eats water-borne plants, which have a high mineral content. It is also particularly high in calcium (the bony parts of fish which can be chewed and consumed) and iodine. Calcium is necessary to keep bones young and iodine for normal thyroid gland function. The thyroid governs body metabolism, including fat metabolism, and therefore is important for weight control.

Fig. 20: Make Sure to have Fish in Your Daily Diet

Importance of Yogurt: Our internal body environment is a convenient habitat for bacteria—both friendly and unfriendly. The friendly bacteria render good service to us by being helpful to our life-sustaining processes, whereas the negative bacteria such as viruses produce illnesses. Negative features of modern lifestyle such as smoking, consumption of alcohol, too many cups of tea or coffee, cola drinks, rich diets, stress and antibiotics can destroy the beneficial bacteria in the intestines. Eating yogurt, from time to time, helps to replace them.

TOTAL CALORIE INTAKE

The total food intake per day must not exceed 1,800 to 2,000 Calories (that is kilocalories); may be less, even around 1,400/1,500 Calories depending upon the level of your energy expenditure as you may be mostly home-bound in old age barring going out for constitutional walks twice a day to the local park.

Calorie Restriction: We are emphasising the importance of the 'calorie restriction' strategy, again and again, for old age health and happiness as it has been a proven and time-tested one. In your case, calorie restriction would mean you ought to consume only around 80 to 85 per cent of what you normally would take.

Implementation of Calorie Restriction: How would you achieve this in our society where people generally 'overeat' (forget about 'break-even' level balanced eating)?

Let us discuss a few ways as you may find it convenient to adopt one of those. These are: (i) take your food in a smaller plate rather than in a large dish and take the dal, vegetable and non-vegetable preparation in the same plate instead of taking them in separate bowls; (ii) don't go for any second help; (iii) while eating out at a party or at a food joint or a restaurant, take in small quantities; (iv) if possible, stand and eat—in fact, buffet style and stand-on eating is the best style for calorie restriction; (v) drink a glass of water, ten minutes before any main meal so that the stomach space is not empty—whenever you feel hungry, have some drinking water—in any case, your drinking water intake should be 3 to 4 litres per day; in summer, increase it by another one to one-and-a-half litre.

MORE TIPS ABOUT YOUR MEALS

- **General:** All your meals should be 'light' to 'moderate' to follow the principle of calorie restriction.
- **Morning Meal/Breakfast:** In the morning time, the body eliminates its toxins produced during the whole night's restful metabolic process; therefore, do not have a 'heavy' breakfast the digestion of which will consume much energy and the toxin elimination work will be affected. Also, avoid taking coffee for breakfast since processing of the caffeine-rich beverage will draw on your limited energy reserves.
- **Night Meal/Dinner:** (i) Firstly, your dinner should be 'light' to 'moderate' as a 'heavy' dinner will take away lot of the energy available to you for its digestion instead of the same energy being used, while you sleep and your brain and body both are restful, for maintenance of vitality in your elderly age and for your physical and mental rejuvenation. This explains why a lot of people don't wake up feeling fresh. At night, despite they are in the so-called sleeping state, their internal physiological systems work hard to digest the food instead of getting rest. (ii) Secondly, for dinner you must restrict yourself to vegetarian items as vegetables are easy to digest. However, avoid fruits at night; these should be had during daytime to supply energy from the fructose form of sugar which ripe and sweet fruits possess in high quantities.
- **Eating Style:** Eat slowly to allow adequate chewing of the food for a thorough breakdown of the inputs to facilitate effective nourishment.

MAINTENANCE OF YOUR BRAIN HEALTH: IMPORTANCE OF DIET

Planning your diet is not only important for your body maintenance but it is also most crucial for the health of your brain. Fatty acids from the diet are the building blocks of the brain as the fat soluble vitamins—especially *Vitamin B12* and *folate* play most vital roles. A diet deficient in one of the essential fatty acids may hamper brain health. An important genetic susceptibility factor for Alzheimer's disease is closely involved with the transport of fat into the brain: slight differences in the structure of this fat transport protein [*apolipoprotein E*] produce major differences in the risk of developing Alzheimer's disease in late life. You collect *Omega-3* fatty acids, essential for brain health maintenance, from bony varieties of fish.

Unrefined grains such as wholemeal bread, pasta, cereals and rice, apart from their being a good source of carbohydrates, vitamins and other nutrients, are also a potent source of minerals, especially of calcium, phosphorus, magnesium, iron and zinc. The high phosphorus content is important for brain tissue, and fruits and vegetables are a poor source of phosphorus.

YOUR DIETARY HABIT MUST NOT BE CHANGED

There is one note of caution for you. If you have been a non-vegetarian all your life, do not turn a total vegetarian in your old age. There is a possibility of shrinkage of your brain due to *Vitamin B12* deficiency. The best sources of this vitamin are liver, milk and fish. *Vitamin B12* deficiency can also cause anaemia and inflammation of the nervous system. Yeast extracts are one of the few food items which provide good levels of the vitamin. Women in their seventies are the most at risk.

IMPORTANCE OF VARIETY OF VITAMINS, MINERALS AND OTHER CHEMICALS

We have just now talked about *Vitamin B12* and its role in your brain health. Let us now look at other vitamins.

People who consume high quantities of fruits and vegetables have high blood *Vitamin C* concentrations. Increased *Vitamin C* concentrations have been repeatedly linked to less heart disease, lower blood fats, less cancer, and fewer cataracts. *Vitamin C* consumption in middle age can also be linked to retention of mental abilities in old age.

Vitamin E is present in plants. *carotenoids (beta-carotene)* are derived from dark-coloured fruit and vegetables in diet.

Vitamin A is derived from the consumption of meat, fish oil and some dairy products.

Selenium and *zinc* are also essential for your brain. *Zinc* is found in high concentrations in the brain, especially in the hippocampus and it is thus important in memory function.

Salt (*sodium chloride*) chemical to be consumed with caution as it heightens blood pressure. Your body's salt requirements are very low and are satisfied by the salt in natural foods, especially vegetables.

FRUITS ARE ESSENTIAL INPUTS

Your tissues must be supplied with adequate high-quality nutrients with a minimum of toxins. Therefore, select fruits (which are eaten raw) as the main food intake instead of grains which have to be cooked (the heat of cooking destroys the good properties and quality ingredients). Fruits are more nutritious, less acidic and easier to digest, less likely to cause allergies and they detoxify the systems. Eat fruit on its own; avoid having citrus fruits with other food since they are acidic. Have them separately.

FATS: HOW MUCH IS GOOD FOR YOU

Have a moderate amount of *unsaturated fats* (obtainable from vegetables and not from animal fats and dairy products) in your diet for optimum health. There is not really any need for you to take any fat separately.

You must be aware of the hazards of fats. About 99 per cent of your fat comes from saturated fat sources such as: animal fats (present in meat and dairy products), coconut and palm oil, margarine, lard (used in frying fish and chips), salad oil and mayonnaise. Saturated fat tends to deposit on the walls of the arteries carrying blood, causing circulation to slow down thus leading to heart disease and possibly a heart attack. If the arteries get narrowed and blood supply to the brain is greatly reduced, a stroke may occur. Reduced blood circulation may affect other normal functions like vision, hearing, reproductive system, and joint movements.

Therefore, as a preventive measure reduce your intake of meat, dairy products, margarine, fast food, sugar (as excess sugar is converted to triglyceride, a type of fat) and take aerobic exercises which increase circulation to all parts of your body. Food high in saturated fat causes an increase in blood cholesterol (cholesterol is a fatty substance essential for formation of cell membranes, nerve sheaths, *Vitamin D*, sex hormones and providing you defence against any infection but too much of it circulating in the blood flow is dangerous). Your body's defence system fights against excess cholesterol but, as a side-effect, it produces free radicals which build up as a 'plaque' in the arterial wall causing reduced blood flow to the heart and other organs. The only solution is in antioxidants to be obtained from natural sources: *Vitamin A* from green/ yellow vegetables; *Vitamin C* from fruits; and *Vitamin E* from whole-grain foods and unsaturated oils.

FIBRES ARE MUSTS

Consume *fibre* in adequate quantities from leafy vegetables, a fibrous fruit (like mango, jackfruit, guava, orange, water melon and banana) as it removes cholesterol from intestines and reduces the blood's cholesterol level. It helps in regular bowel movements and prevents cancer of the colon. It reduces blood pressure and thus the chances of heart disease. It also regulates blood sugar, prevents mood swings, obesity and diabetes, and assists in weight control.

WHAT ABOUT WATER

Our blood contains 85 per cent water and our brain 30 per cent. Have one glass of *water* when you get up in the morning; this will help you in elimination of toxins. And, drink when you're thirsty. Most of your water is needed to eliminate the waste products of meat and to reduce the salt concentration of blood. Concentrate on non-animal protein foods. Collect such proteins from soya, raw nuts and legumes.

APPLICATION TIPS

- You require three main calorie-yielding inputs (namely, carbohy-drates, fats and proteins) plus minerals, vitamins and water. The ideal combination of food items would be: 50 percent fruits, vegetables 20 percent, whole grains 20 percent, and protein 10 percent.

- Make sure to follow the 'Calorie Restriction (CR)' strategy. Go by what you just need and, even on that, you have a cut of 15 to 20 percent. Feel whether your stomach (middle abdomen) is just 80 to 85 percent full.

- Follow the tips provided for your different meals, especially breakfast and dinner.

- *Vitamin B12, folate* and *Omega-3* fatty acids are essential for you.

Chapter 12

Health Care and Physical Fitness Activity and Rest Plan for Old Age

"Live in the moment, enjoy the moment, because if you don't, you'll miss out, and trust me, nothing can bring back time lost."
—Dev Anand, the 87-year-old legendary actor
(In: Ahmed, Afsana, "Forever Young", *Timeslife,*
A *Sunday Times of India, Kolkata Supplement,* 9 January, 2011, p. 3)

PLANNING YOUR OLD AGE HEALTH CARE AND PHYSICAL FITNESS ACTIVITIES

Planned old age health care and physical fitness activities should include, apart from *planned diet*, which has already been discussed in Chapter 11, some 'freehand' exercises to be performed daily at a convenient time. In addition, one should try to burn at least 200 to 250 Calories per day in household physical activities like dusting, removing cobwebs from ceilings and walls, cleaning up pots-pans-utensils-crockery-cutleries, washing clothes, cleaning the car and so on.

WHAT CAUSES ILL HEALTH AND LACK OF FITNESS

For any physical healthy and fit or unhealthy and unfit condition, however, three things are responsible: metabolic characteristics, genetic propensity, and lifestyle.

Two Excellent Examples

Example 1: *Diabetes Mellitus*

It is a problem for which all these factors are responsible. Firstly, genetically, those people who are much heavier in weight compared to their height and do not put any effort to reduce their weight, become easy targets of diabetes.

Secondly, *diabetes* is also due to a metabolic deficiency related to the production and utilisation of *insulin* which controls the level of sugar or glucose in our system. It may so happen that pancreas, which is responsible for generating this hormone, does not produce it in enough quantity or the insulin that is present is not being properly utilised. Due to one of these reasons, the level of sugar in our blood crosses a permissible limit.

And, thirdly, it's a lifestyle disease as the victims do not indulge in physically energy-expending activities; instead, they love to lead a sedentary life as they have unconsciously and subconsciously learnt to live and work within a very restricted 'comfort zone' and their tolerance zone is also narrow. Besides, they use stimulants like tobacco in the form of smoking or otherwise.

Example 2: *Blood Pressure (B.P.)*

It is the pressure that is created on the inner wall surface of the blood-carrying vessels during the circulatory process. BP is measured at two levels: one higher (systolic, when the heart is contracting fully and releasing the blood from all its chambers) and, the other, lower (diastolic, when the heart is relaxed and its muscles are all under expansion). The ideal ratio is 130/85. If your ratio is 140/90 (too high) or 120/80 (too low), then consult your physician. The root causes of high BP are genetic as well as environmental and include: smoking, lack of physical exercise, high degree of fat deposit and high level of bad cholesterol due to consumption of fatty junk and rich food, consumption of alcohol, taking too much of salt, excessive mental stress, diabetes or kidney problems. Remedies are: change in lifestyle, giving up smoking, regular exercise, walking briskly for 30 to 45 minutes, abstaining from alcohol, reducing salt intake (not more than 6 gm daily), taking adequate quantities of fresh fruits, roughages and vegetables; calorie restriction, going in for fatless milk, freedom from mental stress, getting occupied in activities that you enjoy, regular deep breathing. However, your case may be such that some medicine would need to be administered for your BP management. Meditation may be a very useful activity for BP control.

PHYSICAL FITNESS

Physical Fitness means the 330 bones, 230 joints, and the innumerable muscles, tendons and ligaments are all functioning properly without any discomfort, pain, or inflammation. Their combined powers provide us with the load-carrying capacity and make us perform day-to-day activities like standing, running, jogging, sitting, squatting, lying down, and climbing stairs and slopes.

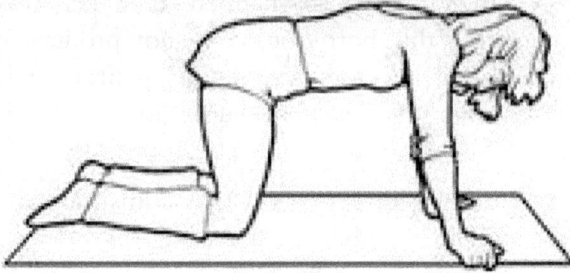

Fig. 21: Free Movements at different Joint Levels

All these together constitute the application of our motor powers. Our such powers get adversely affected when we have painful bone and joint diseases such as arthritis ('arth' means 'joint' and 'itis' means 'inflammation' which together mean inflammation of the joints).

Arthritis produces pain and affects your movements. In *osteoarthritis*, the cartilaginous parts of your joints tend to get damaged (main reasons: heavy bodyweight and sedentary habits).

In *rheumatoid arthritis*, the membranous parts of your joints get inflamed and, as a result, you get stiffness, redness and hotness in your joints (main reason: lack of adequate use which is essential for maintenance of the joints).

Gout, another common form of old age arthritis, is caused by the increase in the uric acid level in the body. Uric acid, when present in disproportionately high quantity, gets crystallised and the uric acid granules get deposited in various locations of the body, particularly, the joints. It generally affects the ankle, knee joint, sole of the foot, fingers, wrist and elbow joints.

There is a strong possibility of *arthritis* if you cannot maintain a steady body weight and your postures and gestures are far from correct and graceful. Regular walking, jogging, stair ascending and descending or swimming constitutes the preventive measures. Eat bony fishes containing *Omega-3* fatty acid. Avoid Poly-Unsaturated Fatty Acid (PUFA)-based cooking oils (such as sunflower, safflower, corn oil); instead use rapeseed or flaxseed oil. Also use ginger and garlic in your cooking.

You might have heard that acupuncture and ice therapy can cure arthritis if applied properly by trained experts.

Cervical spondylosis and *spondilitis* are postural diseases which can also affect your free movements. You can prevent such problems by adopting correct postures such as standing or sitting erect, not stooping to use the computer or laptop for a long period at a stretch regularly (take periodic 'stretch-breaks'), controlling your body weight and diet, and taking regular physical fitness exercises.

Fig. 22: An Old-aged Person taking Physical Fitness Exercise

Check up with your family doctor whether you can take up 'running' as a regular physical fitness activity. If advised by him, go for a *treadmill test*. People who want to live a long and healthy life can take up running, provided after retirement they are fit enough to do so. Apart from reducing the risk of heart disease, running also might keep cancer and neurological diseases such as *Alzheimer's* at bay.

PLANNING YOUR SOUND REST AND SLEEP IN OLD AGE

Men, and not so much women, suffering from sleep deprivation are more likely to die prematurely than those who regularly get a good night's sleep. Researchers at the Penn State College of Medicine, Pennsylvania, found that men with chronic insomnia were four times more likely to die than those with a generally healthy sleep pattern. (1) [(1) "Insomniac Men More Likely to Die Early: Study", *The Statesman, Kolkata,* 2 September 2010, p.4]. The major causes of such insomnia have been found to be: diabetes, high blood pressure, smoking, alcohol use, depression, obesity, and sleeping disorders.

In order to plan for a night of good rest, when you're old, you should try to have an early (and 'light' as already pointed out) dinner between 8.00

and 9.00 pm. After dinner, make it a point to take a slow stroll, if not outside even inside your house or apartment so that blood circulation takes place in the lower half of the body to facilitate your digestive process.

If you lie down straight after your dinner, the blood circulation and blood pressure both adopt a different mode, not helpful for your digestion. And, if you sink into a very comfortable sofa to watch the TV, listen to some music or read something that is also not good for your digestion. Just after you have had your dinner, don't indulge in anything which is very exciting or emotional, particularly where you get angry, afraid, or sad.

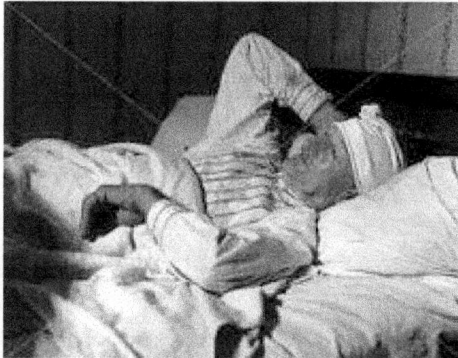

Fig. 23:   Deep, Sound Sleep Gives Rest to Your   Brain

After an one hour gap, you lay your body on the bed in the supine or *sabasana* posture with both your hands kept loosely on the two sides of your body and your head laid on a 1.5 to 2 inches (3.8 to 5 cm) thick pillow (which will allow the blood inside your brain to maintain a balance with the blood inside your body as a thicker pillow will drain out blood from your brain into the body and a thinner pillow will allow more blood than required to drain into your brain). You should avoid sleeping on a thick foam mattress which will make your back and neck muscles work too hard to maintain balance as firm support would be missing. Instead, use a conventional coir mattress topped up with a thin cotton mattress; these will firmly support your entire body and minimise physical energy expenditure.

Now, start deep breathing (all through your nose: breathing in deeply by counting 1,2,3, 4, now hold your breath by counting 1, then breathe out deeply by counting 1, 2, 3, 4, 5, 6, 7, 8—a little longer than the 'in' phase).

Repeat this breathing cycle for 9 to 10 times. Now, get into the next act by starting to do relaxation thinking and feeling. Imagine that the top of your head is getting relaxed and tension-free. Then move your thought to the entire face; then move to the throat-neck-shoulder combination. Once this is achieved to your satisfaction (if not achieved try again), move to your chest-middle abdomen-lower abdomen-waist portions and also your hands—from the shoulder joints to the tips of your fingers, one after another with the same relaxation motive.

Once these parts are also through, move your relaxation thoughts to your hip-thigh-knee-leg-feet region. Your body and brain, both are supposed to get relaxed with these interventions. If you still do not feel sleepy, put up a screen inside your mind. Slowly get the picture of sunny, bright blue morning autumn sky on this screen. Imagine, a few specks of snow-white autumn clouds are slowly moving from the right to the left side of your mental screen, followed by a flock of milk-white pigeons flying around. Concentrate on them......they are flying around and around......around and around. This way, your brain is becoming calmer and calmer....more and more tranquil and poised. Slowly and gradually, your eyelids will become heavy, eyeballs under them steady.....and sleep will take you over. Your brain and body, both adequately relaxed, will now get good rest for quite some time as long as the tranquilising effect of the relaxation thinking/feeling deep breathing and colour meditation (meditation on the blue sky, passing clouds and flying pigeons) remain with you.

As an alternative measure to colour meditation which has just been described, you can switch on a melodious flute recital in an auto stop music system before going to bed. Now lay your body in *sabasana*, practice deep breathing in and out for 9 to 10 times, then concentrate on the music. The slow sound waves of the music will work on your brain and produce brain waves required for sound dreamless sleep.

APPLICATION TIPS

- Perform a set of 'freehand' exercises and also some essential household physical work daily at convenient times.
- Become aware of the symptoms of ill health and lack of physical fitness and also the need for adopting timely preventive measures.
- Go for sound, dreamless sleep daily for 6 to 7 hours which is essential for the rest and relaxation of your tired brain.

Chapter 13

Good Physical Habits for Old Age Happiness

"If it were a new drug that had been shown to do this (that is, increasing your lifespan), it would be a billion-dollar drug. But this is something that people can do for free."
—Dr Dean Ornish,
California-based lifestyle change expert

KEEP AWAY FROM OLD AGE PHYSICAL HEALTH PROBLEMS

Take a vow and try your best to religiously follow the recommendations given regarding planned diet, planned physical fitness activities, and planned sound sleep by making them an integral part of your daily life, and you can keep away from the typical health problems of old age like diabetes, obesity, high blood pressure and high cholesterol, heart disease and stroke.

Telomerase Enzyme: Your Aging Controller

Dr Dean Ornish, head of the Preventive Medicine Research Institute in Sausalito, California, and the well-known author advocating lifestyle changes to improve health, has made a strong claim. According to him, sweeping lifestyle alterations including incorporation of a planned balanced diet, planned physical fitness activities and planned rest can raise your body's level of an enzyme (named *telomerase*) closely involved in

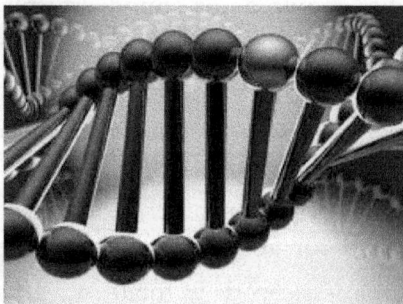

Fig. 24: Inside Our Gene (an Artist's Impression)

controlling the aging process. Ornish had made a statement: "If it were a new drug that had been shown to do this, it would be a billion-dollar drug. But this is something that people can do for free".

Telomerase fixes and lengthens parts of *chromosomes* known as *telomeres* that control longevity and are also important for maintenance of immune-system cells. (Also see Chapter 5, p. 62)

Shortening of *telomeres* indicates disease risk and sudden death in some types of cancer, including those affecting breast, colon and lungs. (1) [(1) "Study: Healthy lifestyle ups enzyme, slows aging process", *The Times of India, Kolkata,* 17 September 2008, p. 15].

Healthy Foods

Foods that are thought to reduce the risk of such diseases and have been researched thoroughly for their benefits to health are:

Monounsaturated and polyunsaturated fats, oils such as olive oil, avocados, olives, nuts and seeds.

Antioxidants: fruits and vegetables with the highest concentrations found in the most deeply and brightly coloured varieties—prunes, raisins, blueberries, other berries, spinach, Brussels sprouts, plums, broccoli, beetroot, avocados, oranges, red grapes, red capsicums, cherries, kiwi fruit, onions, corn, tea, red wine, green leafy vegetables such as lettuce and cauliflower. You would be interested to know that the amount of natural antioxidants produced by the body is largely determined by heredity. This explains why some people may enjoy great longevity, with members consistently living past eighty years of age.

Vitamin B3 (niacin): found in cereals.

Vitamin B12: nutritional yeast; soya; fermented foods; some seaweed products; and modified breakfast cereals.

Beans, legumes and peanuts.

Tomatoes.

WHAT TESTS YOU SHOULD GO FOR

However, we are trying to highlight that *prevention* is always better than *cure*. Therefore, just to ensure your good health and fitness status, go for a few medical tests as follows:

For Men

Blood Tests: blood group identification; full blood counts and peripheral smear; blood sugar test done on empty stomach and after meal; PSA for screening of prostrate cancer; lipid profile; Serum TSH Test: baseline screening for *thyroid* diseases; Liver Function Test; Renal Function Test; Urine Routine Test; Stool Test to screen for gastrointestinal disorders; ECG; Treadmill Test; Chest X-ray; Pulmonary Function Test; Spirometric Test; Ultrasonography to screen for stones in the gall bladder, kidney and to look for aortic aneurysms; Eye Test; Dental Check-up; Dietary Check-up.

For Women

(In addition to those for men)

Bone Densitometry Test: for osteoporosis and osteopenia—apple-shaped women are more at the risk of developing osteoporosis than those who are pear-shaped—heavy cladding of fat does not protect the bones from bone-wasting disease; mammography.

WHERE YOU NEED TO BE PHYSICALLY CAREFUL

As we have already said, prevention is always better than cure. At your age, touch wood, there is a chance of your slipping and meeting with an accident even while pursuing day-to-day activities of living and working.

Walk Carefully

You need to be physically careful while stepping on loose doormats, walking on floors with carpets or rugs, or on surfaces having glossy shiny finish, or on a wet floor in a bathroom or kitchen or in any other area where it has just been mopped or cleaned with water or liquid detergent. You should also remain alert about loose wires or cables which are plentifully present now-a-days because of the wide use of computers and other electrical and electronic gadgets.

Other Precautions

Wherever it is in your hands, use skid-proof floors and slip-resistant mats. Also avoid using footwear which can easily slip. Use a jute rug to cover the floor while taking physical exercise. Floors should be plain and even. Always wear footwear with a firm non-slip sole, inside and outside the house. At door locations, there should not be any door seal which may cause a fall. The underlying causes of fall would be: loss of muscle strength and diminished flexibility. These together results in instability and a decreased ability to control yourself as you lose your balance and start falling.

At house, keep walking paths clear of furniture and other obstacles. Do not leave objects like books, papers, flower pots, decorative items, shoes, slippers, socks, bags, briefcases or blankets randomly on the floor. Make sure wires are securely tacked to the floor or wall. Keep objects off the stairs. Stairways should be well lighted. Always use a handrail while climbing up or down stairs. Use a reading lamp. Have a night light in your bedroom; however, use it only when necessary—otherwise keep it off as it may disturb your sleep. Have a torchlight handy. Store frequently used items in the kitchen, bedroom and bathroom on shelves that you can reach without climbing or reaching high over your head. Never stand on a chair. If you must use a stool, get one with a frame you can hold on to. A solid ladder should have better utility.

Knowledge of Surrounding

Know your surroundings well. Learn where the booby-traps like potholes, uneven surfaces and broken pavements are located and avoid them. And don't be shy about using a walking aid if your stability or footing is insecure.

Dangers of Fall

When older people fall, their weakened bones are more likely to break. As many as one woman in four and one man in fifteen over the age of 60 can expect to suffer a fracture during their remaining years. So the first step is to build *muscle strength* in the thighs and trunk to increase stability.

TRY SIMPLE EXERCISES

You may try simple exercises for strengthening your muscles. We are describing just one of the many.

Lie on your back on the floor and raise one leg at a time with the foot off the floor, holding it there for 10 seconds. Gradually build up to 10 repetitions with each leg and you'll see how much stronger your thigh and calf muscles can get.

Likewise, there are easy exercises to improve balance. Gently holding the back of a sturdy chair, raise one foot off the floor, then try to let go off the chair. Once that is mastered, try it with your eyes closed, and then try it standing on your toes.

Daily stretches, especially of the legs and hips, can slow the loss of flexibility that can result in a fall.

FACIAL MASSAGE

You can effectively cope with age-related problems like stress, insomnia or memory loss by simply massaging your face which has a large number of nerves and blood vessels.

WALKING AND ITS BENEFITS

Walking is a multi-benefit activity. You walk for just 30 minutes a day and cut your risk of falling victim to nearly two dozen illnesses, including dementia and cancer. It is also associated with decreased risk of heart disease and stroke. Walking may protect the aging brain from growing smaller and, in turn, preserve memory in old age as has been observed by the University of Pittsburgh researchers.

Burning up Calories

The first benefit of walking is calorie burning. In medium-pace walking (3 to 4 km/hr), you burn 77 Calories (that is, kilocalories) per km. For fat reduction, walking 13 km per week is reasonable enough. If you want to bring positive change in the quantity of lipid in your blood, you must spend at least 1,000 Calories per week in walking. But the benefit that you'll derive by walking will go down the drain if you consume an equivalent amount of Calories in the form of any solid or liquid or a combination, immediately after you have performed the exercise, to satisfy your feeling of hunger. In most cases, such feelings are psychological, not physical.

Supply of Blood

You have, in total, around 60,000 miles of arteries and veins in your body for circulation of blood to every nook and corner. When a set of muscles are at rest, it does not require much supply of blood as it is not much active. A few of the blood vessels, remaining open and active, would suffice. However, when the same set of muscles becomes active and engaged in work, then it needs rush of blood for which all the blood vessels must open up. When you walk, the involved muscles of your body reach such peak performance condition.

The condition becomes more vigorous when you are running or jogging. You can feel the extra pressure in your system. Since the leg, waist, and lower back and lower abdominal muscles all participate in the walking activity, after retirement and particularly in your old age, you should make it a point to walk regularly. While at home also, you should try and actively stroll from one room to another rather than sitting or lying down most of the time as many senior citizens do.

Other Benefits

Regular walking reduces constipation. Because it contributes fitness to you, you don't get tired easily. Your mind also remains fresh and positively active and agile. You get rid of your mental laziness, sloppiness and depression. It also saves your brain from the common old age problem of loss of memory or dementia.

A Walking Plan for You

Start with a 110-step per minute walk. Then increase it to 130-step per minute. Maintain this pace for 20 to 30 minutes. Those who can walk at a brisk pace have a lot of energy and vigour. They are likely to live longer than who have a slower gait.

Keep your spine erect, breathe in and out deeply using your nostrils, look straight in front of you and walk forward. Walk alone as talking to someone while walking will divide your energy into three separate channels: walking, speaking, and listening. One more channel will get added when you establish eye contact with the person you're walking with.

However, you can use the 'talk test' (that is, testing your walking efficiency while talking and listening) to find out whether you're walking at the right pace. If you do not feel lack of energy while talking and walking then your pace is all right. On the contrary, if you're gasping for breath, that indicates you are walking at a faster pace than you should.

If you can do your walking when the sun is out (but not unbearably scorching) and take the sunshine on your back, you'll get maximum benefit from the solar energy available. Nevertheless, be careful not to look directly into the sun. Of late, health experts are suggesting that going out in the midday sun during Western summer and Indian winter is good for you; 10 to 15 minutes' exposure on the face, arms and legs will help to boost Vitamin D levels. Incidentally, 90% of the body's Vitamin D supply comes from the action of sunlight on the skin.

(2) [(2) "Exposure to midday sun boosts Vitamin D levels", *The Times of India, Kolkata,* 18 December 2010, p. 16.]

Pain on the bottom of the heel: This is a common problem in old age particularly when you are starting your walking regimen after a long gap. One may also suffer from it due to prolonged use of badly designed shoes which do not match with the arch of both feet and put them under strain.

To get relief, perform stretching exercises three times a day. Take a seated position and cross the painful foot over the knee of your other leg. Grasp the toes of your painful foot and bring your ankle up and your toes up. Place your thumb along the *plantar fascia* and rub it to stretch it. The fascia should feel like a tight band along the bottom of your foot when stretched. Hold the stretch for 10 seconds. Repeat 10 to 20 times for each foot. This exercise should be done initially in the morning before getting out of bed and after any long period of sitting.

STAIR CLIMBING: HOW IT CAN HELP YOU

In your day-to-day locomotor activities, not only walking but also using the stairs instead of taking elevators and escalators can be a life-saver for you. Inculcating stair-using habit can improve your health (on the weight management, cardiovascular, respiratory and digestive fronts) and fitness (mobility of your bones, muscles, joints, tendons and ligaments) cutting the risk of dying suddenly within a couple of years after retirement.

Stair climbing has the promise and potential to: increase your aerobic capacity (the amount of oxygen your body can use) by 8.5 to 10 per cent; reducing your body weight and fat levels; dropping your blood pressure by around 2.5 per cent; and decreasing the levels of your 'bad' cholesterol by 4 per cent. (3) [(3) ("Taking the stairs can save your life", *The Times of India, Kolkata,* 2 September 2008, p.15].

WRONG HABITS, NAUGHTY PROBLEMS

Long Stretches of Sitting: Muscle Sprains, Cramps and Heavy Legs

At a stretch, when you continue to sit for long for reading, writing or working on the computer, you may suffer from problems like: muscle sprains, heaviness in legs, or cramp.

These are symptoms indicating that unless you start taking precautionary measures, you may face some big problems soon. Therefore, be conscious about keeping your chest, abdomen, neck and head in a straight line while sitting.

When you are keeping something on the table for studying, reading or writing, try to keep your upper portion of the body (the head-neck-chest-abdomen combination) inclined forward at an angle at the hip joint with your thighs placed at the horizontal level on the seat. Do not maintain this posture stiffly, have it as much relaxed as possible.

Instead of sitting at a stretch, take periodic 'stretch breaks'. During such a 'stretch break', take a few deep breaths and stretch your body in opposite (that is, tension and compression) directions so that the muscles are worked upon.

If you plan to read a book for long on the table, you can use a book stand. If you're working on the computer, keep the keyboard at a height so that while working with the monitor screen and the keyboard both, the upward-downward movement of your eyes and neck should be the minimum. Don't move your neck too much under any circumstances. If necessary, adjust the heights of your table and chair.

Try to arrange for an adjustable support (may be a cushion) near your waist so that your waist muscles are not under strain.

Lying Down and Reading: Strain on Muscles, Bones and Eyes

When you are retired, you tend to lie down and read. This is not a good habit. The problem is aggravated when you lie on a soft foam mattress. The foam is pressed down at the sites where your body weight is more and there is uneven pressure on your spinal muscles and bones. Your neck and back muscles develop pain and then you realise that the problem is the outcome of your wrong postures.

Reading while lying also causes strain on your eye muscles. So, the first remedial step that you ought to take is to ensure that the mattress is not soft. It is always the best solution to have a thick wooden board or plywood sheet as the base of the bed, on which you lay a conventional coir mattress on which you overlay a thin cotton mattress not a spring or foam one.

Plus, there should be enough light available for your reading. You must adjust the distance of the reading material from your eyes to maximise convenience. You ought to ensure a distance of 12 to 14 inches (31 to 35 cm) between the two. If you are using powered glasses, you might have to do further adjustments. It is inconvenient for you to read big bound volumes as they are difficult to manage; handling paperbacks is equally frustrating as you cannot stretch it to open up—so the prints near the inner binding do not become clearly visible.

Dealing with Muscle Sprain or Cramp

It is only natural for you to have a muscle sprain or cramp in old age. However, if the pain lasts for three-four days, then go for an oil (hot) massage. And, if you want to get quick relief, compress the pain site with hot wet cloth/sponge. And, alternate hot and cold compress, four to five times per day, will give quicker relief if the pain still persists with just hot compress. If the pain persists even after that, then you ought to consult your physician.

Sleeping with a Night Lamp on

Sleeping regularly with a night lamp (dim light) on adversely affects the chemical balance and structure of the brain. It interferes with secretion of the sleep-inducing hormone *melatonin* that helps the body know that it is night time. Regular use of dim light at night may result in less dense networks of dendritic spines in the *hippocampus* which is a vital part of our inner or lower brain and is known to be the storage centre of our long-term memory. Dendritic spines are the hair-like growths on brain cells that transmit chemical messages from one cell to another. The *hippocampus* plays a key role in depressive disorders.

Sedentary Habits without Breathing Break

After you've spent some time in some sedentary occupation like working on the computer, reading or writing, leave your desk and deeply breathe in and out as while we indulge in such activities, our breathing is never perfect. We do either half, two-third or three-quarter breathing and, sometimes, even quarter breathing.

And, when you go for such a 'breathing break' look out to a far distance (best if greeneries are there) so that your eye muscles are exercised. Move your neck muscles also, raise and lower them alternately, shake them up to work them out in different ways than when you were working.

Smoking

It may appear that smokers and non-smokers die of heart disease or lung cancer at the same rate, but a 35-year-old male smoker is seven times as likely to die of heart disease or lung cancer as a non-smoker of the same age.

Splitting Pills in Half

Splitting tablets into two or more parts or opening up a capsule and taking out the granulated medicine is potentially dangerous and could lead you taking the wrong dose. There could be serious consequences, especially with the medicines that have a narrow margin between a therapeutic and a toxic dose. Splitting or breaking a capsule into two halves means the parts are often unequal in quantity. Such habits should be forthwith given up.

TIPS FOR TV WATCHING

Watch the TV from a distance of 5 to 6 feet (around 1.52 to 1.83 metres); and don't illuminate your room with very high power lamps while watching the TV. TV screen should be placed at the level of your eyes and you must not bend your neck too much either upward or downward to watch the TV.

TIPS FOR COMPUTER WORKING

Work on the computer at a stretch for 20 to 40 minutes. Thereafter, give a five minutes' break. During that break, you cast your sight to something at a distance of 20 feet (6 metres) and enjoy the experience. Keep the monitor 20 inches (50 cm) away from your eyes. Control the lights in the environment to reduce the strength and reflectivity of the illumination.

Don't rub the corner of your eye even if something has fallen into it. Wash your eyes in clean water. If the discomfort continues, consult your family physician.

EYE PROBLEMS IN OLD AGE

Cataract is a common problem which comes with advanced age. The lens of the eye becomes clouded, smoky and foggy. It can be removed without much hassle. However, if cataract is combined with diabetes, then the problem is really serious.

There is another eye problem, called *glaucoma*, known commonly as the 'silent thief of sight'. Most of us, although familiar with the term *'cataract'*, do not know what *glaucoma* is and have never undergone an 'eye pressure test' or 'tonometry' that determines fluid pressure inside the eye. Increased pressure within the eye is a sign of *glaucoma*. Greater risks of developing *glaucoma* are mainly due to short sight, eye injuries and high blood pressure. *Glaucoma* is a silent disease because most types cause no pain and produce no symptoms. The disease, therefore, progresses undetected until the optic nerve has already been irreversibly damaged, with varying degrees of permanent vision loss. It is therefore advisable for a retired person to get a regular 'tonometry test' done.

With aging, when due to environmental pollution, oxidants get deposited in the macula portion of our retina (which increases the sharpness of our sight), our eyesight gets affected. If you have been consuming fresh fruits (rich in vitamin C and antioxidants) from your early life, the impact of this problem is less. Such fruits include: amla, imli (tamarind), guava, orange, grapefruit, musambi, grapes, and lemon (or lime). The fruits must be fresh and whole (not cut). Fruit juice or stale fruits will also not serve the purpose.

Computer Vision Syndrome

Many of those who are going to retire today, tomorrow and the day after have been and will continue to be computer-users. You may be one of them and may also be a victim of computer vision syndrome. This common problem for computer-users is associated with multiple symptoms such as pain, watering of eye, blurred vision and eye strain and burning sensation, redness of eyes and headache. An affected person can also experience effects like colour fringes and after-images when looking away from the computer screen. Some people develop eye dryness and untreated complications can lead to chronic stages.

The eye blinking rate reduces from 12 to 15 times to 2 to 3 times in a minute when an individual works on a computer. In addition to this change, the air-conditioned ambience in the work environment, with controlled temperature and humidity, makes the eyes dry.

What should you do to reduce the harmful effects of computer use? Try to take a break after spending every 30 to 40 minutes with the computer. Besides, you ought to make it a point to voluntarily blink while working on the computer to help your eyes to produce tears that can help moisten and lubricate eyes. Your monitor should be positioned directly in front of you, about 18 to 24-25 inches (46 to 63 cm) away from your eyes, with the top of the monitor screen placed at your eye level or slightly below it. Anti-glare screen and adjusting the monitor settings do also help.

If the problem still continues, consult an eye specialist who would initially recommend the use of some good eye drops to reduce your eye dryness. Proper and timely precautions will help you to tackle the problem. (3) [(3) Mukherjee, Writankar, "Keep monitoring your eye strain", *The Economic Times, Kolkata*, 20 June 2008, p. 6].

TIPS FOR TRAVELLING

Get yourself medically checked up before any trip. If you had any history of falling ill recently, then the check-up should be proportionately thorough.

If you are taking an air journey, you'll no doubt make sure to have your baggage locked securely and the baggage tags tied up in proper places but also remember to keep your valuables, travel documents, identification cards and, importantly, your medicine with you in your hand luggage.

APPLICATION TIPS

- Take a vow to go for planned diet, planned physical fitness activities and planned sound sleep which will keep you healthy and fit despite your advanced age.
- Follow the do's and don'ts about food and activities of daily living and working.
- Go for the prescribed health status check-up tests.

Chapter 14

Mid-Life Pauses: A Biological Natural

"It's not merely a case of survival waiting for the last day of life to arrive. It is perhaps a case of living as an example of health and happiness at the age of 100 years—projecting a message to the present day younger generation that 'Yes, we can'."

—From the case study of the centenarian
Bibhuti Gupta Bhaya Published in the Bengali popular daily
Ananda Bazar Patrika, Kolkata, 9 January, 2011, p. 19

MID-LIFE BLUES

The physical as well as mental productivity of most common people start declining from the age of around forty-five to fifty-five when hormonal changes take place in a person's body. However, although it is inevitable, hormones do not cause any disturbance if you are healthy and happy despite your age being in that range. In women, this is the period of *menopause* while in men it is the *andropause* which arrives a few years later than in the case of the fairer sex. Members of both the sexes start passing through the *mid-life blues*—a crisis phase. Some may suffer more and some a little less; but it arrives in the life of everyone.

According to a recent report, the malady of mid-life crisis is hitting many 30-somethings as well. (1) [(1) Verma, Varuna, "30 going on 50", *The Telegraph, Kolkata*, 19 December 2010, p.14.] The manifold reasons include: continuous stress; long working hours; addiction to artificial stimulants like nicotine, alcohol, tea and coffee; break-neck competition in the workplace; and the fear of being replaced by younger smarter people. Your commitment to work is not because you enjoyed working; it is out of compulsion owing to other reasons the major one being the ever-increasing rat race, organisational politics and the self-generated pressure to stay on top of one's job. Today, if a working professional does not reach the top of the ladder by the age of 40 or 42, maximum 45, his chances of getting there becomes less. Most interestingly, sometimes having achieved too much too fast could also trigger a similar malaise. If one has achieved things much earlier than their peers, then they come to a stage where he doesn't know what to do with his life as there would be nothing much to look forward to. Naturally, he will start questioning and doubting the path that he had chosen in life.

Diminished energy and motivation, monotony of work leading to growing non-work interest, and the experience of illness (either personal or somebody else's) constitute a set of factors that reduce work output.

In addition, the age-related decline in mental speed and intelligence adds to the decrease in the individual's work efficiency. In most cases, this trend continues till the date when the individual retires from work. The losses in mental powers occur in mental speed of response or response time, the retrieval of recent information from memory, and the use of mental energy to find the ways around.

IT'S MOSTLY IN YOUR MIND: USE YOUR MENTAL LEVERS

However, there is no real reason to worry about it unnecessarily; because, decline in these mental functions may get more than compensated for by the age-rewarded problem-solving abilities and practical wisdom, which open up a totally new area, and which, if pursued seriously, may lead to unprecedented success and also increased earning, respect and prestige.

Some elderly people, who are emotional by nature, do not have the mental strength to brush off losses. They gradually withdraw from society because of some unhappy experiences like the death of a family member or a close friend, feeling of dependence on others. They can get back the normal state of their mind by taking some active steps rather than becoming more and more passive. They should, now, try and develop a few close relationships with like-minded people having similar likes and dislikes. Companionship with people has positive benefits for health and for the integrity of body systems. These benefits extend to mental health and include the preservation of mental ability.

MENOPAUSE AND ANDROPAUSE: ILL EFFECTS

During *menopause* and *andropause*, women and men lose the density of their sleep, suffer from loss of appetite, have burning sensation in their hands, legs and mouth, perspire profusely, and suffer from mental depression. As a result of all this, they may have lowered sexual urge.

This inevitable phase of life continues into further advanced age, that is, pre- and post-retirement. It may bring along a natural 'inferiority complex' or 'low self-esteem' leading naturally to depression to many amongst the elderly, although there may be exceptions who have been high-achievers and have recorded success after success. Those who are affected feel an acute generation gap; many of them, in modern times, suffer from *cyber phobia*. They feel backward and backdated as they are not so much computer-literate, nor they are gadget-savvy (handling mobiles, remote controllers, TVs, CD players, geysers, electric irons and the like).

For men, if they don't keep their male sex hormone *testosterone* and another typically male hormone *androgen* agile and active, they may fall victim of this peculiar syndrome. Keeping the body and brain healthy and fit and being sexually active constitute the answer to such problems. There is a valid reason. Sexually inactive elderly men are more likely to die from heart disease than women of a similar age due to the handiwork of two of the female sex hormones (*estradiol* and *estrone*, called together *estrogens*) which are also present in males along with the male sex hormone *testosterone* and are linked to increased levels of *bad cholesterol* and low levels of *good cholesterol* in men. (2) [(2) "Sex hormones up heart risk in men", *The Times of India, Kolkata,* 2 September 2008, p.15].

However, there is a note of caution attached. Although men, unlike women who are born with all their eggs in one go right from birth, make sperms throughout their adult life and the process of making *semen* (which involves copying *DNA*), is prone to error as men age. In aging men, successive germ cell replications occur and *de novo* (not passed from parent to offspring) mutations accumulate monotonously as a result of *DNA* copy errors. Therefore, children born out of men aged more than 55 years, have a high probability to be born with the propensity of having *bipolar disorder*—a severe mood disorder involving episodes of mania and depression. (3) [(3) "Bipolar Disorder: Older Fathers to Blame?" *The Statesman, Kolkata,* 3 September 2008, p. 8]

After your retirement, the resulting loneliness may add to such problems. Therefore, spend much of your time with your spouse; try to involve the partner in most of the plans and decisions. This may help you to overcome the hazards of menopause and andropause.

From this point of view, it would be wiser for you to involve your spouse in your retirement planning. You may have certain ideas which may be different from your spouse's. However, there should be a very good understanding between the two of you to go for the best alternative. Make minimum 3 and maximum 5 alternative plans. Both of you can contribute your ideas. Now, evaluate each alternative's Plus Points (PP), Minus Points (MP) and Most Interesting/Important Points (MIP) and select that particular alternative which has maximum PP and MIP and minimum MP.

Decision/ Solution	Plus Points (PP)	Minus Points (MIP)	Most Interesting/ Important Points (MIP)
Alternative I			
Alternative II			
Alternative III			

Select the one which has maximum PP & MIP and minimum MP

Fig. 25: The PP-MP-MIP Technique of Decision-Making/Problem-Solving

SENSORY LOSSES

The powers of all your anatomical and physical systems reduce with aging very fast, if you had not been maintaining them properly during your pre-retirement days.

One of the most important set of powers pertains to your sensory system. Your sensory powers (sight, sound, smell, taste, touch and kinaesthetic sense) provide you with two major applications: attention and awareness. These two faculties go hand in hand.

'Selective attention' is the ability to throw the spotlight on to a limited range of stimuli; whereas 'divided attention' is the ability to do several things at once. These two abilities may not exist in the same individual in equal quantities. However, whatever may be the degree or level of these abilities that you had possessed when you were young you may not be lucky to have them in the same quantities when you retire. And, you should be prepared to face that reality; otherwise frustration will make you unhappy.

Your cognitive abilities may decline due to inadequate attention, poor concentration, and lack of patience. These are deficiencies which can be overcome to a considerable extent by practicing attention and concentrated listening with positive eye contact and total abstinence from periodic interruption.

Developing a deficiency in hearing starts from the mid-thirties and, as aging proceeds, perception of higher frequencies (usually in the 4000-6000 Hz range—but most marked over 8000 Hz) is reduced. Then noises start sounding to you louder than they really are. Such problems may impair your capacity to take part in conversations unless you concentrate with some special effort (by establishing and maintaining eye contact and refraining from the bad habit of interruption from time to time). Impairment of your ability to appreciate music or a movie in its true form may not be as serious as the communication-related problems that you may face.

Sight is also impaired by aging. The most common example is the clouding of the lens of the eye that begins at around the age of twenty to twenty-five and becomes noticeable as a cataract in some elderly people. This clouding of the lens reduces the amount of light falling on the retina at the back of the eye, and scatters the light that does get through. As the brain slowly ages it has plenty of time to adjust to the changed properties of the image relayed to it by the retina. However, vision once impaired by bilateral cataracts can be restored by replacement lenses.

The capacity of your eyes to adjust themselves to different light levels may become less efficient with age. Colour vision and changes in visual acuity also worsen with aging: it becomes more difficult to distinguish blues from greens, and both near and distant visions are affected. Such problems take away your confidence to drive a two-wheeler or a car.

Your reading and computer operational speeds may be slowed, especially if the print is small. Secondly, your visual search strategies may become less efficient.

The senses of touch, pain sensation, your positional orientation, and balance are also diminished after retirement.

You should not forget another important point that your sensory and mental faculties get affected if you have been on some medication, especially for neurological or psychological treatment.

TAKE CARE OF YOUR GLANDS

Your six *glands* are the source of your vitality and happiness. You must get acquainted with them. The *pituitary* and *pineal* glands are situated inside your brain; the *thyroid* is in the neck region, the *adrenals* and *pancreas* in the mid-abdominal area and the *sex* glands in the lower abdominal region.

The *Pituitary* Gland

It is a small oval endocrine gland lying deep inside the lower structures of your brain. Its behaviour is most interesting and versatile. The frontal portion of the *pituitary* secretes several hormones, having an effect upon other endocrine glands whose general overall function is to regulate growth and metabolism. The back portion of the *pituitary* secretes *pituitrin*. The *hypothalamus* regulates the release of hormones from the *pituitary*—hormones amongst whose major function is the regulation of the release of other hormones from the *adrenal glands, testes* and *ovaries*.

As you advance in age, there is a rise in your blood of a hormone secreted by your *pituitary*, called the *thyroid-stimulating hormone (TSH)* and a fall in the concentration of an *adrenal hormone* called *dehydroepiandrosterone sulphate*. Periodic 'fasting' increases the lifespan. The simple reason is that it raises the level of the growth hormone secreted by your *pituitary* which stimulates the production of *T-lymphocytes* from the *thymus gland*. *T-lymphocytes* play an important role in keeping up the body's immunity to disease. Reduction in the immunity response triggers the possibility of age-related diseases like *arthritis*. The level of growth hormone is raised with the help of physical activities including exercises. Regular exercise and periodic fasting are thus some of the measures that prolong life. The level of growth hormone, secreted by the *pituitary,* rises during sleep as well. However, fasting should not be carried too far as there is a possibility of protein-calorie malnourishment and weakening of the immune system.

The *Pineal* Gland

It secretes *melatonin* which is the sleep-inducing chemical also having a few more beneficial properties.

The *Thyroid* Gland

It secretes the *thyroxine* hormone which, if secreted inadequately, you tend to become sluggish and fat; whereas if it is secreted in too much quantity, you suffer from nervous tension and become thin. *Thyroid* gland problems are quite common.

The *Adrenal* Glands

These again, like the *pituitary*, are responsible for the secretion of a variety of hormones. These are connected to the *medulla* inside your brain's *adrenal cortex* area which secretes the 'fight-or-flight' hormone *adrenalin.* Another hormone that it secretes is *cortisone* or *cortisol* which plays a key part in metabolism and is also vital to the functioning of the immune system.

The *Pancreas*

It secretes two hormones, called *insulin* and *glycogen* which help to balance the body's sugar level. Dysfunction of *pancreas* may lead to *diabetes*, which is the result from a failure in the production of *insulin* causing an increase in the level of your blood sugar.

The *Sex Glands: Testes* and *Ovaries*

The *sex hormones* secreted by the *sex glands* are important not only for sexual virility but also for sparkling eyes, smooth skin and a pleasant and attractive personality.

General Tips about the Care of Your Glands

Adherence to the good lifestyle rules of planned diet, planned physical fitness activities and planned sound sleep will help you to maintain the functions of your glands which, in turn, will give you a happy life.

IMPACT OF AGING AND STRESS ON GLANDULAR FUNCTIONS

The human brain may shrink as much as fifteen per cent between the ages of fifty and sixty five. This shrinkage problem might have affected you already. Much of this loss is due to cells themselves shrinking as they lose water, and ventricles and sulci enlarge, although there are also some neuronal loss in particular brain regions. The extent of cell death is affected by neuronal processes. Such shrinkage, in turn, will also naturally affect the glands located inside the brain and their functions.

Which glandular functions get affected by *stress*? Chronic *stress*, for instance, increases *cortisol* production, and chronically increased *cortisol* in turn accelerates cell death in regions of the brain like *hippocampus*, whose neurons carry receptors for the hormone. Such factors may help explain why neither shrinkage nor the cell loss is uniform across the brain, but particularly prevalent in parts of the *frontal lobes*, *hippocampus*, *cerebellum* and *basal ganglia*.

Both fear and pleasure involve whole body hormonal responses including *adrenalin* generated in the *adrenal* glands and 'steroids' (such as *cortisol*).

These hormones interact directly with the brain. The neurons of *hippocampus* are packed with receptors able to interact with *steroid* hormones to help cognition. *Adrenalin* interacts with the brain via *amygdala*, triggering neuronal pathways which also activate *hippocampus*.

There are changes in the immune system and hormone levels, including both *cortisol* and steroids such as *oestrogen* and *testosterone*. Such fluctuations will affect their interaction with neuronal receptors in the brain, notably the *hippocampus*.

APPLICATION TIPS

- Tackle your mid-life blues (which are most natural biological phenomena), if you are affected by them, with your mental levers.
- Fight your loneliness by spending much of your time with your spouse if your family now constitutes only the couple, and involve the partner in all the plans, programmes and decisions.
- Learn to face and accept your sensory slowdowns which are a natural part of your aging process.
- Be conscious about the functions of your glands and take as much care of them as you can.

Chapter 15

Mind Care for Old Age Happiness

"Worry about getting old—and you'll start experiencing the effects of old age."
—Kevin Hogan, Dave Lakhani, Bob Beverley and Black Warren,
The Secret behind the Secret Law of Attraction,
Eagan, Minnesota: Network 3000 Publishing 2007

TWO CASE STUDIES ON AGED MINDS

Worry means a wandering mind and wandering mind means an unhappy mind, according a global study of happiness conducted with iPhones. (1) [(1) Nadkarni, Vithal C. "Goof off, be blue", *The Economic Times, Kolkata*, 25 November 2010, p. 8].

Most aged people's minds, of both sexes, tend to be filled with all kinds of wandering thoughts, particularly worries. In the crowd of their mental worries, the three most predominant groups that stand out are: first of all, those regarding their own health and fitness and how the process of aging is affecting them; secondly, those related to economic problems— for the rich and affluent amongst them how and where to invest so that they get a safe and secure high return on investment over a short period of time as they feel they do not have much time and life left—and for the economically backward amongst them, wherefrom they will arrange funds for their subsistence; and, third and lastly, those related to their dependents, particularly their children—their future.

Meet Nagendra Nath Basu, 57, who works as a commercial executive in a private family-managed firm. His place of work is at least 12 km away from where he lives in South Kolkata and he takes the Calcutta Metro rail for his daily to-and-fro travel. Basu has been suffering from rheumatoid arthritis for the last twenty years and it has attained such a worse condition at present that his daily living and working are being severely affected. He feels tremendous pain in climbing up and down stairs, getting up from a seat once he sits down, getting down from bed and, worst of all, while walking. He recently consulted a reputed orthopaedic surgeon who after some investigation told him that the fluid in both his knee joints have dried up and the joint cartilages have also thinned down so much that he has to go for knee replacement surgery very soon;

otherwise, he will be totally disabled. Basu's mind carries a heavy load of worry every day not only as he has to climb up and down the stairs at the metro stations at both ends of his journey, twice every day, but also mainly because he has to go up and come down four floors in an old building where his office has shifted in a residential area of North Kolkata after their original office in a central commercial area of the metro city was damaged badly by fire six months ago. He feels he will be much happier if he can get another job (which may not pay him as much as he is getting at the moment) nearer his home. But would he really be happy even if that happens—may be only a little, relatively?

Meet Jamunesh Banerjee, 79—a widower. He left his chartered accountancy practice in the hands of his two junior partners at the age of 70. His only son, who is still single at the age of 49, is also a chartered accountant and is an executive director in an international chartered firm, being posted in New Delhi. Jamunesh lives alone in his compact well-decorated flat in Kolkata, and is mobile having a well-maintained car with a driver. His movements are, however, restricted because of his bone and joint problems. He suffers from acute waist and lower limb joint pains at the hip, knee and ankle levels. Until about two years ago, he was terribly depressed because his son was not getting married. On top of his joint problems, he had developed 'Irritable Bowels Syndrome (IBS)' which is a direct outcome of unhappiness and stress. Besides, during his high stress period, if someone would ask him how he was keeping, his answer would be most cynical. Recently, his mind has taken a U-turn. He has reconciled with his son's decision that he will not marry and remain single all through, and this has helped him to put up with his loneliness. Although he has irreversible macular degeneration in both his eyes and cannot read anything without strain (he can read well with the help of magnifying glasses but he finds it most inconvenient), he is not unhappy as he has accepted it as a natural consequence of the aging process. He spends his time talking to friends and relatives using his cell phone, and also likes to receive and send e-mails. He has minimised his worries and has control over his mind which was evident when we got some instances of his cognitive powers and live memory. His mind does not wander now as it has attained a happy state compared to what it was like even only two years ago.

Why mental worries increase with age will be easier for you to understand when we tell you how old age affects the powers of the mind.

A simple technique for 'stilling' your mind to develop your powers of concentration and information processing which reduce as you age, is provided a little later in this chapter itself.

MENTAL POWERS: NATURAL SLOWDOWN

Each Brain is Different

Your brain is different from everybody else's. The connections between the *neurons* in your brain have been fashioned as you have lived out your life and pursued your working and living habits to provide you with a totally individual and unique brain, different from everyone else in this world. That way, every human being is a very special thing!

To what Extent Aging Affects Your Brain's Processes

However, as you had attained middle age, some of the processes inside your brain started slowing down a little. One example is with respect to acquisition of new skills such as driving. "Statistics from the British School of Motoring suggest that the average number of hours tuition (the number of hours a person pays for at the school to learn to drive) roughly matches the student's age."(1) [(1) Greenfield, Susan, *The Human Brain: A Guided Tour*, London: Phoenix, Sixth Impression, 2000, p. 151]

Although your brain continues to slow down in certain ways, as you advance in age, in a few other ways, it still adapts and changes its profile. By the age of seventy, although there is a 5 per cent loss in brain weight, you can still process an astonishingly large amount of information. There is also little evidence that learning ability decreases with age. On the contrary, vocabulary generally improves with age. Heads of business, top professionals, political leaders and other highly successful people are observed to be at the peak of their powers during the post-sixty phase of life as we'll see from a few examples highlighted elsewhere in this volume.

Even at the physical level, not all of us are destined to become invalid. Take the case of Hilda Crooks, the lady who climbed Mount Fuji in Japan at the ripe old age of ninety-one. Although a little different, let us talk about the retired schoolteacher V L Bela of Aizwal, Mizoram—one of India's least developed hilly States in the north-east. He and his family members celebrated his birth centenary at his Aizwal home in November 2010. Around five years ago, when angiography showed 70 to 80 per cent blockage in one of his major coronary arteries, Bela himself gave the green 'go ahead' signal to the famous intervention cardiologist of Kolkata Dr Tarun Praharaj to carry out a stent angioplasty which was most successful. Dr Praharaj made a visit to Aizwal recently for a check-up on Bela and he is very happy with his present state of health. Bela still walks unassisted. (2) [(2) Yengkhom, Sumati, "Surgery at 95, ticking on at 100', *The Times of India, Kolkata,* 26 November 2010, p.4].

Two more cases of old age achievements have recently hit the headlines and both are from the state of Assam. The first case is about centenarian Bholaram Das who is the oldest research scholar in an Indian university—Guwahati. The same university has got another feather in its cap with septuagenarian Sarojini Bhagawati having cleared her MA in political science in 2011. Don't these cases inspire you? I get immensely motivated when I find elderly people are breaking records or setting trends. I set new goals for myself and drive towards them with all my hands and legs and heart and soul

Impact of Your Social Environment

The impact of post-retirement aging on your mind powers is not necessarily merely a plain and simple biological phenomenon. It has to be recognised as an impact of your lifestyle and social environment on your biology.

When you retire, at that age you can no longer perform things you had achieved as a younger person; for example, reading the small print without glasses. The more advanced you are in age, the greater is the possibility of people close to you—family and friends—being no longer there in this world any more, thus increasing your loneliness. In today's society, where there is a heavy focus on work outside the home, retirement, particularly for men has been, for many, a period affecting one's sense of self-worth. It is not surprising therefore that one observes an increase in incidences of post-retirement mental depression or anxiety neurosis. One big attributable cause is the frequent crowding of our mind by the fearful images of growing old, invasion by different sorts of diseases, some disabling, and senility. Such negative visualisation results in many of our powers, particularly mental powers, getting affected. These are consequences of the social learning and conditioning processes and the consequent value system that paints a gloomy picture of our greying years. It involves attitudes passed on to us from family, friends and society at large since our early childhood.

The Extent of Slowdowns

After retirement, for many, there is a reduction in your brain's sensitivity and slowdown in responses to external stimuli. In addition to such adverse changes, as a result of the neuronal depreciation (that is diminution in the powers of the neurons), a number of metabolic processes slow down.

Most of the functional changes are brought about by physical and social contexts and factors, some of them are context-independent such as *reflexes* (for example, the 'eye-blink reflex').

Years of Routine Work Stagnate Your Unused Brainpowers

One very important yet unrecognised aspect is there for you to reckon with while talking about your mental powers.

If you have been a knowledge- and not a physical worker, a couple or three decades of experience doing the same type of routine job is equivalent only to one or two years of experience as you have been repeatedly using the same set of brainpowers. It would normally have brought stagnation in your brain's potentials. In fact, there is a strong possibility that lot of your brainpowers would have almost snoozed off or disappeared due to lack of their periodic even occasional use as it happens in the case of any machine or electronic gadget, because of the biological 'use it or lose it' principle. These unutilised powers would have been easily restored had you been in the dawn or morning hours or even the noon of your career. Now that you are approaching the dusk, getting those powers back may be possible because of the plasticity of the brain tissue, but with great difficulty—lot of hard work and committed practice.

However, if you had a varied experience throughout your career or would have used some of your diverse mental powers outside your work role by indulging in activities like music composition, creative writing, directing or acting in drama, choreography, interior decoration, fashion design, or original painting, much of your brainpowers would have been productively and positively utilised to a greater extent. This state of your brain health will give you confidence to continue working even after you have crossed your chronological retirement age.

Look at Sudhin Gupta, who had held a clerical position all his life in a govt. ordnance factory and had been engaged in almost the same types of jobs all through his career. Immediately after his regular retirement, he joined the MA classes in history at the Rabindra Bharati University, Kolkata, completed it in the regular course and has again joined MA (Economics). He was never good academically and had only completed his BA without any major or honours before he joined the ordnance factory job; so completing his MA at the age of sixty as a regular student was a really commendable feat for him. On asking him how he could make it, he was very honest. He said that he studied on his own regularly everyday at least for 6 to 8 hours and practised by writing answers to test paper questions.

Are You Mentally Fit for a Post-Retirement Job Assignment

But, how do you ensure that you are mentally fit to take up a post-retirement job assignment? Check up your mental abilities with a few day-to-day practical things.

If you are able to follow any TV programme, then you are audio-visually and cognitively capable. Instead of TV, if you're able to listen and enjoy radio news, a talk, a play or some group discussion, your auditory powers and their relationship with your cognition seem to be of a satisfactory level. Similarly, if you're able to read and follow newspapers and magazines and derive satisfaction, and follow others' conversation and interpret them properly, then you should not have any reason to worry. Along with these, you should check on the status of your 'working memory' and your abilities on the creative front (should you possess any such inherent talent) and if you find all those are generally O.K., then you are mentally fit.

PRACTICAL EXAMPLES OF MENTAL SLOWDOWN

A few practical examples pertaining to the post-retirement 'mental slowdown' phenomenon are being cited below.

Mental Speed

After retirement, you may find that your mental speed does not appear to be as fast as it used to be when you were younger. Don't get scared; don't you feel that you have some neurological or psychological problem. This kind of slowdown is quite natural with aging.

Mental speed is the 'response time' or 'reaction time' between your experiencing something (that is, receiving a 'stimulus') and coming out with a 'response' or 'reaction' after your brain has processed all the information associated with the event. You may not face so much difficulty with 'one stimulus at a time' situations as much as you may feel with 'multiple stimuli at a time' where you might have to discriminate between the various stimuli and choose one or a selected few from them. Decreased speed of nerve transmission/conduction of the information, impaired sensory functions (see 'Sensory Losses' discussed in Chapter 14) and slowed reactive muscle movements are all responsible for slowing down your 'simple' as well as 'multiple choice' response/reaction time.

For some people, the slowing down happens soon after retirement due to *stress* arising from the sudden change in activities and lifestyle whereas for some others, who have been preparing themselves well for such changes, the slowing down process may be slower.

Powers of Concentration and Information Processing

We have talked, in the beginning of this chapter, about the 'wandering mind' problem which is related to these two brainpowers: concentration and information processing.

At any point of time, the events you are interested in (for example: reading a paragraph in a book or a newspaper, watching a TV programme, or listening to someone's talk), take place in groups of inter-connected brain cells. This occurs against a background of many other parcels of information being shared between brain structures.

Your brain thus focuses itself on the set of information that you are interested in while there would be a whole host of information present in the background, just ignored by your brain. The more developed or stronger your power of concentration (opposite is restless hyperactive wandering mind or, at the other extreme, very slow, dull hypoactive mind) is, the better will be the quality of your information processing and perception or understanding development about the event.

While you have, due to your advanced age, a lot of experience stored in your brain against which the freshly received current information will be weighed to give a much better ultimate perceptual judgement than a much younger inexperienced brain, your powers of concentration and information processing (by which your brain evaluates the inputs received against every type of information acquired from your wide experience and exposure rather than storing it in your memory) may deteriorate due to the aging process, leading to 'hyperactivity' or 'hypo-activity' or both in a bipolar form.

These powers are present in your brain's 'executive controller' function located in the front portion of your frontal lobes, which is known as the pre-frontal cortex (PFC). The PFC is not present in the brains of chimpanzees who happen to be our closest ancestors living today, having 98.4 to 99 per cent genetic properties shared with us, human beings. (3) [(3) Rose, Steven, *The 21ˢᵗ Century Brain*, London: Vintage Books, 2006, p. 92]. The PFC is actively stimulated if you had held a position or pursued a profession that required systematic planning and programming, frequent weighing of pros and cons, cost-benefit analysis, opportunities-and-threats studies, making judgemental decisions, managing resources effectively, and guiding people. These activities are all electrical in nature.

You can reduce your problems arising out of hyperactive or hypo-active or bipolar thought processes by 'stilling' your mind.

How to practice 'stilling' your mind to increase your power of concentration: In order to 'still' your mind, sit in a relaxed erect posture on a chair (preferably armless) with your hands laid on your lap having your fingers interlocked and with your feet kept loosely on the floor— one foot placed across the other.

Now, start breathing deeply using your nostrils by keeping your lips loosely shut: breathing in to fill your breathing vessel, with air from the bottom (that is, lower abdomen) moving to the top (that is, the throat level).

Once you have breathed in deeply to fill your breathing vessel with air, hold your breath for 2-3 seconds so that the air collected can get dispersed and distributed evenly throughout. Finally, breathe out through your nose, releasing the expired air from top downwards. Repeat this cycle nine to ten times in order to slow down your brain's activity by allowing the brain to pick up your slow and regular respiratory rhythm. Now, concentrate on an imaginary picture by putting it up on an imaginary mental screen for a couple of minutes. After spending four to five minutes altogether, come back to your real senses.

Your Diverse Memory Powers

Men in their 70s and 80s are more likely than women to get affected in their memory power and have difficulty thinking. Mild Cognitive Impairment (MCI) involves a level of mental decline which is a normal impact of aging.

Your *long-term memories* (in terms of knowledge, experience, skills, habits, information, know-how and so on) were laid down over many months and many years and would remain accessible throughout much of your life. Such memories are expected to last indefinitely and believed to be permanent as when they are first stored in your young age, your brain feels the need of having firm impressions and storing them in case you need them some time in future for your sustained survival and security. Therefore, mind you that forgetting is not erasure, but some temporary inability to access the stored memory. Your short-term memories (lasting minutes to hours) are *'working memories'* that constitute the current account of your daily living and working.

Working memory is what is called into play when one is actively engaged in the work of recall, and may last only for seconds. It is the memory of the ever-disappearing present as it fades into the past. *Working memory* involves a dynamic flux across many cortical regions (that is in the outer and upper structures of your brain). We'll talk about your *working memory* a little later.

The *hippocampus*, which is located amidst the lower structures of your brain, can contain some 36,000 distinct memories.

Regarding the classification of memory types, different experts have put forward different proposals. However, for general purposes, we can classify them into the following types: (i) *declarative memory*—memory of something that you had most firmly declared; (ii) *procedural memory*—memory of how to do things, such as how to ride a bicycle, how to do a work assignment, how to work on the computer and so on; (iii) *episodic memory*—memory of events and episodes; (iv) *semantic memory*—memory connected with the meanings of words and sentences. *Reference memory* is the hypothetical 'store' of *semantic* and *episodic* data located in the left *infero-temporal cortex*—a region which becomes active when memory is called upon.

Loss of memory, during your post-retirement days, may follow a sequence like this: first in the series is the loss of *episodic memory*, followed by *semantic*, followed ultimately by *procedural memory*.

All the new information that you capture using your sensory systems through sight, sound, touch, taste and smell is placed in the temporary *'working memory'* store where it is available for short-term use. The short-term use can provide data for an immediate reaction in response to very recent sensory inputs. However, some sets of data, even from the short-term acquisition, are transferred to the long-term memory store.

Both your 'visual' and 'auditory' channels contribute to your *verbal memory*—the memory that is responsible for your vocabulary building and retrieval of words from your word-power storage. In your post-retirement days, you may find problems in understanding and production of language as your *verbal memory* may get adversely affected although your verbal knowledge increased with age, as you would have already noticed. However, although you may have a strong vocabulary, you might face a problem of accessing that storage and may not get the right word at the tip of your tongue at the right time at the right place. As a result, you may substitute the right word by describing its function in a round-about way. For example, instead of using the word 'comb' you may describe it as 'the thing for grooming my hair' or instead of 'butter knife' you say 'the thing for applying butter on toast'. Sometimes, you may also ask for the wrong thing (such as: you ask for 'sugar' instead of 'salt' when 'soup' is being served). This will happen although you know exactly what you want, but you just cannot get the right verbal input. Those amongst us who have a strong *working memory,* which should help us in tackling the immediate past, and present, are much happier than those whose long-term memories are much stronger than the short-term *working memory.* Happy people have plastic brains which help them to remain firmly in the immediate past and future whereas unhappy people, while aging, live more in the distant past and have a relatively weak *working memory* compared to their *long-term memory.*

If your case is a worse one, you may not be able to follow the TV or radio programmes as your language processing faculties might have deteriorated.

So what is the remedy? To cope with such depressing situations, first of all, you must be prepared for such slowdowns with aging and sudden change from active life to a life of idleness and vacuum. Although you might have retired, you should try to follow the same daily schedule (to the extent feasible) as you had been following before your retirement.

Secondly, you should not give up facing situations (like conversation with others, reading, watching the TV, listening to the radio, or going to movies) where you have difficulty to follow and correlate. Instead, you should try to expose yourself to such situations and put in a little extra effort to comprehend as much as possible.

With the advancement of your age, in the post-retirement phase of your life, there are adverse changes in your immune system and hormone levels (including both *cortisol* and *steroids* such as 'testosterone' and 'oestrogen'). Such fluctuations affect their interaction with the brain's neuronal receptors, especially the *hippocampus*, located in the lower structures of your brain, which happens to be the seat of your memory. *'Episodic'* (event-based) memory may get more affected than *'semantic'* (related to words, their meanings and proper usage) memory. *'Procedural'* memory (how to do things) may be the least affected.

Going a little deeper into the other kinds of memory that your brain is empowered with, you have the *'implicit'* (non-declarative) memory which occurs unconsciously when you are just not aware about the learning. *'Explicit'* (declarative) memory builds up when you learn with a purpose. The latter always involves the *hippocampus*. The former involves diverse brain circuits. You are likely to have your *'explicit'* memory affected due to aging whereas your *'implicit'* memory continues to give you service.

In any case, mild difficulties faced with your memory should not be considered a very serious problem as these are inevitable with aging.

The 'executive controller' power of your brain is helpful in tasks involving your *'prospective'* memory which provides strategies to remember to switch off appliances before going to bed, locking up on leaving the house, shutting the windows during a heavy downpour, remembering birthdays and other anniversaries, or taking medicine.

A happy elderly person will not suffer on this front at all and will remember to prospect every thing before leaving the place

If you have an impaired *'prospective'* memory, it may be very annoying for others as you tend to forget that you had already told somebody something. You may go on repeating the same message to the same person which may be most disturbing for him. This is a common problem that most retired people face. One effective way to solve this problem is to note down things that you are likely to forget in a memory pad.

Eating salmon, tuna and other fatty fish may help prevent memory loss in addition to reducing the risk of stroke. A new study suggests a *vitamin* commonly found in meat, fish and milk may help to keep you away from the possibility of memory loss due to aging. This memory-friendly chemical is *Vitamin B12*. (4) [(4) "Vitamin helps fight memory loss", *The Times of India, Kolkata*, 11 September 2008, p. 17].

Common problems related to memory in old age include trouble finding words—difficulty in retrieval from the memory store. Root cause is possibly gradual neglect and atrophy of the brain's attentional system. One good remedy is to keep the habit of new learning continuously even in the ripe old age which keeps the concerned part of the brain active by secretion of the neurotransmitter *acetylcholine* which is the brain chemical essential for learning.

A good brain exercise to keep your brain fit would be on 'self-organisation': (i) how would you reorganise your desk and drawers for time-saving; (ii) how would you reorganise your clothes for time-saving. Another good exercise would be on 'kinaesthetic perception': how would you recognise objects by touch rather than by sight.

Learning Ability

Learning and memory development are inter-linked. We have an intense period of learning in childhood. Every day is a day of new stuff for a kid. And then, in our early employment, we are intensely engaged in learning and acquiring new skills and abilities. And, more and more we progress in life we are operating as users of mastered skills and abilities.

During middle age, activities such as reading newspaper and magazines, practicing a profession for many years, and speaking the prevailing languages are mostly the replay of mastered skills, not learning by understanding (learning mechanically never produces the same beneficial developmental effect as in the case of learning by understanding and developing a clear perception). Any new learning by understanding engages the system in the brain that regulates *plasticity*. By the time we hit our seventies, we may not have systematically engaged that and associated systems that regulate plasticity for forty to forty-five years— may be even more.

Anything that requires highly focused attention will help the control system for plasticity to keep up its production of *acetylcholine* and *dopamine*. Those may include: learning new physical activities that require concentration and which you enjoy (such as swimming or playing badminton, table tennis or tennis, or dancing), solving challenging puzzles (such as sudoku), or making a career change that requires that you master new skills and material.

Learning and training can increase your brain weight—generally by 5% and up to 9% in areas that the training directly stimulates. Trained and stimulated neurons develop 25% more branches and increase their size, the number of connections per neuron, and their blood supply. These changes can occur late in life, though they do not develop as rapidly in older persons as in young ones. When you are motivated and interested to learn, the brain responds by having the specific areas getting bigger. When motivation or 'passion', 'potential' for development and 'practice'—all the three are 100% present, the skill development is very fast and high—it can take place within a short 'period'..

Everything that happens in a young brain can happen in an elderly brain provided there is motivation.

The Power of Intelligence

Intelligence can be defined as the combined powers of reasoning and judgement which, when exercised, help you to make accurate appraisals of circumstances, study problems and come up with appropriate solutions and act always with a purpose.

Intelligence can, most safely and conveniently, be divided into two broad categories: 'crystallised intelligence' and 'fluid intelligence'. The former is the collective knowledge and experience accumulated over time to sharpen your combined powers of reasoning and judgement. The latter signifies your mental flexibility and willingness to adapt to changes, to seek novelty, and to try to make appropriate adjustments.

In fact, some parts of intelligence gather momentum with age. These are: vocabulary, practical judgement, information power, and proper composition of sentences. It happens provided, of course, you have been using the powers during your active career in the pre-retirement years.

Mental Flexibility

Your upper brain's front portion located just behind your eyes in your forehead, shown as *frontal lobe* in Fig. 26, is the seat of your mental flexibility, which helps you to adjust with changes, develop new insights, generate new ideas and novel solutions, remain creative, and display innovativeness across the lifespan. This power of yours may also tend to get adversely affected after your retirement whereas at that stage of your life you need it desperately if you are in a nuclear family situation and there is nobody else senior or junior to you whom you can consult while in doubt.

You can try out a simple exercise to test the level of your mental flexibility. This exercise involves word generation tasks where you try to name as many words as possible, within a minute, beginning with the

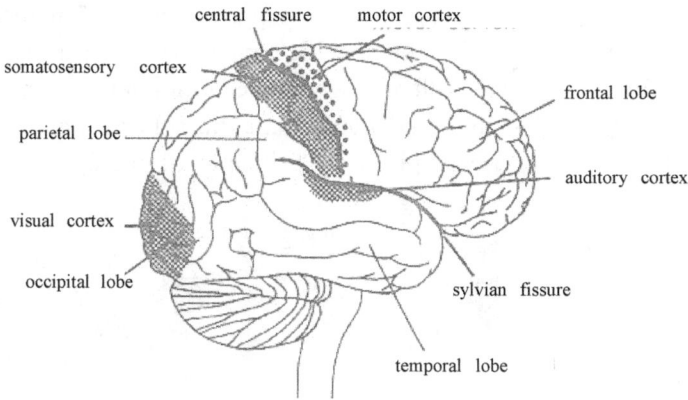

Fig. 26: The Human Brain's Right Side View

letter 'S' (such as: sugar, science, scenery, Satan, since, serious, serve, small, short, stalwart, sometimes, severe etc.). A satisfactory score will be ten in a minute. This exercise challenges your 'verbal fluency'. To keep your mental flexibility well-maintained, despite the impact of the aging process on you, you can practise such exercises regularly. One such common exercise is solving crossword puzzles.

Your Brain's Plasticity and Self-Organising Power

During the springtime of your life, one of the most remarkable properties of your brain was its plasticity. A young human brain achieves its plasticity by the wide spreading out of the dendrites (or branches of the brain cells) for inter-cellular transactions and also for alteration of potentials in the cells' biochemical functions. Such plasticity gave your brain its power for quick internal reorganisation with more experience and newer and newer exposures.

See in Fig. 27, how the upper and outer brain structure of ours has two different areas, adjacent to each other, known as the *sensory cortex* (where all our sensory organs have representative spaces allocated) and the *motor cortex* (where all our motor parts/organs have representative spaces allocated). The allocation of representative space, whether it is in the *sensory* or in the *motor* cortex, has been done according to the importance of the organs or parts; and, the importance is decided upon according to the frequency of the organ's or part's use. For example, if you are a right-handed person, the representative spaces for your right side organs and parts provided on the left half of your brain would be relatively more than the corresponding spaces of your left side organs and parts provided on the right half of your brain.

In a profession like machine operation, or playing a musical instrument, where the fingers are used, if some specific fingers are used more than the others then the brain map will change correspondingly to show larger space for the fingers that are used more than the others. This is possible owing to the 'use it or lose it' plasticity principle of biology.

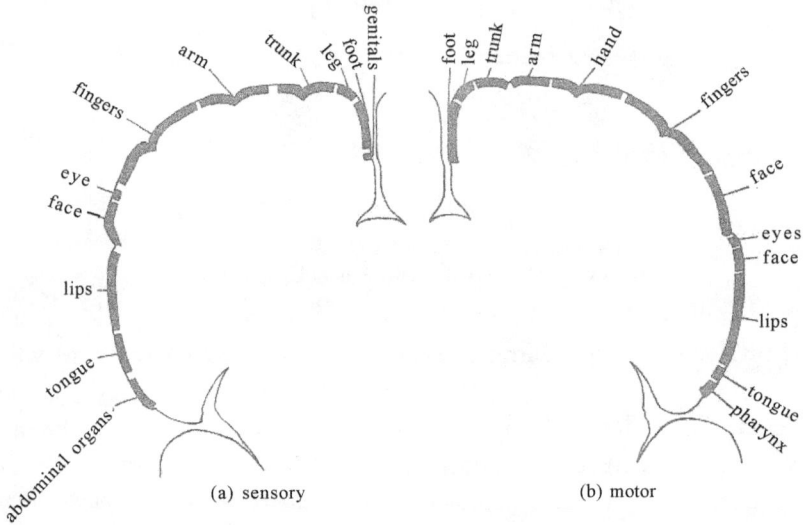

(a) sensory   (b) motor

Fig. 27: (a) The Sensory Cortex and (b) Motor Cortex, where respectively all our Sensory and Motor parts/organs have representative spaces allocated according to their importance/frequency of use

Those of you who had, knowingly or unknowingly, utilised the powers and potentials of the upper and outer structures of your brain in course of your pre-retirement years would find that the plasticity and self-organising abilities of your brain are better retained even after your retirement than in the case of those whose work roles consisted of routine tasks and assignments taking away the motivation to perform due to the drudgery.

CHANGE IN A FEW OTHER ABILITIES

In your post-retirement days, due to lack of retention of some regular habits, there may be deterioration in some other abilities like perceptual linguistic skills (reading and understanding the correct meaning, speaking and writing with good command over word power, grammar and composition).

Your Brain's Blood and Oxygen Supply

Your body is the vehicle and brain, the engine. Blood is the fuel. Your brain cells need continuous flow of blood and not only just one or a few, but millions and millions of them. When the normal blood flow (with the blood in its normal mood of pressure and temperature) stops, the cell breathes its last within a few minutes. Blood is the carrier of oxygen, which is the life-giving force to the cell. With the stoppage of oxygen supply, the cell suffers and eventually dies.

Brain needs glucose and oxygen for its proper functioning. These are transported through the blood flow inside the brain. The brain's blood circulation process is also responsible for the removal of all the waste material. Every brain cell relies on a constant supply of oxygen to convert its primary energy source (glucose or sugar) to brain cell energy. Without oxygen and the removal of cellular waste material, the brain cell is dead within ten minutes of a stoppage of blood flow. Fat-rich diets and high blood *cholesterol* levels during your post-retirement days might land you into such problems, post retirement. The affected arteries may diminish the supply further and consequently increase the chance of a *stroke*—the sudden temporary shutting off of glucose and oxygen to particular brain regions leading to cell death.

Aging slowly and gradually affects the blood flow to the brain. There is also a corresponding drop in the use of oxygen by the brain as those brain cells which die with age would neither require the supply of blood nor the supply of oxygen. However, brain blood flow is directly proportionate to the brain's metabolism (which is its working). Therefore, if you continue to keep yourself busy with brainwork even after your retirement, you may not face the 'brain cell death' and 'brain shrinkage' problems like those who just retire to remain idle and free from any kind of serious mental work.

One of the few unique features of your brain is that if you maintain good physical and mental health, it is protected from extremes of high or low blood pressure. High pressure might change the properties and may even rupture the blood vessels of your brain; and low pressure might diminish blood flow to the point that respiration in brain cells would be compromised. Cerebral auto-regulation is the mechanism ensuring that brain blood flow is reasonably constant in the face of a wide variation of blood pressures. Thus, your brain itself controls the blood flow inside it, in its own private environment. It makes it possible by changing the diameter of the blood vessels, contracting the muscles around the vessel when pressure is low for increasing the flow or relaxing the muscles when pressure is high for decreasing the flow. These movements take place in medium-sized blood vessels with high efficiency. They ensure, for example, that during the large and rapid changes in blood pressure accompanying normal daily activities including mood swings and emotional changes, you do not lose your consciousness or burst a blood vessel due to a high-vibration brain wave (that is, 25 to 32 cycles per second). For such a high level self-defence mechanism of your brain a few neurotransmitters are responsible. For example, *acetylcholine* can dilate blood vessels in the upper structures of your brain, whereas *serotonin* can constrict large vessels in the brain stem (located in your brain's inner and lower portion) or dilate the smallest blood vessels in your brain. These chemicals are secreted by the endings of the nerves, the network of which is present inside your brain connecting your brain cells to the muscles around the blood vessels.

If you are a victim of high blood pressure (hypertension), you'll be treated with pressure-lowering drugs some of which can disrupt the auto-regulation mechanism and cause many side-effects including reducing the brain blood flow. Raised blood fat levels (hyper-lipidaemia), heart disease, cigarette smoking and a few other factors also reduce the brain blood flow. However, to prevent such possibilities when you retire, don't forget to perform planned physical fitness activities (including physical exercises) regularly. People who continue to work after retirement or perform regular physical exercises show much more constant cerebral blood flow values than others who retire and engage in little if any physical activity. Mentally and psychologically also, members of the former group are much better-off than those belonging to the latter group. However, as far as mental work is concerned, it will increase blood flow only to that part of the brain doing the work. Therefore, basically post-retirement physical activities would be equally, if not more, important as mental activities for maintaining a healthy flow of blood as well as supply of oxygen to your brain. Neglect of these post-retirement ground rules may also lead to some cerebro-vascular disease which would eventually affect the brain blood flow and, instead of being smooth and regular, the flow of blood through the vessels become turbulent, with pools and eddies replacing the straight flow in the blood vessel. This would cause the delivery of essential nutrients and removal of waste products from the brain to become progressively less efficient.

Different Types of Dementia

The older you get, the higher is your risk of developing *dementia*. This old-age illness is characterised by confusion and intellectual impairment. The symptoms include loss of memory, judgment and reasoning, changes in behaviour and communication abilities, mood swings, depression, irritability and trouble learning new things, making a decision or remembering facts. Non-vegetarians (poultry, meat and fish-eaters) consuming high levels of cholesterol and saturated fats (both found only in meat and hydrogenated vegetable oils) are more than twice as likely to become demented as their vegetarian counterparts and those who have been regular non-vegetarians were worse-off.

Binswanger's disease is a dementia characterised by damage to small blood vessels in the brain as a result of hardening of the arteries to the brain. *Lewy body dementia*, which accounts for about 20 per cent of all dementia cases and is characterised by the presence of abnormal structures called *Lewy bodies* in the brain; and *vascular dementia* is caused by several small unnoticed strokes in the brain. *Alzheimer's disease* is the most common cause of dementia. People with a diet of unsaturated, unhydrogenated fats and low cholesterol foods decrease their risk of developing *Alzheimer's*. Foods high in cholesterol should be avoided; these include meat fat, full fat dairy products and processed foods such as cakes and biscuits.

Shrinkage of Your Brain

The human brain, the cranium, has taken 2 million years to grow to its peak size of 1,500 cubic centimetres in proportion to the gradual increase of the powers of the brain which took place due to the challenges that our cave-dwelling ancestors faced. However, over the past 20,000 years, the average volume of the male and female brain both have shrunk by about 150 cubic centimetres, losing a chunk the size of a tennis ball once the human species started getting civilised. (4) [(4) "Shrinking making humans dumber", *The Economic Times, Kolkata,* 3 January 2011, p. 1]

This is what has happened over the thousands of years. But even in one life and one generation, your brain shrinks with age, as much as fifteen percent between the ages of fifty and sixty-five; this happens due to both the cells themselves shrinking (due to the loss of their water contents) and actual loss of brain cells in some regions. Chronic stress increases *cortisol* production and chronically increased *cortisol* in turn accelerates cell death in regions of the brain like the *hippocampus* which is the place where our memory is largely stored. Cell loss is prevalent particularly in parts of the frontal lobes, hippocampus, cerebellum and basal ganglia. (5) [(5) Johnson, S.A. and C.E. Finch, 'Changes in gene expression during brain aging: a survey' in Schneider, E and J. Rowe, eds. *Handbook of the Biology of Aging,* New York: Academic press, 1996, pp. 300–327].

The Blood-Brain Barrier/Diabetes/Alzheimer's Disease

Your brain has an impenetrable protective layer around it in the form of a thick *blood-brain barrier* which does not allow it to be affected easily by the chemical changes taking place elsewhere in the body. The barrier, composed of tightly packed cells, insulates the brain from an overload of undesirable chemicals that circulate in the bloodstream while still allowing the essential metabolic functions.

This is thought to be true in the case of *blood sugar* as well. Diabetes patients, who have high levels of *glucose* in their blood because of faulty *insulin* production, normally have near-normal *glucose* levels in the blood circulating through the myriad blood vessels in the brain. Yet, recent findings indicated that 30 to 65 per cent of diabetics run the risk of developing *Alzheimer's disease*. In fact, the densely packed cells of the *blood-brain barrier* are often exposed to the flooding of the high blood sugar. As a result, the blood vessels of the brain get damaged and the availability of nutrients in the blood is reduced. Many of the weak nerve cells in the early stages of *Alzheimer's* die prematurely due to the poor nutrient supply thus increasing the possibility of the disease to progress faster.

To sum up: the general changes that are likely to take place in your mental abilities after your retirement would include: slowing down of your mental speed (applications: judgement, decision-making, problem-solving); slowing of your information processing power (applications: perception, idea generation); reduced ability to divide attention and shift attention from one thing to another (applications: alertness, awareness); reduction in mental dexterity or fluidity and mental flexibility (applications: coping with change, calculated adjustment with unexpected situations); reduction in your brain's blood and oxygen supply sometimes leading to the shrinkage of the brain; frequent increased blood sugar level exposure in the case of diabetics damaging the defence mechanism of the brain's blood-brain barrier leading to cell death thus increasing the possibility of fast progress of the deadly Alzheimer's disease.

However, if you had been born only ten to fifteen thousand years ago (and not one or a few million years) before the dawn of civilisation, you would have faced acute survival problem having reduced abilities for food-gathering and personal physical safety. Today, you're much better off, with your food, clothes, shelter, means of transportation and, above all, your kith and kin. This changed scenario of human existence should itself provide you with adequate solace and security.

Finally, we may say that put the belief 'use it or lose it' into your brain and stay with it all the time. Chant it, practise it, preach it, eat it, drink it, and sleep with it. You'll simply not believe what'll happen to you—something totally unexpected, totally impossible!

BE CONTEMPORARY FOR MENTAL WELL-BEING

If you enjoy, then keep up with the popular culture by listening to modern music, watching current films and attending the latest plays. Also, stay in touch with computers, and iPods, send text messages, and read contemporary literature. Read newspapers and attend to the TV news channels to update yourself with the latest information; and, if you have good company, discuss whatever you feel like—open your heart and feel free. And, if you can continue learning something new—may be a language or a new subject, music or dancing, there is nothing like it to keep your brain cells charged and vibrating with positive waves.

APPLICATION TIPS

- You'll age faster if your habit is to live with worries and self-destructive negative thoughts. It's not only aging that will take you over but you'll provide the housing for some old age diseases for which you may have genetic propensities.

- Like your physical and sensory losses, your brain's processes and powers will also undergo a natural slowdown as you age; and the degree of slowdown will depend to a large extent upon what kind of work you used to do before your retirement for the last few years—routine or non-routine and what kind of pursuits you would indulge in outside your work life.

- While you'll have to accept such slowdowns, you ought to feel joyful that you're your experienced brain is now enriched with knowledge, information and wisdom compared to those who are younger in age.

- Test yourself, if you wish, whether you're mentally fit for any post-retirement job assignment, professional self-employment or entrepreneurship. Check yourself up on a few mental powers including your mental speed, cognitive abilities, intelligence, learning skill, power of concentration and diverse memory powers which all would provide you with the base for planning, decision-making and problem-solving.

Chapter 16

Retirement and Your Mental State

"You have to take a different view of age now. People are living longer. Age just gives experience. Besides, it takes you until about 50 to know what the hell is going in the world."
—Lee Iacocca
Former Chairman of Chrysler Corporation
(who turned the ailing company round)

MENTAL POWERS THAT COME AFTER RETIREMENT

Despite the physical and cognitive abilities diminishing as part of your natural aging process, you may possess extensive knowledge and experience (see under "Years of Routine Work Stagnate Your Unused Brainpowers" under 'Mental Powers: Natural Slowdown' in Chapter 15) and for your aging-related deficits often by filtering out 'noise' and irrelevant distractions and focussing on the essential points thus facilitating prompt decisions or actions. Compared to mid-career or younger generation employees, you would work smarter. The dominant features observed in employees of your age group are: commitment, reliability, performance and basic skills.

Slowness in decision-making power, which is likely to happen to you once you retire due to lack of regular decision-making habits which you had during your pre-retirement days, in fact, has a bright side. It allows time for better decisions to be made. This is what is called *wisdom*, which helps you to earn respect of people.

However, today's retired people, as a group, have very different life histories from those who will retire ten or fifteen years from now and, therefore, the contexts and contents of their *wisdom* are also expected to be different.

It is thus healthy for you to indulge in reminiscence with members of your age group which will trigger recall and make you take stock of and share your life's experiences.

Health and Fitness: Main Determinants for Post-Retirement Occupation

In any case, health and fitness are the two most predominant factors prompting the elderly employee to continue working even after crossing the official retirement age. If his economic need is strong, he will explore the possibility of part-time or home-based assignments. On the other hand, it is seen that people who continue to be engaged in some economically rewarding or even voluntary job, remain healthier and have a longer lifespan than who retire for good. Apart from their physical involvement, they enjoy the psychological benefits of contribution and self-esteem and their social needs of working together get satisfied.

Health risks usually stem from too little physical or mental activity, not too much. Therefore, today's less physically strenuous jobs in automation- knowledge- and service-oriented economy offer greater health hazard potentials than the physically and mentally arduous work activities of yesteryears. So, people who can keep themselves physically and mentally much active outside their work roles can continue performing their work activities even up to an advanced age of their late sixties and, in some cases, even early seventies.

Lee Iacocca, who shot to fame, after holding the reins of the ailing Chrysler Corporation, had once said:

"I've always been against automated chronological dates to farm people out. The union would say, make room for the new blood; there aren't enough jobs to go around. Well, that's a hell of a policy......I don't know if the Internet will .....change stereotypes, but I hope so. I had people at Chrysler who were 40 but acted 80, and....80-year olds who could do everything a 40 year-old can. You have to take a different view of age now. People are living longer. Age just gives experience. Besides, it takes you until about 50 to know what the hell is going in the world." (1) [(1) David Wallis, "Act 2.0" *Wired*, May 2000].

When You Never Retire

You never retire or the question of retirement does not arise if you enjoy your *profession* and are passionately in love with it. What do we mean by the expression *"love for your profession"*?

Your 'work role' normally has two sides. Firstly, it has the 'technical' or 'functional' side for which you were trained—in your college, technical or professional institute, or university. It may be production or manu-facturing, it may be engineering design-development or maintenance, or materials manage-ment, quality assurance, financial or cost accounting, human resource management, company law and secretarial practice, sales or marketing. Secondly, it has the 'trans-technical' or 'trans-functional' side, which is beyond the purely technical or functional realm and boundary where you have to deal with people, plan, chalk out programmes, organise, direct, motivate and influence people to get things done which may be described as 'general management'.

So, depending on your job-mix and the duties and responsibilities at your level, you may have more to do with the 'technical' or the 'trans-technical' part or you may have to handle them in equal proportions. So, by your 'profession' we mean your job content from this angle. If you're totally sold and dedicated to your job content from this angle, then you have *love for your profession* and you would enjoy every moment of your performance.

You never retire or the question of your retirement does not crop up if you enjoy your 'job' and are passionately in love with it. By your 'job' we now mean the kind of work activities that you're engaged in. *Work,* as such, can be of three types. One type is *Self-Engagement (SE)* where you're engaged in some work activities, typically 'solo' (that is, involving only yourself and nobody else) which means using your brain or 'cerebral apparatus'. There is another type of work *People & Social Engagement (PSE)* where you indulge mostly in speaking and listening, sending and responding to e-mail, chatting through the Internet, all involving your 'communication apparatus'(that is larynx, pharynx, windpipe, palate, tongue, mouth cavity, nasal passage, eyes, ears, hands and fingers), in the foreground, the brain being in the background. The third and the last category of work is *Physical Engagement (PE)* where you're utilising your 'muscular-skeletal apparatus' (that is, bones, muscles, tendons, ligaments and joints) for doing physical work and for outdoor and indoor movements.

People who enjoy all these three types of activities are indeed a rare species. Individuals like one type of work with another type as the next most preferred and the remaining one to be least preferred. So, each person has a characteristic *Working Personality (WP)* and the principle is called the *Working Personality Principle (WPP).* If an individual's job-related work activities match with his *WP*, then there is a task-talent fit (or, task-talent matching) and both will enjoy each other's company and there would not be any question of any boredom or stress. If this match happens most of the time, then the person is on the top of the world; he never thinks of retiring. He becomes an *ageless* person.

One example is that of Bob Lutz who took over as vice chairman of product development at General Motors Corporation in September 2001 and by January 2003 unveiled five fantastic prototype vehicles at the Detroit Auto Show as a part of his strategy for GM's attempt at a marketplace turnaround. (2) [(2) Welch, David, "GM's Design Push Picks up Speed", *Business Week*, July 18, 2005]. Lutz started his career as a Marine Corps pilot; he entered the automobile sector at GM Europe, shifted himself to BMW, and then to Ford Europe. He rose to the position of executive vice president of Ford US, and then joined Chrysler in 1986 to work for Lee Iacocca. In 1998, he retired from Chrysler breaking the company's rules regarding official retirement age. He did not have to relax and enjoy his retired life as he was soon picked up to become the chairman and CEO of the sick battery maker Exide Technologies. In less than two years, he turned the company around and showed a profit for the first time in three years. Lutz's passion is for 'turnaround management' and his every assignment was so well-matched with his natural propensity that he succeeded every time, increased his worth so much in the employment market that there was no question of his retirement.

In India, the first such example that comes to mind is that of N Sridharan, the MD and CEO of Delhi Metro Railway who had taken up the challenge of spearheading the complex high-tech project from scratch and kept his word by starting up and commissioning the project in record time, all well past his mandatory retirement age. His passion for project management got adequately fuelled in this most prestigious assignment. In the country's government sector, such examples are perhaps just one in a million.

These are two examples, from two different worlds, of people who have remained as executives all their lives being employed in organisations. Amongst members of the employer class, we have umpteen examples of stalwarts who have waged wars against the tribulations of aging. From the first world, we have the examples of Rupert Murdoch and Warren Buffet and from the third world India, B K Birla and R P Goenka—all still going strong. Amongst self-employed professionals also, there are examples galore. For instance, among stars in the US, we have Clint Eastwood who got the Academy Award as the best film director at the age of seventy-five and in India, we have the grand old man Dev Anand who, as the media report from time to time, is planning a brand new production.

Therefore, if you enjoy your job from the *professional* as well as *WP* angles or if not both at least one of them, you never think of retiring. Even after your official retirement, you explore and spot opportunities as to how you can continue.

THE VITAL ROLE OF SELF-AWARENESS/ CONSCIOUSNESS IN EASING THE IMPACT OF RETIREMENT

In case you're not so lucky as to be in a profession or a job that is most enjoyable for you, and as a result you never retire, there are other ways for you to ease the impact of retirement.

It is most vital for you to remember that we, humans, are the only creatures on earth that can change our biology by what we think and feel. One concrete example is our breathing. Breathing is a regular life-giving activity for us which goes on involuntarily, freely all the time. And, just like our heart's activities get influenced by the fluctuations in our physical and mental conditions, breathing also gets affected. However, we can control our breathing voluntarily to regulate our biological processes.

You and I, who are members of the human species, possess the only nervous system that is conscious about our post-retirement physical and mental changes. Even the head of the animal kingdom, lion, does not realise what is happening to him when he ages, but you and I do. This is the very special mental power, our *self-awareness* (or, shall we say, *consciousness*) that you have to evoke and utilise while planning for retirement so that you do not allow physical and mental depreciation to take place abruptly when you retire. And, you can practice *self-awareness* by following your breathing—what kind of breathing style you have and how it fluctuates.

YOUR ATTITUDE TOWARDS RETIREMENT

Endocrinologist and medical researcher Chopra says: "How you perceive yourself is causing immense changes in your body right now. To give an example: In America and England, mandatory retirement at age 65 sets an arbitrary cut-off date for social usefulness. The day before a worker turns 65, he contributes labour and value to society; the day after, he becomes one of society's dependents. Medically, the results of this perceptual shift can be disastrous. In the first few years after retirement, heart attack and cancer rates soar, and early death overtakes men who were otherwise healthy before they retired. 'Early retirement death', as the syndrome is called, depends on the perception, but for someone who holds it firmly, it is enough to create disease and death. By comparison, in societies where old age is accepted as part of the social fabric, elders remain extremely vigorous—lifting, climbing, and bending in ways that we do not accept as normal in our elderly." (3) [(3) Chopra, Deepak, *Ageless Body, Timeless Mind: A Practical Alternative to Growing Old*, London: Rider, an imprint of Ebury Press, Random House, 1993, p.12]

Normally, we picture a 'career path' as an ascending line or curve in terms of responsibility and rank—up the corporate ladder. In a traditional sense, retirement means a sudden stoppage to that ascension and a drop into the abyss of non-performance. Those who are ambitious and want to grow higher and higher, it is a wrong mental model. On the other hand, it is the right mental model for those who had got stuck at a certain level of the hierarchy, for whatever may be the reason, and have been stagnating there for quite some time suffering from *stress*—some of them even developing some chronic ailments.

The first group thus consists of a few, a handful of people in different fields whom we may describe as *Sustained Winners (SW)*. They would like to continue doing something meaningful even after crossing their official retirement age and may reach higher and higher peaks of progress at the ripe old age of 75 and beyond. The members of this group are most valuable as *human capital*.

The second group consists of *Sustained Losers (SL)*, who have been counting how many days are still left until they retire. These are the employees who would love to retire and put an end to their career in the organisation where they have been employed for many years. Their main goal is to reduce the frustration and *stress* which overpowers them particularly in the company of those who used to be their juniors or colleagues and now are sitting above them as their seniors and bosses. These people never analyse the reasons for their lagging far behind those who have superseded them to occupy the limited few rooms above. Let us, therefore, count them out from the manpower that could still be considered as *human capital*.

There is yet a third group whose advocates try to influence the concerned corporate authorities to adjust their roles, responsibilities, schedules, and other work arrangements as they approach retirement. They want to downshift into a lighter, less intensive but still adequately rewarding task-time schedule, so that they can continue with the same nature or pace of work even after their retirement either in the same organisation on a retainership or some other basis or somewhere else. The members of this group may be called *Downshift Adjusters (DA)*. In terms of economic productivity and human capital management, this category of employees, the *DAs*, makes the least sense in the immediate pre-retirement phase of their employment career.

You'll have to analyse which group you belong to. You'll face no hurdle at all, if you belong to the first group, under any circumstances as you'll never retire from active life. And, if you belong to the second group, it's for you to choose what would make you happy after a long phase of unhappiness.

If you happen to be in the last group of *DAs*, you would like to take up something meaningful after retirement and, in principle, you have a few choices. You may continue to do the same work as you used to do before retirement, maintaining some loose or tight relationship with the same organisation like some retirees do. Or, you may like to do some entirely different work for the same organisation provided you get such an opportunity and you're considered suitable. Or, you may like to shift to a smaller organisation where you'll feel more important, taking up the same type of assignments as in your mother organisation. Or, you may want to do totally different type of work in a different organisation to have a new flavour and a fresh taste. Or, you may want to provide service to a voluntary, non-profit organisation or set up your own enterprise in a small way.

You must have realised by now that it's the *SWs* who make the maximum contributions to the society, economic or non-economic or both.

PRE-RETIREMENT JOB-PERSONALITY ADJUSTMENT

Your physical and mental well-being, after your retirement, would also depend upon what kind of job-personality adjustment pattern you had displayed during your pre-retirement days.

There is a very common type of person who adjusts with his job situation even though he may find it boring and uninteresting and not matching with his personality. Or, his circumstances compel him to adjust with and accept even such drudgery. This kind of forced *suppression/repression* would affect his physical and/or mental health due to the *stress* that is being continuously generated and allowed to remain unmanaged.

There is yet another kind of person who is so confident and positive-minded that he does not find routine work boring. He adds creativity even when handling repetitive work. Such people have the excellent flair for making even mechanical work interesting and fun-filled.

There is another type of individual who has the guts to look for a job that he likes. He does not worry about financial security when his happiness is at stake. Once he finds a job that satisfies him, he keeps at it without thinking of retirement. He finds everything at work: growth, progress, prosperity.

A fourth type of person is desperate for leisure as work is not satisfying for him. On the contrary, it is killing him. This person cannot wait for retirement; the moment an early voluntary retirement scheme is announced, he desperately opts for it.

YOUR MENTAL HEALTH MANAGEMENT

Once it was widely thought and discussed that, with age, brain cells generally get lost. Such loss results in shrinkage of the brain tissue and this process starts at around the age of fifty (from 1.4 kg it may become 1.2 kg at 65 years of age) due to loss in the water content of the cells. But it has now been proven to be wrong. A healthy brain may not shrink as much as loss of brain cells with aging is not as extensive as once thought and is certainly not generalised throughout the brain as brain cells, like the cells in any other part of the body, follow the universal 'use it or lose it' law. The work done by the brain cells (although the brain may constitute only 2 per cent of the body of a 70 kg man it consumes 20 per cent of all the energy) may also not decrease with age if positive mental activities are regularly maintained just like physical work. The blood circulation throughout the brain must be maintained for achieving this end. If these observations are true, then there seems to be some real prospects of slowing or even preventing some of the worst effects of brain ageing.

Tips for Overcoming a Mild Mental Loss

You may observe a decline in some mental performance abilities but a gain in others. For example, you may come up with fewer alternative solutions to everyday problems (as your brain might have lost its ability to think absolutely logically and rationally—one solution at a time) and none of these may be the best solution for you. However, this should not pose a threat to you. You can merrily use the PP (Plus Points), MP (Minus Points), MIP (Most Interesting/Important Points) technique discussed in Chapter 14 and illustrated in Fig. 25 to evaluate every alternative solution that you have chalked out (better to chalk them out in writing than just mentally working out) and select that particular alternative which will provide you the maximum MIPs and PPs and minimum MPs.

Example of a Mental Gain in Old Age

That was the example of a loss whereas a gain in your mental performance could be a different and deeper perception (than younger people) of many things for your wider and longer exposure and experience which have made you wiser. However, unless this gain of yours is combined with calmness and patience, you may face problem due to the mental block created by your own professional ego, which may prompt you to disagree and argue with those whose ideas, opinions and views may not totally tally with yours.

Other Mental Losses with Strategies for Remedy

Other mental losses for you could include: deterioration in your mental speed of response, the retrieval of recent information from memory, and spatial ability (finding your way around with the help of mental imagery or visualisation).

Lessons derived so far from keen scientific studies in the physical and mental health of middle-aged people (45 to 55 years) well into their ninth decades of life point to some simple lifestyle rules which, if followed, certainly improve the chances of keeping mental abilities and psychological well-being intact. These are: keep fit, keep mentally active, eat a balanced diet, interact with people as and when such opportunity arose (and do not isolate yourself from others and turn into an island), and don't smoke.

Let Us Imagine Your Story

Just as in the case your physical health, as regards your mental health also, with your age advancing, you have been (like most post-50 people) avoiding complicated mental work involving critical decision-making, problem-solving and taking up light routine work to which you have been habituated.

This habit of yours has reduced the work on your brain putting your brain health into jeopardy. Your brain has been relaxing for some time in the 'comfort zone' thus losing its immense powers to face the sudden changes of your retired life many of which you might not have expected or vividly visualised in your mind in advance. Therefore, when you confront the situation face to face, it may make you mentally traumatised leading to unhappiness as you feel it is happening to you only and not to anybody else that you know—as if you're the most unlucky person.

A phase of sudden depression or loss of self-esteem due to a feeling of loss of self-worth can damage your *immune system,* whereas self-love can boost it. Despair and hopelessness raise the risk of heart attacks and cancer thereby shortening your lifespan. Joy and fulfilment keep you healthy and extend your life.

An unhappy mind is a restless, turbulent mind. In order to make it normal and steady, you can try out this approach: find out the wealth of resources that you have (that is your 'strengths' or 'plus points'). Also, make a list of all the good things that have happened to you and all the prize possessions you have. Add up these two. Now, make a list of the things that you wanted to have but you do not have which others have. Add to that what unexpected unhappy situations you're facing now, specifically point by point. On analysing these four, you'll certainly find that you're no worse off compared to those who make you feel inferior.

NEGATIVE THINKING IS THE MAIN VILLAIN

Aging is not primarily responsible for the depletion of your mental strength and capabilities. Negative thinking, inability to cope with the uncertainties of the highly competitive modern life, most unexpected threat-ridden situations and getting carried away by the sudden flooding of hijacking emotions like anger, anxiety or despair, all these create havoc and not only shake up but, to a considerable extent, erode the strong foundation of your mind—the confidence, the self-esteem that you had especially built up when you were younger.

It is true that beyond your late-forties, your brain starts losing some cells but that happens only in the case of those which have not been in regular use. For example, the 'intelligence' area of your brain (located in your Pre-Frontal Cortex or PFC) just above your eyes and before the forehead which helps you in decision-making, problem-solving, and coming out of critical situations, will lose its cells and shrink if you have no opportunity of or yourself avoid using in your day-to-day living and working as you feel there are others who would handle such situations. You ought to remember always that our cells—whether they are in the body or the brain invariably follow the 'use it or lose it' principle.

MENTAL HEALTH PRESERVATION

Even if you have not been in the habit of using some of your brain skills, how would you preserve your mental health? Your daily diet should contain plenty of fruits, fibrous leafy vegetables and other fresh green vegetables which can be consumed in the raw form like cucumber, tomato, radish, carrot and onion. Among non-vegetarian items, concentrate on bony yet less oily fishes which contain the *Omega-3* fatty acid good for your brain. *Omega-3* arrests to a great deal the negative impact of aging on your brainpower like short-term memory, stress resilience, common sense and presence of mind.

Inability to face the traumatic experience of the death of a near and dear one, separation from somebody very close to you (like your life partner or an offspring), lack of adequate preparedness for retirement, critical illness of a family member and such other sudden jolts increase the age of your cells at the genetic level.

Brain cells communicate with each other through chemical messengers—the neurotransmitters. So far, more than 500 different substances have been found naturally in the brain, and many of these meet the criteria for a neurotransmitter. Neurotransmitters involved with the control of movement, attention, arousal, the sleep-wake cycle, eating and aggression are found in quite separate brain structures. With aging, the amount of specific transmitters may gradually decrease. In normal aging, the amount of the neurotransmitter *acetylcholine* slowly declines in the hippocampus which is our memory store. The number of brain cells in the hippocampus is usually preserved in people with an advanced age. However, the loss of *acetylcholine*-containing cells from the aging hippocampus is one of the most likely explanations of memory deficits in otherwise healthy people.

At your age, the memory that plays an important role is the *practical* or *working memory* which helps you in your day-to-day activities. One important aspect of that is keeping track of time; remembering what work activities you have to take up at what time and in what sequence; remembering where you have kept the items essential for your use, such as your glasses (and their case), your watch, your wallet, your mobile, handkerchief, comb, car keys, cabinet keys and so on. The other type of information that you need to remember includes: the names, addresses, land and cell phone numbers, e-mail, wedding and birth anniversary dates. Another category includes what all you have read or heard—trying to remember those things for some time. One good way to sharpen your *working memory* is to use both your eyes to vividly photograph the items that you wish to remember along with their locations; and, then shutting your eyes and see whether those pictures are appearing on your mental screen when you want to see them. Practising a few times will give you such photographic memory power. If you want to remember some factual information, you identify the 'key points' representing some 'key ideas' and click their photographs with your camera eyes and again ensure if you can make them appear on your mental screen.

APPLICATION TIPS

- If you continue to be engaged in some economically rewarding and even voluntary job after retirement, you'll remain much healthier and have a longer life span than who retire for good.

- If you have a love for your profession, you'll never retire. You'll also never retire if you had loved the work you did—the job itself. It is very important for you to assess your attitude towards your profession and also towards the work that you do as that would decide your physical and mental health conditions after you retire.

- Practice self-awareness by following your breathing style and its other characteristics.

- Assess your attitude towards retirement—what do you feel about the stage of your life called 'retirement'.

- You may face some practical problems owing to the aging-related mental deficiencies but following the mental health management tips should help you to remedy them to a reasonable extent.

Chapter 17

Brain Care for Old Age Happiness

"I am not afraid of dying but I am really scared that one fine morning I find, or my wife finds, that there is something wrong with my head. So I allowed Kurt Wallander to enter the world of Alzheimer's and think about life and aging."

—Henning Mankell, Swedish writer
(On his Swedish detective character Kurt Wallender,
In: 'Millennium trilogy will be forgotten after 20 years',
The Times of India, Kolkata, 3 February 2011, p. 12)

".........feeling is a definite force or energy. When controlled by intelligence, it can be a force for good, but also it has the capacity to destroy. Since we know that feeling is associated with every thought we think, and that we can sense events only through feelings, it is time we realised that our only protection against wrong use or wrong influence of feelings is the developed ability to control and direct them."

—Harold Sherman
(*How To Make ESP Work For You*,
New York: Fawcett Crest, 1964, p. 55)

THE AGE OF YOUR BRAIN

Wrinkled skin may be a main sign of your physical aging but in order to know the current age of your brain, you have to track the brain's lactic acid level. *Lactic acid* is a normal product of metabolism so age-damaged DNA in the mitochondria could be affecting the metabolic processes. However, why should you bother if you feel your mental powers have not deteriorated to the extent that you need to worry? And, to know which of your mental powers you should be concerned about, didn't you get tips in the last chapter—the chapter that you've just scanned through?

A COMMON BRAIN-RELATED PROBLEM IN OLD AGE

Loss of 'Gross Motor Control'

'Gross motor control' is a brain function that declines as we age. The outcome is loss of balance; the victim tends to fall and faces difficulty with mobility.

Apart from the failure of the vestibular processing mechanism of the victim's ear, this decline is caused by the decrease in sensory feedback from his feet to his brain.

The root causes are: dependence on footwear; use of footwear of wrong design not taking cognizance of the natural arch of the foot; regular use of two- or four-wheelers—self-driven or just ridden which does not allow the natural sensory motor function of our feet to be utilised; very little barefoot walking.(1). [(1) Doidge, Norman, *The Brain That Changes Itself: Stories of Personal Triumph from the Frontiers of Brain Science*, New York: Penguin Books, 2007, pp 90-91/123-124]

If we went barefoot, our brains would receive many different kinds of inputs as we went over uneven surfaces. Shoes are a relatively flat platform that spreads out the stimuli, and the surfaces we walk on at home, workplaces, shopping malls and other public places are increasingly artificial and perfectly flat. Therefore, as we age, we gradually lose the ability to differentiate between various types of surfaces *vis-à-vis* the soles of our feet. Then, at a more advanced age, we may start to use and become dependent upon canes, walkers or crutches or rely on other senses to steady ourselves. By resorting to these *compensations* instead of exercising our failing brain systems, we hasten their decline. As we age, we want to look down at our feet while walking down stairs or on slightly challenging terrain, because we're not getting much information from our feet.

Our brain contains the atlas of our entire galaxy of functions which allow us to live and work. Different functions and the parts associated with them have different maps. Just like the physical location of India is at a particular place with specific latitudes and longitudes, whereas you find the map of India on a particular page number of the school atlas copy that you have, similarly the soles of your feet are located at the bottom end of your lower extremities whereas the map of these soles are in your brain. As the function of the soles of your feet change with your lifestyle, correspondingly the shape and size—the profile of the sole map in your brain will also change. (For a clear understanding, refer to Figs. 26 and 27 of the human brain in Chapter 15).

Preventive Solution

The preventive solution to this problem is to use your bare feet as much as possible. In case that is not feasible for you, go for regular massage of your feet using your own hands. During this massage, you have to consciously press the muscles on top and under the arches of both your feet.

THE PROBABLE POST-RETIREMENT BRAIN DISEASES

First of all, you must note that fitness and exercise have been shown to slow age-related changes in the brain in healthy people.(2) [(2) "Fitness protects brain in Alzheimer's", *The Times of India, Kolkata*, 30 July 2008, p.15].

The probable post-retirement brain diseases include:

Cerebral Stroke: Cerebral stroke is a sudden loss of brain function caused by brain blood vessel abnormality which would have been building up for some time but reached its peak and snapped off. Increased blood pressure, cigarette smoking, irregular contractions of the heart input chambers (atrial fibrillation) and diabetes are all well-established risk factors. Stroke may be caused by haemorrhage (that is, rupture of a blood vessel) or by blockage of blood vessel by clotting. The actual picture will be revealed by a brain scan. Preventive measures include control of risk factors like smoking, taking regular exercise to maintain satisfactory brain blood flow, reducing blood fat levels by drug treatment, and improving control of diabetes. British scientists have made substantial progress in developing techniques to help stroke patients regain their speech. (3) [(3) "Human brain can learn a new word in less than 15 minutes.", *The Times of India, Kolkata*, 16 December 2010, p.16.] (Also see Chapter 9 for more information about 'Stroke'.)

Neuronal Death: The inevitable path to neuronal death starts with reduced cerebral blood flow, which in turn rapidly depletes the energy available for brain cells to sustain life. Because oxygen is unavailable, lactic acid accumulates in the cell (refer to the beginning of this chapter to understand why lactic acid formation takes place) and causes failure of the brain cell pumps that maintain the mineral salt balance across the extra-cellular membrane. The membrane rapidly deteriorates, and calcium floods into the body of the cell, activating proteins that will digest key cell components. The only possible outcome is cell death.

Dementia: *Dementia* is a mental disorder of adult life. It is now becoming a major problem in developing countries where it did not exist fifty years ago. It is a lifestyle-related neurological disorder, usually caused in the elderly by Alzheimer's disease, vascular disease, or a mixture of the two.

By 2025, the *dementia*-affected people in developing countries are likely to rise to 71 per cent of those likely to live thus making it a very serious forthcoming problem. Typical signs of *dementia* include: presence of 'plaques' (protein deposits) and 'tangles' (twisted nerve fibres). The common forms of *dementia* involve very slow progressive deterioration, and eventually all powers of memory and reasoning are lost.

There are considerable changes in the *dementia*-affected person's outlook. Emotions in the early phase are coloured by feelings of inexplicable fear, bleakness, a sense of powerlessness or notions of dread, loathing or shame. The symptoms include: confusions; loss of memory; difficulty in judgment and reasoning; changes in behaviour and communication abilities; mood swings; depression; irritability and trouble learning new things, making a decision or remembering facts. One in five people with *dementia* will become aggressive and can pose a danger to himself or the people he lives with.

There is no cure, only a slowdown in the progression of symptoms. Diet is one factor in reducing the risk of *dementia*. Non-vegetarians are found to more likely to be demented compared to their vegetarian counterparts. Other dietary attributable factors include: eating of high levels of cholesterol and saturated fats; both are found only in meat and hydrogenated vegetable oils. Cholesterol aids the production of beta-amyloid protein, which is one of the chemicals thought to cause damage to the brain in Alzheimer's disease. Foods high in cholesterol (such as, meat fat, full fat dairy products and processed foods such as cakes and biscuits should be avoided *Statins*, the so-called 'wonder drugs' taken for lowering the high cholesterol level in blood, which have saved millions of people from heart disease, may have an additional role in protecting the brain from *dementia*. A recent research study has shown that if a person takes *Statins* over a course of about five to seven years, it reduces the risk of *dementia* by half. (4) [(4) Laurance, Jeremy, "Statins 'Halve' the Risk of Dementia" *The Statesman, Kolkata,* 30 July 2008, p. 6]. *Statins* were established as the most effective preventive treatment against heart disease more than a decade ago and are considered so safe that in UK some of the branded *statins* are sold in drug stores even without a doctor's prescription.

Alzheimer's Disease: This ailment is associated with the loss of cortical neurons. Surviving cells show reduced dendritic sprouting and synaptic formations. This disease is typically of gradual onset and slow progression, in which three main phases are usually distinguished. The first phase, which lasts up to two years, witnesses: memory impairment, poor concentration and awareness of everyday difficulties. Route-finding is impaired. In the second stage, there may be some facial weaknesses and an abnormal foot withdrawal response. Delusions or hallucinations may take place. In the third stage, language is much impaired and soon lost completely. Many patients do not recognise themselves or their relatives. They soon become confined to bed and lose control of one's urination and defecation.

The second and the third stages of the disease last usually for four to five years.

However, people in the early stages of Alzheimer's disease who are more physically fit are generally observed to have less shrinkage in areas of the brain that are important for memory. In the words of Dr Sam Gandy, chairman of the Alzheimer's Association's Medical and Scientific Advisory Council: "The message is essentially if you have Alzheimer's disease, it's not too late to become physically fit." (5) [(5) "Fitness protects brain in Alzheimer's", *The Times of India, Kolkata,* 30 July 2008, p. 15].

If we assume that the life expectancy is up to the late 80's, then when one is 85, there is a 47% chance that you'll have Alzheimer's disease! So modern life blessed by science and technology has created this bizarre situation in which we are keeping people alive long enough so that, on the average, half of them get the black rock before they die. We've got to do something about the mental lifespan, to extend it out and into the body's lifespan.

Our neglect of intensive learning as we age leads the system in the brain that modulates, regulate, and control plasticity to waste away. The common brain powers that get age-affected and ride a downslide are memory, thinking—both logical and imaginative, response time and processing speed.

The main thing is to understand the role of what is required to develop a new skill in the brain and to *sustain* normal skills and abilities that we acquire in the brain at some young age just deteriorate as the physical brain deteriorates.

Let us take the case of memory loss with aging. The main attributable factor is the slowing down the S-R or stimulus-response process which starts with stimulus receiving, stimulus transmission to the brain for processing, following the different steps of processing, coming out with a response strategy and ends with implementation of the response action. However, keeping yourself exposed to new information, knowledge and skills to be internalised will certainly help you not to lose your brain's data processing and memory-building- storage-and-retrieval powers.

Parkinson's Disease: This disease where the patient develops tremor in the upper and lower limbs is caused by deficits in the brain neurotransmitter *dopamine*. It could be prevented by keeping up regular rhythmic activities like walking, jogging, stair climbing and dancing and visualising past achievement events and also planning future achieve-ments as *dopamine* is the reward chemical produced inside the brain; and, once already affected, made good by giving patients large doses of *dopamine* supplements.

BRAIN WAVES

This is perhaps the time to talk about brain waves. Your brain, like your heart and lungs, is a vibrating instrument generating waves. During wakefulness, you have *beta* waves: 14 to 32 cycles per second (c/s). As long as you're happy and poised, you've *beta*-positive waves, that is 14 to 24 c/s. When you're unhappy and tensed, you're in *beta*-negative, which is 25 to 32 c/s. If you continue in *beta*-negative for quite some time, your brain would have lost substantial amount of mental and emotional energy.

7 to13 c/s is the *alpha* wave condition which normally you get inside your brain early in the morning after a good night's sound restful sleep. This is the time when creativity flashes appear and your brain is in the idea generation/problem solution mode. **We can attain this state by means of slow and steady *deep rhythmic breathing* and, once your mind has become steady, coming out of its usual restlessness, followed by *colour meditation* (concentrating on some serene scenic picture imagined on your mental screen).**

4 to 6 c/s (*theta*) is attainable only during deep sound sleep. Sleep comes in two phases: Rapid Eye Movements (REM) when dreams arising out of the suppressed emotions—both good and bad, bottled up inside the subconscious mind are released and ventilated in symbolic forms thus disturbing the sleep's restful state; and Non-Rapid Eye Movements (NREM) when we have sound, undisturbed deep dreamless sleep. During REM sleep, we may get *beta*-negative brain waves, whereas *beta*-positive is representative of the sound, dreamless sleep.

Delta, 0-plus to 3 c/s, is obtained during the trance state when the body and brain are both spending minimum energy. Negatively, it also represents a critical patient's coma condition.

ACQUIRING ENERGY AND BRAINPOWER THROUGH BREATHING

There are 72,000 nerves in our body which need to be cleansed and purified regularly and, in these tasks, our breathing activities play a vital role. While breathing, the air that we're taking into our system is much more important than our food and drink inputs for good health and long trouble-free life.

Breathing is a twin-purpose activity. On the one hand, it is essential for internal cleansing and, on the other, it is very important for acquisition of energy. The former purpose of breathing lays more thrust on breathing out while the latter focuses on breathing in. The breathing cycle (in and out) is going on incessantly and you do not concentrate on that at all. If you had concentrated, you would have noticed that because of the in-built tensions that you carry, your breathing is not defect-free. That is the reason why we go for auto-reflex activities like occasional sighing to breathe in or out or yawning when we have run out of energy.

We are going to introduce you to a very simple (yet to be performed regularly) breathing exercise which will reduce your greed as you'll be allowing more than usual energy to get into your system through breathing and, as a consequence, your appetite and food intake will be controlled. One of the main responsibilities that effective breathing fulfils is that of adjustment of the energy flow in our body. Proper breathing also improves our mind power, memory and concentration.

According to *Hathayoga,* the ancient Indian science, there are eight types of *pranayam* or breathing exercise. However, you need not be concerned about following any complicated breathing technique; it's good enough for you to go for a very simple breathing exercise which will be described now.

A Special Energy-Boosting Breathing Technique

Stand erect. Relax all the muscles of your body one by one. Start from your feet. Imagine all the muscles, bones, ligaments and tendons of your feet have become relaxed and thus light and tension-free.

From your soles and toes, come up to your knee level and feel absolutely relaxed. From thereon, move up to the thigh level and feel relaxed. This way, come up to your head.

Start breathing in deeply through both your nostrils, when your whole body feels light and tension-free. Your mouth will remain lightly closed. Don't move your chest. This type of breathing is being made possible by your diaphragm which constitutes the muscles below your lungs. Your lungs are taking in and releasing breath with the expansion and contraction of your diaphragm. Try to feel what's really happening and enjoy the activities.

While breathing in fill the lower, middle and upper portions of your lungs from the bottom to the top. While breathing out, empty the upper portion of your lung first, then empty the middle portion and, lastly, come to the bottom portion.

This entire set of activities has got to be performed with total ease so that there is not an aorta of tension. After performing in this manner, you'll be conscious about your chest and the respiration department. You'll realise how softly your diaphragm is coming up with breathing in and going down with breathing out. However, if your entire chest gets involved then you are over-exercising; that should be avoided. When you practise this breathing exercise you can play some soft instrumental music in the background.

By pursuing such breathing exercise regularly, your brain is stress-free and relaxed. You can also keep yourself away from Cardiac-Arterial Diseases (CAD) and respiratory disorders in comparison to those who do not have such habit.

DOMINANCE OF CREATURLINESS

It may so happen that, throughout your career, you have been performing by and large routine work. Same type of work activities and assignments were filling eighty per cent of your time; non-routine (change from routine tasks) constituted only around twenty per cent of your workload. You would be an exception to this very commonplace phenomenon if you had been intellectually very active having held a senior to top management position or having been a top scientist, poet, painter, music composer, dance choreographer, fashion designer or a front-ranking self-employed professional.

As a consequence, the inner and lower structures of your brain responsible for all your basic instincts and sensory-motor powers were being stimulated much more than the outer and upper structures which house your mental powers like thinking (logical, analytical, rational, imaginative and creative), evaluating, judging and planning.

The former structures contain your *creaturliness* (or 'creaturely' nature) thus giving you your: strong desire to 'win' by making others 'lose'; need for 4-As (attention, acceptance or acknowledgement, affiliation and appreciation); and dislike for attack (or direct criticism—even constructive ones). Any one of these features, if not satisfied, manifests your reactive or negative behaviour ('fight': disagreement, argumentation, confrontation, direct criticism—or 'flight': suppression, avoidance and trying to escape, deception, and so on).

The latter structures contain your *humanliness* (or your 'rational-economic human' nature) as well as *godliness* (or your 'compassionate-forgiving-spiritual godly' nature). *'Humanliness'* stands for proactive behaviour (that is, behaving wisely after judging the situation which represents a 'planned' rather than 'emotional' response). *'Godliness'* stands for a higher order of behaviour, transcending the mundane materialistic level. At this plane, lot of tolerance and patience are displayed.

If you have been pre-occupied mostly with your creaturely nature in your career which you have just left behind, then with the lack of adequate use, the upper structures of your brain are likely to shrink with age, whereas the lower structures would remain intact and active. As a most likely result, any 'stimulus' received by your sensory receptors will be transmitted straight to your inner and lower brain rather than being sent to your upper and outer brain structures. This will tend to make you more 'reactive' when in your retired life and old age you face any stimulus which is not to your liking—may be physical, may be chemical, may be behavioural (that is, somebody else's behaviour).

This possibility has got to be averted by trying to use your upper brain more and more by going in for planned and programmed activities and, if you have a knack for it, indulging in imaginative-creative pursuits also. It could be either of this two also since not all are equally equipped with both the potential brain powers.

DECISION CRISIS AND ITS SOLUTION

Many a times, you may be suffering from a decision-making problem. You're confused and unable to choose which of the alternative solutions available you should opt for and implement. Under such circumstances, you must use a technique that we have already presented in an earlier chapter, to evaluate each alternative separately and exclusively—its 'Plus Points (PP)', 'Minus Points (MP)' and 'Most Interesting Points (MIP)'and select the one which has maximum 'PP' and 'MIP' and minimum 'MP' (refer to Chapter 14 and Fig. 25). In complicated cases, each alternative's pros and cons must be weighed from the technical, economic, social and human factors angles.

THE THOUGHT-PILL TECHNIQUE FOR MENTAL REJUVENATION

Your mind can be compared to an iceberg. The tip of your mind is the 'Conscious Mind (C)'. Immediately underneath this (C) is the 'Subconscious Mind (SC)' which contains in a submerged form, the memory of your past (both pleasant and unpleasant) and your future dreams, hopes and aspirations (which could be positive or negative or a mix of the two).

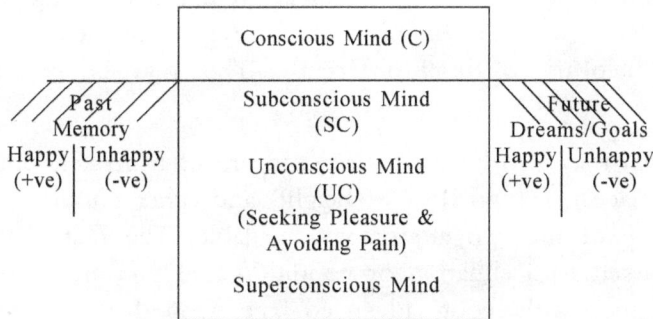

Fig. 28: The Iceberg Model of the Human Mind

Many a times, when you're lonely and depressed out of boredom, your SC may have negative self-talk, such as, 'I'm not O.K.', 'I'm distressed', 'I'm under stress', 'I'm unlucky' and so on. Negative messages emerge spontaneously as you subconsciously compare yourself with others or with your previous positive state when you were younger. Immediately below the SC is the 'Unconscious (UC)' which is running your body's internal automatic processes involuntarily. Once your SC is adversely affected due to negative charge, the same charge will affect your UC negatively and you may start suffering from some health problems.

How do you rejuvenate your mind to free itself from the negative charge? Reverse the mental self-talking process by dropping thought-pills from the C level of your mind, passing it through the SC and moving it into the UC part of your. Thought-pill messages must be positive-affirmative and superlative-positive, such as "I'm great", "I'm absolutely O.K.", "I'm extremely fine", "I'm terribly lucky", "I'm most fortunate" and so on. While dropping such thought-pills into the depths of your mind, think out what great things and connections/links you have got which your friends and relatives with whom you are comparing yourself have not got.

EXPOSURE THERAPY FOR KEEPING YOUR BRAIN HEALTHY AND ACTIVE

Your brain continues to rewire itself as long as you live provided, of course, you expose it to diverse knowledges and experience even at the advanced stage of your life that you have reached now. The biological brain hardware undergoes changes as new cells get born to replace dying cells with newer and newer exposures. Moreover, all those newly acquired knowledge and experience develop into more recent software. Knowledge and experience for you, unlike in the case of the computer, really does change your brain circuits. New knowledge and new perspectives help us to think differently. This may be called *exposure therapy*.

Exposure therapy may also be used for getting relief from xenophobia (fear of crowded places), vertigo (fear of height) and other phobias where you can adopt one of the two alternatives available. The first alternative is exposing yourself to a situation or condition that you are scared about. Let us imagine, with your advanced age, you have started losing confidence in a crowded place like a cinema hall, a fair, a shopping mall, a church congregation, a puja pandal, a circus tent, or an overcrowded metro rail compartment or a thickly crowded railway platform. You feel (although there is no valid reason for you to feel as it has never happened to you) if something goes wrong, like a sudden fire, or earthquake, or a stampede, you'll be subjected to oxygen starvation and faint. The problem is called xenophobia. The remedy is for you to face such a situation in reality, on a small scale again and again. The second alternative, of course, is to visualise that you're exposed to such an adverse situation instead of a real-life physical exposure. By doing this negative visualisation again and again, you can condition your mind to restore your confidence to face such situations squarely.

PAST ACHIEVEMENTS AUDIT FOR SELF-MOTIVATION

There is another remarkable technique available for motivating yourself and removing depression from your mind; and, that is, your past achievements visualisation.

Every individual's life is a combination of 'achievements' and 'failures'; so is yours.

An 'achievement' represents an event where you received appreciation—formal or informal from others whereas a 'failure' is represented by another event where you might have had to face adverse criticism. Our achievements are due to unconscious, semi-conscious or conscious application of our 'strengths' or 'plus points' while our failures are either due to non-application of our 'strengths' or for unknowingly becoming victims of our 'weaknesses' particularly those which are insurmountable (which we describe as 'constraints').

So, when you vividly remember or visualise your past achievements and you stay on such visualisation exposure for some time, you generate the positive 'feel good' chemicals *dopamine* and *endorphin* and *beta*-positive electrical waves in your brain which creates a positive ambience.

CREATING YOUR DESIRED FUTURE

In order to create a future that you desire to have, you may visualise what you want vividly with all your sensory-motor powers and, along with deep rhythmic breathing. If you practice such positive futures visualisation, you have a very good chance of reaching very close to it.

BRAINPOWER UTILISATION

Even with advancing age, the brain cells are not lost. On the contrary, they remain most active if you stimulate them by learning, thinking (logically as well as imaginatively), planning, decision-making, problem-solving and innovating. Practical activities like reading, information collection, chess playing, solving crossword and sudoku puzzles and playing other brain-teasing games will keep your brain young despite your reaching an advanced age.

PERFORM BRAIN GYMNASTICS

To keep your brain active, play guessing games. Try to guess the time without looking at your watch. Try to guess how distant is your opposite neighbour's boundary wall from your house; how wide is the road separating his house from yours. Try to guess the height of the floor of a flat that you are visiting for the first time. Try to guess the prices of the products on display when you go to the daily market or for shopping in a mall once in a while. Try to figure out the title of the movie and the name of the singer when you hear an old melody.

Record something impromptu in your cassette recorder. Then switch it off and try to write down what all you had said. Now try to compare both—what you could remember and what you could not. After watching a programme on the TV or listening to one on the radio, once it's through, brainstorm randomly to think out and question anything that you like; for instance, what did happen, how did it happen, why something else did not happen, what could have been the other possibilities, what impressed you and what else didn't. Try and keep a diary regularly; still better for you to write stories or articles or compose poems if you can. If you can act, act. If you can paint, paint. If you can compose music, compose. Or, go to a museum, a zoo, or an art gallery; move about and make notes about the things on display which interests you specially. Prepare and use checklists even for simple tasks and for organising things.

A SPECIAL BRAIN FITNESS EXERCISE: EXTENDING YOUR *MIND*

So far, in brain science, our perception of the *mind* had been that its location is inside the head—in the *brain*. In 1949, philosopher Gilbert Ryle was the first person to challenge the idea (6) [(6) Ryle, G. *The Concept of Mind,* London: Hutchinson, 1949.]

Of late, the idea of the mind not being confined to the head has been reinvigorated by philosophers and cognitive scientists who see the mind as 'spreading out' or 'extending into the world' (7) [(7) Menary, Richard Ed. *The Extended Mind,* Cambridge, MA: MIT Press, 2010.]

In order to prevent the brain cells from becoming victims of the 'use it or lose it' law, aged people can practise the brain exercise of stretching the mind to any place to where they had been to and still possessed a vivid, joyous memory which is indeed rejuvenating. One can also visualise any experience with an object, an individual, or a movie, a music or a dance recital. This sort of reliving of a past memorable occasion can stimulate the right half of the upper brain or cerebral cortex positively. Now, if the same experience which is remembered is put into writing, then it is the left cerebral cortex which would be exercised.

BRAIN HYGIENE MAINTENANCE

Like body hygiene and dental hygiene maintenance, you have to do brain hygiene maintenance by not taking up smoking and other ways of tobacco abuse, alcohol consumption, drinking too many cups of tea and/ or coffee or cola drinks, and taking pharmacological drugs without doctor's advice or going for narcotic drugs. All these listed things contain substances which are extremely harmful for the brain and would definitely contaminate your brain and you'll be able to feel the serious consequences of such wrong habits. With the help of such stimulants, you get relief for a moment but at what cost—have you ever posed this question to yourself?

WHICH CULTURE DO YOU SUBSCRIBE TO

If you find from the discussion here that you subscribe to the 'wrong' cultures, analyse why shouldn't you move over to the 'right' cultures.

There are twelve commonly practiced cultures listed here—each negative one with its positive opposite. They serve as the twelve pillars of your personality and contribute to your social image.

'Culture of dark criticism' is wrong. 'Culture of bright appreciation' is right.

'Cultures of total dependence/total independence are wrong'. 'Culture of inter-dependence' is right.

'Culture of shame' is wrong. 'Culture of confidence' is right.

'Culture of inter/intra-team competition' is wrong. 'Culture of inter/ intra-team cooperation' is right.

'Culture of blunt assertiveness/straightforwardness' is wrong. 'Culture of assertiveness with tact/diplomacy' is right.

'Culture of "I win, you lose" (or "Win-Lose") communication/ behaviour' is wrong. 'Culture of "You win, I also win (or "Win-Win") communication/behaviour is right.

'Culture of comparison' is wrong. 'Culture of co-ordination' is right.

'Culture of inaction/procrastination' is wrong. 'Culture of action/ promptness' is right.

'Culture of reactivity' is wrong. 'Culture of pro-activity' is right.

'Cultures of rudeness and accusation' are wrong. 'Cultures of politeness and forgiveness' are right.

'Cultures of hatred and jealousy' are wrong. 'Cultures of understanding and love' are right.

Forget what cultures you had been following during your pre-retirement days, prepare for a happy retirement in advance much before the last month, week or day at the workplace, by subscribing to the right cultures. This practice will change the orientation of your body and brain cells and, if there are any negative vibrations killing the energy of your system, those would change in quality and quantity, and bring happiness in your retired life.

APPLICATION TIPS

- Are you happy with your mobility or you have some difficulty in maintaining your balance during locomotion? Please check up as it is a very common old age problem. If you have some problem, you can cure it yourself to a large extent by using your will power and using your limbs and their different parts rather than depending upon sticks and walkers.

- Guard yourself against old age brain disorders like cerebral stroke, neuronal death and dementia by having more vegetarian inputs (fruits, vegetables, and vegetable protein) in your food. Also try to maintain your brain hygiene by following the do's and don'ts prescribed.

- Be sensitive about any sign of Alzheimer's disease and, to prevent it, do not give up the habit of learning anything new which will stimulate your brain cells and keep them healthy and active and perform brain gymnastics. Be watchful of the symptoms of Parkinson's disease also and take timely preventive actions by keeping up rhythmic physical activities like walking, jogging, running, dancing and so on.

- Incorporate energy-boosting breathing exercise into your daily activity schedule. And, whenever you need a charge of positive energy, use the thought-pill and past achievements visualisation techniques for mental rejuvenation. You can also try out other brain fitness exercises recommended.

- Be aware of your creaturely mind's propensities and take actions to consciously rise and remain above them to become more humanly and godly being proactive, planned, imaginative and innovative.

- Also ensure that you do not subscribe to any wrong culture.

Chapter 18

The Old Age Financial Plan

"When the German philosopher Eugen Herrigel was studying traditional Japanese archery, he was having a tough time learning to let the arrow leave the bow at 'the right moment'. Even after three years he just wasn't getting it. Finally, his instructor drew his attention to a bamboo leaf in winter. It bends lower and lower with the weight of the snow, he said, till suddenly the snow slips to the ground without the leaf having stirred. One has to stay like that at the point of highest tension till the arrow leaves the bow like snow leaves the bamboo leaf. Herrigel still didn't leave the arrow properly for a long time but that day at least he knew what had to be left. And it wasn't the arrow."

—Mukul Sharma,
"Knowing what one has to leave",
The Economic Times, Kolkata, 11 January 2011, p. 6.

You'll never suffer from the tension of economic insecurity if you keep yourself cool and use your numerical skills to chalk out your old age financial plans in advance and review the plans against the actuals regularly. However, once you are ready with the plans to start with, you have got your basic tools like arrows. These will help you to take confident actions to hit your targeted goals for satisfaction of your needs.

WHAT MAKES THE FUTURE TENSE

Just as a person's physical and mental health and fitness are products of habits, so are his financial health and fitness.

Too many of us neglect our health and fitness during the young and middle ages of our life when they really needed regular care to lessen our worries in old age. Since we do not recognise the value of our personal potential assets and spend the years and decades without utilising them properly and, sometimes, even using them wrongly, one day we suddenly discover that we are not well-off physically or mentally.

In the same manner, we deal with our economic assets—the money that we earn—our income. We do not plan our spending; on the contrary, we handle our money at random, carelessly; we buy items (sometimes, fancy ones) which were not really essential for our living and working. Suddenly, one day we discover that we are short of funds; and then we go for credit. Such a situation makes our future tense. It could have been prevented if we had handled our finances with wisdom from beforehand.

One glaring example, where both our biological (body and brain-related) and economic neglects meet at a common point and have a far-reaching multiplier effect, is our smoking habit. Just one packet of cigarettes would not kill a person and it is also not a drain on our pocket; but a packet a day for thirty-six to thirty-eight years (starting at the age of 22, continuing up to 58 or 60 when you retire) may have a fatal end (the adverse effects of smoking will take place inside you and the outcome would be 'indirect') and it would turn out to be a big money-waster 'directly', leaving aside the expenditure to handle the medical problems that crop up due to your bad addiction.

Most unfortunately, it is not always obvious to us that the quality of our physical, mental as well as economic lives in our retirement years will depend upon how we plan and prepare for it in our youth (25 to 35 years) and middle age (35 to 55 years). Today, when you're waiting for your sun to set, just take a break and travel 15 to 25 years backward in your life's time space. You'll find that neither did you consciously enjoy nor did you save any sunshine and store them up in solar battery form to be able to bask in it during your greying years. In other words, if you're suffering and living a most painful existence in your senior adult years today, you must have lived month-to-month with no investments between the ages 35 and 55.

HEALTH-WEALTH COMBINATIONS

You should be able to put aged people into five 'health-wealth mix' categories, once you are familiar with their personal information. These five categories are:

(1) Good health and no financial wealth;

(2) Good financial wealth and no health;

(3) Good financial health and robust health;

(4) No financial wealth and no health; and

(5) Eroding financial wealth and health.

Category (3) is the best amongst the five and you should be lucky to find a place in it. And, category (4) is the worst of all. Category (1) is the one which has good scope for improvement as the 'health' front looks good; and Category (5), where the 'wealth' and 'health' are both eroding, one should target the 'health' to be perhaps improved first through special health and fitness improvement programmes within a short time frame by consulting the family doctor and wellness experts and, once these have improved to a certain level, one should concentrate on the financial status improvement—or, otherwise, if there is an indication that the health and fitness status improvement will take some time and financial status improvement is of a higher priority, then contact persons who are more knowledgeable in this field should be consulted.

For some people, loss of financial wealth and deterioration in financial status can lead to loss of health and fitness because of the inherent lack of mental strength in them. However, a mentally strong spouse with counselling skill can help build up confidence to face and eventually get over the problem.

AN EXERCISE FOR YOU

If you are about to take a break from your working career or have already retired, just think coolly, with respect to the above five categories of people: (i) where are you today; and (ii) where will you be tomorrow and the day after.

What level of health and fitness resources you have today, you might have already assessed as a part of the 'Resourcefulness Audit' which had been explained in Chapter 3. If you had not done this audit already, why don't you do it now?

Now, make an assessment of your financial health and fitness by making calculations on the following basis:

1. *How much funds you already have:* (i) in deposits (commercial banks/ post office/company/any other kinds of deposits; (ii) savings accounts (commercial banks/post office); (iii) invested in shares/stocks; (iv) invested in mutual funds; (iv) life insurance schemes; (v) public provident fund; (vi) in liquid cash; (vii) others (like jewelleries/ commodities etc.)?

2. *How much money you are going to get on retirement (applicable only in case of people who are going to retire) from different sources:* (i) provident fund; (ii) gratuity; (iii) leave encashment; (iv) other claims including pending salaries after all adjustments, arrears in medical reimbursements/tours and travel expenses; (v) miscellaneous heads?

3. *What would be the money value (at current rates) of your other assets:* (i) fixed (such as land, buildings etc.); (ii) movable assets (like car, computer, furniture, gadgets etc.)?

4. *Do you have any other income from:* (i) rent; (ii) agricultural activities; (iii) business activities; (iv) royalty payments for creative work such as

books published, music recorded and sold commercially, screenplays written etc.; (v) private tuition offered; (vi) miscellaneous?

5. *What is the wealth status of your spouse* (work out the details on the same lines).

6. *Are you getting any funds:* (i) capital—one-time; and (ii) recurring—regular from your kith and kin like: brother/sister; son/daughter; uncle/aunt; anybody else? If your answer is 'yes', then you will have to work out the details.

This exercise of your fund inflow calculation will be discussed once again in a relatively more organised form a little later when we discuss the 'Financial Planning and Fund Management' aspects for you. So don't get confused.

Once you are ready with a rough assessment of your planned financial resources, ask yourself the following questions (as applicable to you since different people have different dreams and desires and different worries) and find out the answer—a simple 'Yes' or 'No':

• Will I have the financial resources I would like to have?

• Will my old age be no better than just a struggle for survival?

• Will I be financially sound enough to do the things that I would like to do?

• Will I be able to travel and see all the places I want to see?

• Would I have to spend my later years worrying about catastrophic medical expenses and inadequate insurance coverage?

• Shall I have to regret wishing you had done something about your future earlier?

• Will I and my spouse become a burden to our children?

THE PRACTICE OF BUDGETING

You are in an 'Instant' Society

The society that we live in is an 'instant society'. We are inundated with credit and debit cards, the Internet and cell phones, fast food joints, e-booking of rail, air and ship tickets, electronic banking and money transfers, 'any time money' counters, choice of hundreds of TV and radio channels, departmental stores and shopping malls, one-day cricket and so on. These changes have taken place over the last two decades to provide immediate satisfaction of all our wants and needs. It has led to a very destructive 'get-rich-quick' way of thinking. Who wouldn't love to get rich—why in a few days—why not in a few hours as we can see there is a huge craze for big money-linked TV shows? So, we shove our tasks of financial prioritisation and planning to the back seats.

The 'instant satisfaction' or 'immediate gratification' route can never be taken for our health and fitness status improvement. You can't lose 15 kg of your weight or reduce your waistline by 10 cm overnight. Nor can it be taken for attainment of economic security or wellness in your old age. Success in both the things rarely comes to one instantly.

Practice of Budgeting is Recommended

For your old age financial soundness, we recommend the practice of *budgeting*.

Imagine, you are well into your retired life and journeying along the aging process, one of the few essential habits that you ought to inculcate is maintenance of a financial discipline. And, preparation for acquiring that habit must start a few months, preferably a year prior to your retirement. However, you will be economically safer if you start practicing the financial discipline well ahead of your scheduled retirement—may be from five years beforehand. What you have to do is nothing complicated. It is called *budgeting*. The dictionary defines 'budget' as 'an estimate, often itemised, of estimated income and expense for a given period in the future'.

Budgeting *vis-à-vis* Financial Planning

But when it comes to *financial planning*, making a budget doesn't just stop at listing out your income and expenses; a saving plan goes hand-in-hand. Then there is the aspect of discipline about sticking to your allocations for different heads and limiting your expenses accordingly.

We'll assume here that you're not yet retired but going to within a year or a few months' time.

YOUR RETIREMENT FINANCIAL PLANNING AND FUND MANAGEMENT

Why Planning

Your planning depends upon when you are going to retire and how are you going to behave financially after retirement. These are important considerations because in most cases there is no proper financial management and economically disciplined lifestyle in the case of the would-be retiree well in advance before retirement as we have already discussed.

This means that for a long period of time there has been little savings and even improper borrowings to fund various expenses. Once having got used to a certain standard of living, it becomes very difficult for a person to change the habit overnight after retirement. Thus, for many, it becomes a compelling need to continue searching for some source of income (through another employment, or self-employment, or through an own mini enterprise) even after official retirement for post-retirement sustenance. Therefore, it is most desirable for a would-be retiree to start chalking out some plans and programmes for post-retirement financial management, well in advance.

There is also another very important reason as to why you should go for the anticipatory planning exercise. As a person becomes older, there is a higher chance that some illness can impact him or his spouse or both with the consequence of his normal working being adversely affected directly or indirectly and, at the same time, there is an additional expense involved to meet the medical costs.

The Goal of Retirement Financial Planning

For the individual, the goal of retirement financial planning is to assure a stream of income that maintains, no matter how long one lives, one's standard of living during retirement.

Income from all sources should be taken into consideration and one's goal must be that it should replace between 65 to 85 per cent of the pre-retirement income.

What all are to be Calculated

(i) Expected Fund Inflow

Total Fund to Be Available on Retirement: First of all, you have to calculate what total fund you will get from your organisation on retirement. This may include: provident fund (PF), gratuity, leave encashment, any other outstanding claims (such as: salary, medical expenses reimbursement against bills already submitted) after adjustment of all your loans/advances taken), and, if applicable, social security fund, cooperative fund, and any other payments due to you.

Total Income from Your and Your Spouse's Personal Sources: Such sources may include: regular monthly income from property rentals, from bank fixed deposits/post office deposits (monthly)/interest on loan(s) given/agriculture/farming/private tuition/ any other source; one-time income (to be invested further) from life insurance policy/ mutual fund/bank fixed deposit/company deposit/govt. securities attaining maturity; any other form of investments which can be liquidated if required (such as company shares/mutual funds etc.). If you are going to receive some regular monthly allowance/payment from any other sources such as one or more of your children who is/ are well-settled, that should also be considered.

(ii) Expected Fund Outflow/Capital and Recurring Expenses

Well in advance, you would have done, we presume, your capital and recurring expenditure planning so that you don't face any financial problem after retirement. In order to make such advance financial plan, you have to make certain assumptions based on what are actually going to happen. For instance, you have to consider important aspects like: making provisions for (whichever is applicable): your property purchase/property renovation; two/four-wheeler purchase; any other machinery/equipment purchase (like fridge, air-conditioner, dish TV, washing machine, geyser, computer, laptop, ceiling/table fan/ microwave oven for household use); your children's education (in case you have your children continuing their education even after your retirement); their education abroad (in case they are very keen); your children's marriages; your and your spouse's healthcare and medical cost; costs for your property maintenance; costs of looking after your old parents; cost of travels for holidays and sightseeing; cost of hobbies; cost of daily necessities like food, toiletries; cost of periodic necessities like clothes, footwear, seasonal clothes (for winter), entertainment and gifts; cost of trans-portation (if you're going to maintain a car, that provision has to be made). Like this, all possible costs and expenses have got to be anticipated and estimated. In the total calculation, some *contingency amount* would also need to be added.

In the items, you might have to include: income tax; insurance premium; children's annual fees; sight seeing/travelling/tourism expenses; club's annual charges; cost of children's books and stationeries.

In the regular half-yearly expenses, you might have to include: property tax; insurance premium; cost of clothes/apparels/soft linens and furnishings; cost of children's books and stationeries.

In the regular monthly expense items, you can include; wages/salaries of household employees/security guard/sweeper/driver; telephone charges; mobile recharging; insurance premium; cable TV expenses; computer maintenance expenses; internet/broadband charges; monthly provisions; children's educational expenses; tutors' fees; medicine and health expenses; electricity charges; newspaper and magazine charges; guest entertainment; LPG cost; club expenses; maintenance of your old parents; cost of toiletries.

In the regular daily expense items, you are going to include: the daily household expenses; your personal expenses (if any); travel and transportation; pocket money to be given to your children.

(iii) For Setting up Your own Enterprise

In case you are going to have your own business/manufacturing set-up after retirement, the list of equipment to be procured along with their costs would need to be prepared along with the working capital requirements and also the possible sources of funding.

Similarly, on the other side, you have to anticipate and estimate the channels and amounts of your income. Some fixed sources of regular income for you may be: property rental income; income from investments; income from other sources. Fund available with you may include: public provident fund (PPF), some investments undergoing lock-in period, multiple/double bank deposits/company deposits/ company shares/mutual fund investments which you can possibly encash now at any time you like (please check up if encashment is possible or not). By doing this kind of a planned expenditure-income budgeting, you should be able to determine whether you need to take up a job or set up practice as a self-employed professional or set up your own organisation for generating some income.

(iv) Investment of Your Surplus Funds

Your available funds should be invested in different channels in such a way that you get the maximum return on investment. Possible channels could be: public provident fund; post office savings scheme; term deposits in commercial banks; government bonds and other schemes; mutual funds; company shares and deposits; commodities like gold and silver. It is always better for you to consult a knowledgeable professional (like a chartered accountant or a financial investment analyst) who can guide you regarding the investment channels where you would get maximum income-tax relief and so on.

Further Questions to be Asked

You also ask yourself the following questions and be prepared with your answer to each:

- Have you categorised your expenses into two types—'fixed' and 'variable' and, thereafter, the 'fixed' expenses into 'fixed mandatory' (such as home rent, home loan repayment, car loan EMI and medical insurance) and 'fixed voluntary' (such as newspaper and magazine subscription, club membership, membership of professional associations etc.); and the 'variable' expenses into 'variable mandatory' (such as groceries, clothing and healthcare among others) and 'variable voluntary' (such as eating out and watching movies, going for other kinds of entertainment)? (Yes/No)

- Have you crystallised any plans for controlling your expenses, particularly the 'fixed voluntary' and the 'variable voluntary' items? (Yes/No)

- Are you monitoring your budget regularly against the actual on a monthly basis? (Yes/No).

- Do you have any *debts* (on account of credit cards, property loans, vehicle loans and so on) to be paid up before you can think of seeing the face of some *income* on the *credit* side of your balance sheet? (Ans. Yes/No)

- Have you already made plans to organise your funds to have a 'bullet-proof' retired life? (Yes/No).

- If your answer to this question is 'no', then have you ever thought of organising your funds to be 'bullet-proof' after retirement? (Yes/No). 'Bullet-proof' means you have multiple streams of income: from rent, dividends, interest, liquidity, and reasonably good return from funds invested in any business.

YOUR POST-RETIREMENT WISH LIST: TO BEGIN LIFE AFTER RETIREMENT

Prepare your post-retirement wish list by choosing from the following:

(particularly those you had little or no time to do before your retirement)

- Library/availability of books to choose from

- Domestic help
- Medical assistance
- Respite from cooking but healthy food at doorstep
- Place to meet people of similar age and with similar interests
- Attending absorbing discourses and social gatherings
- Freedom from worries
- Comfortable travelling to the city centre and occasional shopping
- Banking
- Placement opportunity (full/part-time)
- Going for sightseeing and on vacation
- Go adding on to this list.

YOUR NUMBER SKILLS HAVE MADE YOU FINANCIALLY SECURE

According to a brand new study of married couples in the US, couples who scored well on a simple test of numerical ability accumulate more wealth by middle age than couples who scored poorly on such a test.

'Numerical ability' is the power to reason with numbers and other mathematical concepts, and are skills typically learned during school and college. So if at your old age today, you are financially secure, in all probability it is due to your numerical skills which got sharpened during the schooling phase of your life. (1). [(1) "Couples' number skills linked to family wealth", *The Times of India, Kolkata*, 11 November 2010, p.14.]

Regular practice of maths puzzles and playing number games may help in keeping such numerical skills active and fresh despite age. (2) [(2) "Electric brain stimulation boosts maths ability", *The Times of India, Kolkata*, 6 November 2010, p.12]

I am giving below two examples.

Example 1:

The date today is 4th December 2010. If we express it numerically, we get: 04. 12. 2010 which is equal to 4 (= 0 + 4) + 3 (= 1 + 2) + 3 (= 2+0+1+0).

If we add up 4 + 3 + 3, we get 10 = 1+0 = 1. Now, name a few things that you know of which are unique and unparalleled.

Example 2:

Question: Can you identify a few things where the number '7' is playing the most dominant role?

Answer: (i) The 'spectrum'—7 rays of the Sun: VIBGYOR; (ii) 7 days of the week: Sunday-Monday-Tuesday-Wednesday-Thursday-Friday-Saturday; (iii) 7 *swaras*—sa-re-ga-ma-pa-dha-ni; (iv) The word *'Mahatma'* which has 7 alphabets; (v) 7 Nobel laureates who had some connection with Kolkata: Sir Ronald Ross, Rabindranath Tagore, Dr C V Raman, Dr Hargovind Khurana, Mother Teresa, Dr Amartya Sen, and Gunther Grass; (vi) the name *'Kolkata'* itself; (vii) the sacred river *'Hooghly'*.

IT'S ALL IN THE GENES

If, for your frugal habits and controlled nature, you are criticised by your children and grandchildren, never mind. Play it cool as thriftiness, generosity and altruism are all in the genes. Researchers at the University of Bonn, Germany, have got such indications. (3) [(3) "Blame It on the Genes", *The Times of India, Kolkata,* 11 November 2010, p. 16.]

APPLICATION TIPS

- Ascertain which category of the 'health-wealth mix' you belong to. In any case, however, first assess your financial *resourcefulness*—what funds you already have with you—invested in various schemes and channels, and what more funds are likely to flow into your kitty.

- The practice of *budgeting* is most important for you if you have been subscribing to today's Instant Society's *instant/immediate gratification culture.*

- Follow the tips given and make plans for your post-retirement fund management and get to know where you stand *vis-à-vis* your post-retirement wish list.

- Also develop your number skills which, once developed, will be one of the keys for you to feel confident and not confused in making financial calculations.

- Ascertain if you are thrifty, frugal and controlled or unbalanced and impulsive in your economic behaviour. If your nature is of the latter type, you need not worry if you literally follow what tips are there in this chapter.

Chapter 19

Other Wellness Factors

"20 minutes of an individual's time should be spent on meditation, 20 minutes for exercise and 20 minutes for pondering over what one should do for someone else."
—This 20:20:20 principle has been coined by Professor Nitin Nohria, Dean of Harvard Business School—the Mecca of Business Management (reported in *The Times of India, Kolkata,* 10 January 2011, p. 18.)

"The [prison] cell is an ideal place to learn to know yourself……..
The cell gives you the opportunity to look daily into your entire conduct, to overcome the bad and develop whatever is good in you."
—Nelson Mandela, Nobel Laureate,
In: *Conversations with Myself,* New Delhi: Macmillan, 2010.

YOUR DAILY SCHEDULE

Here, I'm tempted to quote the whole of a short piece by the ace columnist Mukul Sharma to highlight the initial time-structuring problems of a freshly retired person. It reads like this:

"A friend retired a year back and almost immediately—within a matter of weeks really—hit the skids. He used to be a high roller in the hierarchy of the organisation where he had worked for over a decade, getting respect, fear and perhaps some friendships now and then along the way, but then, overnight, it was all gone, vanished. Or so he believed, because the first thing he thought was he had become worthless and, who knows, may be his worth had declined drastically as far as his former colleagues were concerned since he no longer counted or mattered in their daily preoccupation with employment.

As a kind of compensation, therefore, one of the first mistakes he made was exult in the thought that he didn't have to wake at six, seven or eight in the morning to arrive in time some where a little letter. That was heady and, in fact, it went straight to his head. Much to the chagrin of his spouse and other members of his nuclear family who were all still busy wage-earning their way through life, he would rise close to noon and listen to music, make some passing reference to lunch and grab another nap in the afternoon that often stretched to the evening when the others started trickling back. Did he care that they seemed to be frowning on this sort of a thing? No, he had enough money.

The only problem with this lifestyle, however, was what to do with weekends. The ones he ran into initially merely amused him. Thereafter, they became a source of irritation. Everyone was home, waking up late after watching television or partying into the night, then making plans to visit people, see a movie may be or just generally hang around at home. But for our friend, time suddenly hung heavy. So he decided that was the day he would catch up on his correspondence, sort out some personal papers and—yes, why not?—begin learning yoga since the course classes were open through the afternoon on Sundays. Pretty soon, he had totally reversed his earlier life and made a mess of it in the process.

Six months later when he was admitted into an institution for a mental breakdown, he knew the *asanas* well enough to look after his body—if not his mind. Now this is a true story about a real person, so there can obviously be no moral here without moralising, but perhaps it might be a good idea to keep weekends free to do nothing when you think you have nothing to do during the rest of the week."

—"Lots of time, yet nothing to do",
The Economic Times, Kolkata, 13 July 2010, p. 12.

Now, how should you structure your daily schedule?

If your sleep breaks early, get up early; don't toss around on the bed. Get ready after freshening up to go for a morning walk after taking a cup of tea and two biscuits or a handful of germinated wet grams or pea nuts, if it is not difficult for you to chew and digest them. If the gram or the peanuts make you feel heavy, don't go for them.

After walking a mile, come back, put on light clothes—move to an airy space and start breathing and freehand stretching-bending exercises. Thereafter take bath in lukewarm water if that makes you feel good and have breakfast. All this should be over by 9.30 am.

After breakfast, if you have no other important work to do (such as reading, writing, accounts work, practising music if you're musically skilled, going to the bank or post office and the like) read the newspaper or some light magazine. Weather permitting, you can again go out for a stroll or to a friend or a relative's place, or for shopping between 11.00 am and 1.00 pm. Getting the mid-morning winter sun on your body is an excellent freshener and energizer. If it rains or there is gusty wind or snowfall if you are resident at a cold place, stay indoors and spend time alone (read the quotes from Nelson Mandela provided in the beginning of this chapter).

If you remain at home, do some light household work or sit at your desktop computer or laptop; or spend some time solving crossword or sudoku puzzles. If you have your own or your neighbour's little grandchildren, you can have your free time beautifully spent with them.

Have your lunch between 1.00 and 1.30 pm. You'll feel sleepy immediately after lunch, but you should not go for sleep. Engage yourself in something (like reading, watching TV, listening to music, sketching, writing) before you go for your siesta after a one hour gap. You rest for one hour only. At 5.00 pm, you have some tea with a light snack. The best choice would be to go for some non-citreous fruits. Again, you may go for a stroll or to the market or you can go to meet friends at a club or at their places or visit relatives or spend time with little children or other people visiting you.

After you come back, you and your spouse can talk together or watch the TV together, or if your grandchildren are staying with you, spend some time with them before you have you dinner between 9.00 and 9.30 pm.

Don't go to bed immediately after your dinner. Walk a little inside or outside the house. Don't read or watch anything exciting like a horror story or a movie. You may, if you can, listen to some soothing music (like flute) which will absorb your tensions, if you have accumulated any and make you ready for a restful sleep. Never delay your sleeping time beyond 10.00 to 10.15 pm.

OTHER *MAGIC* LIFESTYLE THERAPY *MANTRAS* FOR BEING HAPPY

There are several *magic* lifestyle therapy *mantras* available to choose from. These include:

- *Colour Therapy:* Different colours have different vibrations. Violet, Indigo and Blue are most soothing colours. You can meditate on natural scenic pictures (real or imaginary) to bring relaxation to your brain. For violet, you can choose violet flowers like aparajita, neelkantha, dhatura or violet chrysanthemum. For indigo, you can choose the dark blue ocean where it meets the horizon. For blue, you can choose the bright and sunny blue sky with some white autumn clouds passing across. Green, yellow and orange are vibrant colours.

For green, you can meditate on a green paddy field, or a green hillside, or a huge green tree, or a lush green tea garden. For yellow, you can imagine a sunflower garden. For orange, you can imagine you are looking at the beautiful sunset. Red is the most powerful colour; it has its good as well as bad properties. In order to get benefit of its good qualities, you have to meditate on the picture of sunrise where the sun is rising as a red ball of fire. For relaxation, meditate on violet, indigo or blue. For being practical, meditate on green. For cheering yourself up, meditate on yellow. For practising self-control, meditate on orange. And, for increasing your stamina and enhancing action orientation, meditate on red.

- *Art Therapy:* It is nothing but applied colour therapy. Instead of exposing yourself to real scenic beauty or colour meditation, you stand or sit in front of a coloured picture which has the most dominant colour or a combination of colours that you need for being happy.
- *Music Therapy:* For getting sleep, listen to soft flute music. For getting relaxation, listen to Indian classical music in strings (sarod, sitar, santoor or guitar)—only the *alap* portion. For energising yourself, listen to percussions, moderate to fast beats and follow the beats by tapping with your hands or feet.
- *Laughter Therapy:* Smile, laugh, enjoy whenever you feel like. However, avoid monstrous laughter or sarcastic smile.
- *Pet Therapy:* Keeping a pet like a dog, a cat, or some birds, or even an aquarium with specially chosen gold fishes in it will help you to pass time happily.

SEVEN SIMPLE *SUTRAS* FOR RESTORATION OF POSITIVE ENERGY

Positive energy dwindles in old age. Self-healing is the process to restore energy balance inside the body using seven simple *sutras.*

- Feel the earth—our mother planet, beneath your feet for a few seconds. (Usually we are not conscious about our constant touch with mother earth—you have to feel it consciously.)
- Establish a connection between your soles and the ground and visualise roots going downwards. Barefoot walking on grass will provide you with the best experience.
- Take 10 deep, slow breaths using your nose. The mouth should be kept lightly shut. It will help you to send more oxygen to your brain,

your blood pressure will drop and, a sense of calm will envelope you. Do it as often as you like, anywhere and anytime. Feel relaxed with every phase of exhalation.

- Rub your palms together for a little while then have your fingers interlocked to make a closed circuit so that energy leakage, which is maximum from our palms and fingertips, is arrested.

- Bring into your mind affirmations and positive thoughts which will heighten your self-confidence and increase your self-esteem.

- Don't miss your daily bath. While having a shower or pouring water on your body, think that all mental impurities (like anxiety and ego) and all physical deficiencies (like frailty and fatigue) are being washed away being replaced by seeds of potential strengths.

- Wear clean and well-pressed (not crushed) clothes. You can use white or any other colour; but the top and the bottom wears should be well-matched and harmonious so that your appearance has a soothing yet attractive effect on the beholder.

FRAUD PREVENTION TIPS: USE OF *PRACTICAL INTELLIGENCE (PI)*

There are umpteen opportunities for application of your *Practical Intelligence (PI)* so that you do not get entangled in any fraudulent transactions.

Be assertive to say 'No' to people calling or wanting to meet you. Remember, you aren't being impolite; you are only making sure that your time is not wasted. Don't be afraid to say 'No' to any offer made to you when you're at home or are taking a round at your local park.

Don't give any personal information, particularly your 'debit' or 'credit' card numbers or bank account details to anyone over phone or in person, unless the request is from the manager or somebody else from your bank or your financial adviser.

Do not seek any "help" or let any stranger "help" you with cash withdrawal at an ATM by offering to keying in the PIN (Personal Identification Number) or in any other way.

Try to use an ATM close to the place of your residence where many local people are known to you. Even for traditional cash withdrawal from the bank cash counter, use your bank account in a bank next door—never far away from your home. At the time of depositing cash, do not take the help of any stranger to count your money; you should always try to take somebody close to you to the bank. Have your savings bank account passbooks updated every month and after every deposit/withdrawal event. Put all your 'debit' and 'credit' cards as well as bank cheque and pass books in a safe place under lock and key. Report about any lost or stolen cheques, cheque books, pass books and bank cards without any delay.

Don't be fooled by deals that seem too good to be realistic. Stay away from any deal, including for house purchase that asks for a lot of money in the beginning.

Any confidential information written on a piece of paper must be destroyed once it has been used up.

Be careful when buying things online. Common websites making attractive offers may not protect your credit card or bank account information. Check if the website is a safe one before you enter details of your account or credit card for any online transaction.

APPLICATION TIPS

- Your wellness depends upon how well you structure daily schedules.
- There are other lifestyle therapy *mantras* for being happy which are worth your consideration.
- You should also think seriously about restoration of positive energy by following the seven simple *sutras* suggested.
- You should also use your *Practical Intelligence (PI)* to prevent getting involved in any fraud particularly in any capital asset purchase or financial investment transactions.

Chapter 20

Retirement: Different Nations, Different Outlooks

"Retire from your career—be it employment, self-employment, trade or industrial business. But never retire from life. Then you'll be missing all the fun."
—A retired chief executive officer of a reputed company
who is still enjoying a fun-filled life in his mid-eighties

RETIREMENT: WHERE PRACTICED

There are three common ways of generating income: by being an employee, that is working for others; by being a self-employed person—a trader or a travelling sales person, a skilled craftsman or a high-powered high-end professional like a doctor, an architect, a lawyer, an accountant, a management consultant or a fashion designer; or, by being an employer who employs people for getting work done.

An employee again may be engaged in any one of the following three types of sectors—an unorganised sector (as a security guard in somebody's place of residence or as a cook or a bearer or a governess or a nurse); a semi-organised sector (like a sweet shop, a small workshop or a drug store); or, an organised sector (like a business house or an industrial set-up coming under the purview of industrial laws).

An employer never retires unless he is forced to retire due to ill health or the pressure of his successors who are interested to take the reins from him to turn around a static and stagnant organisation into a dynamic and fast-growing one. An employer not having any worthy successors may sell the business off to some interested and deserving parties so that he can retire in peace.

A self-employed professional also does not normally retire. He continues as long as he is fit and senile. He may groom his next generation (may be own children or some kith and kin) to take over or may hand over his mantle to some capable juniors as is common in many trades and professions.

An employee in the unorganised or semi-organised sector also does not generally retire because of the knowledge and experience-based value that he has added to the organisation's human capital assets. His employer tries to retain him for his worth. The question of retirement crops up only in the case of the organised sector as it attracts different legal provisions which do not allow any employee to continue to work on a whole-time basis beyond a certain age, normally 58 to 60 years in Indian government, business and industry and 62 to 65 and, in some cases, even 70 years in the organised educational sector.

THE THIRD WORLD SCENARIO

In a vast third world country like India, every year thousands, may be even millions, of people are retiring from different types of organised sector establishments including the Central and State Governments. In the absence of any valid statistical data, we can surmise that following the Indian tradition, most of them would retire from active life and live with their grown-up children and their families. Those who have no such choice or are a little independent-minded, may decide to maintain their own separate identities and establishments.

Professionally Qualified and Experienced Retirees Continue having Post-Retirement Career

However, those retirees who are professionally qualified and experienced including women who have spent their working life in teaching, nursing or medical fields may choose to continue in their field of specialisation on a whole- or part-time basis. We know of several managers who are qualified accountants and have set up their professional practice; law degree holders who have gone for advocateship; engineers and architects who have gone for freelance consultancy; teachers and professors who have opted for lecturing assignments; medical doctors and nurses who have joined group practice or private health care units. But compared to the huge workforce who retires every year, the percentage of such post-retirement economically engaged persons is very insignificant.

Those who Retire for Good: Where do they Stand

We should be concerned more about people who retire for good and not those who take up something for economic return. Among the complete retirees, we know of people who have started giving voluntary service to NGOs, joined some academic or professional courses again, or have started pursuing training in music, fine art, or creative writing. There are also cases where the retiree has gone for entrepreneurship.

Today's elderly members of the organised sector workforce are relatively well-educated and well-off. They are graduates or technically professionally qualified and have had the highest incidence of being qualified and having the highest average household incomes and investments in fixed and movable assets compared to members of their previous generations—their grandparents and parents, their spouses' grandparents and parents. In big metro cities and industrial townships, away from their home base, they have also had the opportunity to intermingle with seniors, peers and juniors from different communities, cultures and language backgrounds. So, as regards socio-technical exposure also, they are way ahead of their parents, elders and other ancestors.

However, having grown up with long-hand working and not being married to latest information technology, some of them shy away from computers and latest devices. Even if they adopt the latest, they restrict themselves to their routine and elementary applications. Very few of them enjoy working with new technologies as much as their younger and mid-career colleagues. So, if they want to be hired again after retirement, they have to train themselves up in latest technologies and such preparation has to begin at least two or three years before they are due to retire.

If such retirees were married and had children early in their lives, as would be the case with those born in the 1950's, while approaching retirement they will have fewer hassles with their children's education or even with their marriages. And, it is not unlikely that some of them would have also become grandparents and would be looking forward to spending quality time with their grandchildren after retirement. Like the good old days of joint families, very few of them would have to serve as caregivers of an elderly relative or an adult dependent like an unmarried or widowed sister or an unemployed and dependent brother, sister, niece or nephew. In other words, today's Indian elderly belonging to an organised sector of business and industry is more independent compared to the previous generation employees. For most of them, work comes before their presently limited family responsibilities. Only those having growing or unsettled children or responsibilities of getting their brothers, sisters or some relatives settled in life would put family before work.

THE FIRST WORLD SCENARIO

In a first world highly developed country, the situation today as had been predicted by management guru Peter Drucker just as we stepped into the second decade of the twenty-first century is well described by his words:

"In the developed countries, the dominant factor in the next society will be something to which most people are only just beginning to pay attention: the rapid growth in the older population and the rapid shrinking of the younger generation. Politicians everywhere still promise to save the existing pensions system, but they and their constituents—know pretty well that in another 25 years people will have to keep working until their mid-70s, health permitting.

What has not yet sunk in is that a growing number of older people—say those over 50—will not keep on working as traditional full-time nine-to-five employees, but will participate in the labour force in many new and different ways." (1) [(1) Drucker, Peter F., "The Next Society", *Economist*, November 3, 2001]

Three Categories of Employee Population

In USA, the employee population is divided into three categories: *mature* (55 + years old); *mid-career* (35 to 54 years old); and *young* (18 to 34 years old). Today, many American employees belonging to the first group want to remain productive, even after the traditional 'retirement' age. There are books written to show you how to keep their capabilities, company knowledge and customer connections work for you. (2) [(2) Dychtwald, Ken, Tamara J. Erickson and Robert Morison, *Workforce Crisis: How to Beat the Coming Shortage of Skills and Talent*, Boston, Mass: Harvard Business School Press, 2006]

The 1940s-Born Generation

The social, political and economic implications of increasing lifespan, and the aging of the 1940s-born generation in the world's industrialized nations is enormous. Currently, for every US federal tax dollar spent per senior citizen, only 14 cents goes to a child. The average senior receives $7,000 annually in medical benefits; in 1965, it was only $1 per year. Politically also, the US is turning into a *gerontocracy* (a special word coined by combining 'gerontology'—the 'study of the aged' with 'democracy'). There, the elderly have the lowest poverty level; constitute the richest segment of the society; and dominate the political arena as over 70 per cent of the seventy-year olds cast their votes as against the less than 33 per cent voting response from the twenty-year-olds. Politicians, therefore, have learnt to devote more time, effort and energy to woo the senior citizen class. 80 per cent of the consumer growth comes from the fifty-plus age group. On the family front, couples have to divide their time between their living elderly parents and the children. In organised business and industry, big names like General Motors have far more retirees than young or mid-age employees on their active rolls.

Such a reversal in the human resource management strategy indicates a thrust on knowledge and talent management by retaining retiree employees or by not limiting the age for retirement for those who can contribute more meaningfully for their acquired maturity than those who are younger and have quite some time left to reach their retirement age.

Earlier, people went for their education and professional training, got a job, climbed the ladder and retired. But that pattern is becoming more cyclical with periods of education, work and recreation overlapping or running in parallel across a lifetime.

Today, younger employees want more time off, middle-aged workers are making radical career changes, and many older employees are sitting on boards, starting new businesses, and giving back to their communities as never before. Two-thirds of today's employees plan to work at least part-time in retirement. Their professional aspirations are also numerous and diverse. Opportunities for post-retirement working have also opened up to a large extent. (3, 4) [(3) *The New Employee/Employer Equation* survey, conducted in 2004 by Harris Interactive for the Concours Group and Age Wave, found that 66 per cent of employees plan to work, at least part-time after retiring. AARP reports similar findings in (4) "Staying Ahead of the Curve 2003: The AARP Working in Retirement Study", September 2003].

The generations born after World War II have lived lavishly and saved little. Not surprisingly, saving rates are generally low and consumer debt high. Many investment and retirement funds exploded a few years ago when the dotcom burst-out took place, huge companies went bankrupt and global markets got shaken up. There is thus a lot of pressure on public pension schemes like the Social Security which rarely pay enough to maintain pre-retirement lifestyles.

People in their late 40's and Early 50's: Where do they Stand

Truth is, many people in their late forties and fifties today might have to work well beyond the age of sixty or sixty-five, just to make both ends meet. And, this is the fastest growing age segment, and large-size organisations can expect the percentage of employees over fifty-five during 2010-2015.

According to the AARP poll, the top four reasons for one to continue working in retirement were: staying mentally active (87 per cent); staying physically active (85 per cent); being productive or useful (77 per cent); and, having some fun and enjoying (71 per cent). As expected, in an affluent country like the US, working after retirement purely for economic reasons and for entitlement to health benefits got a score of 22 and 17 per cent respectively. (4) [(4) AARP, "Staying Ahead of the Curve 2003: The AARP Working in Retirement Study", September 2003].

A QUESTION TO BE ASKED

In a developing country like India, we must not forget to address ourselves a question: can we ever progress in educational and human resource development infrastructure and business and industry as fast and as much with our relatively younger population (mostly first-generation organised sector employees) and the standard traditional retirement policies?

POINTS TO PONDER

Although such bigger issues are beyond the scope of this book, a would-be retiree reader, glancing through these pages may like to explore the possibility to reconsider his plan for retirement. He should seriously think whether he can, health and fitness permitting, continue to play some role in the ball game of the nation's social and economic growth by pursuing a professional practice, or by being a small entrepreneur, or by continuing his employment career, if not in the same but in some other outfit. It would be an important area for him to consider in the planning for his happy retirement. Besides, he should persuade his organisation's concerned authorities to allow him to join in-house and external training programmes which would equip him in some way to chalk out a better plan for happy retirement. Normally, retirees are kept outside the purview of such HRD activities and the obvious reason cited is: retirement on the horizon but it is not a fair practice. Such commonly prevailing practices ought to be reviewed from a broader perspective. If a retiree gets trained which helps him to settle down happily and contribute something meaningful even after his retirement, it is better for the society and better for the nation. The organisation must not abdicate all such intangible responsibilities in the case of retirees; on the contrary, it should take such steps in respect of retiree relations that the employee's loyalty, faith and trust in the organisation continue to be reinforced and strengthened and he continues to serve as a brand ambassador and evangelist spreading good words about the organisation all around.

APPLICATION TIPS

- First assess if the question of retirement is applicable in your case or not. Even if it is not, just read on as we feel you can play the important role of an advocate in propagating whatever we are trying to promote through this book.

- And, if you happen to be a retiree or would-be retiree, please consider it seriously if you would like to do something of social value even after your retirement as you, possessing a reasonably good health and fitness both in body and mind, must not allow your energy and powers to go to waste just by retiring fully and spending your life like the idle-chatting elderly whom I meet whenever I'm in town and go for morning walk in my local park.

- Tips on *Old Age Happiness* are changing people's lives. You may, if you like, draw inspiration from one of them who says: "Thanks a lot for waking me up from my post-retirement slumber!. I had been limping with a half-brain and a quarter self-confidence before I got the happiness tips from you. Now, I have abandoned my walking stick and made myself posturally erect to maintain a decent gait. None of the people who know me ever believed that I could do it. Many many thanks once again!"

> —Nikhilesh Chaturvedi (name changed),
> a septuagenarian retired top executive.

Standard Height-Weight Chart for Persons of Medium Frame

Normal Range of Weight in Kg for Men	Height of the Person in Feet and Inches (cm)	Normal Range of Weight in Kg for Women
Men	Height	Women
50–56	5'–0" (152.4)	45–51
52–57	5'–1" (154.94)	47–52
53–58	5'–2" (157.4)	48–54
55–60	5'–3" (160.02)	50–55
56–61	5'–4" (162.56)	51–57
58–63	5'–5" (165.1)	53–59
59–65	5'–6" (167.64)	54–61
60–66	5'–7" (170.18)	56–63
63–69	5'–8" (172.72)	59–65
64–70	5'–9" (175.26)	60–66
66–72	5'–10" (177.8)	62–68
68–74	5'–11" (180.34)	63–70
70–77	6'–0" (182.88)	66–72
72–79	6'–1" (185.42)	68–74
74–82	6'–2" (187.96)	76–79

Note: Recent research studies have indicated that stereotypes about body size/weight can be misleading. An individual can be extremely balanced to look at and still have a heart attack waiting to happen. And, another individual can also be overweight but otherwise healthy. It has been observed that about half of overweight people have normal *blood pressure* and *cholesterol* levels, while an equal number of trim people suffer from ills usually associated with obesity.

WHO IS OVERWEIGHT

The most practical method of determining whether a person is obese is by referring the weight to the standard charts based on weight and height relationship. A person is considered overweight if he exceeds the upper range of ideal weight for his body frame. He can also be considered as obese if his weight exceeds by 9 to 10 kg. of his ideal weight. The amount of body fat can also be estimated from whole body specific gravimetric determination or from measurements of the thickness of subcutaneous fat folds (fat beneath the skin) with skin fold callipers. These methods are of only academic interest.

Ten (10) Powers of the Body

Serial No.	Power Description	Full Score	Your Present Score	Remarks (Highlights of Your Problems)
1.	Health	100		
2.	Fitness	100		
3.	Gait (Style of Walking)	100		
4.	Postures (Standing/Sitting/Lying)	100		
5.	Gestures (Hands & Fingers/Eyes/ Legs & Feet/Whole Body)	100		
6.	Voice (Softness/Strength/Steadiness/ Sonorousness)	100		
7.	Power of Observation	100		
8.	Power of Hearing	100		
9.	Stamina (Capacity for Hard & Long Hours of Work)	100		
10.	Action Orientation (Physical Promptness & Timeliness)	100		
	Total Score:	1000		

Ten (10) Powers of the Brain

Serial No.	Power Description	Total Score	Your Present Score	Remarks (Highlighting of Your Problems)
1.	Logical/Analytical/Rational Thinking; Intelligence; Questioning / Planning / Programming/Passion for Details	100		
2.	Powers of Calculation & Measurements/ Numerical Skill	100		
3.	Science/Scientific Bent of Mind / Systems / Procedures	100		
4.	Language; Grammar/Composition/ Spelling / Vocabulary/Reading/ Speaking/ Writing	100		
5.	Factual Memory (Names/Addresses/ Tel. Nos./E-mail Ids Etc.)	100		
6.	Emotional Thinking/Feelings/ Sentiments	100		
7.	Imagination/Visualisation/Creativity	100		
8.	Motivation	100		
9.	Leadership Quality (Capacity to Motivate Others)	100		
10.	Impressionistic Memory (Images / Sounds/ Other Sensory Experiences/Emotional)	100		
	Total Score:	1,000		

Tips on Diet

"Would you please think about declaring one day every year, perhaps January 12....., to celebrate vegetarianism and compassion towards animals? Such a declaration would save countless animals, reduce environmental devastation caused by the meat industry and help participants clear their arteries and their consciences."

—Paul McCartney of the Beatles fame,
urging the Indian Prime Minister Dr Manmohan Singh on January 12, 2010, the foundation day of People for Ethical Treatment to Animals, India (PETA)

DIET MUST BE PLANNED

Dr Robert Atkins, America's most famous "diet guru" made millions by recommending consumption of more meat and cheese by restricting the intake of carbohydrates. His dietary advice has raised a lot of controversy as long-term study has shown that such dietary habit paves the way towards heart attack, congestive heart problems, hypertension and obesity in individuals prone to fatty deposits and cardiac arterial dysfunctions.

Impact of Zero-Carb/Low–Carb Diets

Let us look at a few altogether different schools of thought, which have come into the limelight recently.

According to the **first** one, propounded by Dr Richard Wurtman, director of the MIT clinical research centre, consumption of carbohydrates should not be given up totally as these have an effect on our mood. Stoppage of carbohydrate inputs leads to the stoppage of *serotonin*, the chemical in the brain that elevates mood and suppresses appetite. Individuals, whose brains produce less *serotonin* as a natural part of their metabolic process, have an inherent desire to consume more carbohydrates. They are the 'carbohydrate-cravers'. They experience a change in their mood, usually in the late afternoon or mid-evening. And, with their mood change comes a yearning to eat something sweet or starchy. The brain makes *serotonin* only after a person consumes carbohydrate. It will not make *serotonin*, however, unless little or no protein is eaten at the same time.

Diet must Contain 'Good' Carbohydrates and 'Good' Fats

The 'South Beach Diet', a **second** school, divides carbohydrates into 'good' carbohydrates (whole wheat based stuff and high fibre cereals such as brown bread and brown rice) and 'bad' carbohydrates (milled rice, pasta and biscuits). It also differentiates between 'good' fats (monoun-saturated such as olive oil, lean chicken/fish) and 'bad' fats (saturated such as in red meats). It recommends you to eat three healthy balanced meals a day, which even includes snacks. By eating right, you'll feel fuller for longer and lose weight. This diet is not suitable for those with kidney problems.

Diet that is Good for the Elderly

According to a **third** school of thought, we should focus on 'micronutrients' rather than on fats, carbohydrates and proteins, which is the old school of thinking. Nutrient-rich low-calorie foods help to stop damage at the cellular level that can develop into disease, and make you look better and have more energy. **This may be a better choice for the elderly than the others already discussed.**

This school recommends consumption of: beans, berries (particularly blueberries), broccoli, oats, oranges, grapefruit, pumpkin, soy, spinach, tomatoes, walnuts, salmon (as 'fish' item), turkey (as 'bird' item), yoghurt (as a 'milk product'), and tea. Both recommendations are based on sound logic. But the problem is: which one to follow or recommend to others.

Fibre in Diet is Essential

Therefore, rather than trying to join the Atkins or any other conceptual bandwagon, as many social climbers attempt to do, it'll be wiser to go in for a time-tested simple planned diet. However, before we move into the details, let us share a general observation. Some specific sources of dietary fibres (such as 'wheat') significantly cut the risk of death from heart disease. 10 grams of fibre per day would be good enough. A slice of whole wheat bread contains 1.5 grams while a standard size *roti* or *chapatti* would contain about 3 grams, equivalent to the fibre content of one apple. The latest recommendation to consume a diet that includes an abundance of fibre-rich foods to prevent coronary heart disease is based on a wealth of consistent scientific evidence.

Fibre-rich cereals are also known to put the risk of diabetes away.

Why Meat is not Good

Look at another recent finding. Eating a meat-free vegetarian diet, researchers say, may reduce the risk of colorectal cancer. The fat in red meat increases the excretion of substances called bile acids, which in turn produce other substances that encourage tumour growth.

Furthermore, meat contains natural compounds and substances formed during processing and high-temperature cooking that can disrupt the normal balance of cell growth in the colon, potentially triggering the cancer. Alternatively, substances in fruits and vegetables, contained in the vegetarian diet, may inhibit these adverse effects. Frequent fruit-eaters —consuming more than 5 servings of fruit per week—are over 40 per cent less likely to develop colorectal cancer. **All such observations obviously lead to the conclusion that diet must be planned.**

Rice *vs. Atta*

Both rice as well as *atta* contains sufficient carbohydrates. *Atta* is higher in protein, fibre and certain micronutrients. However, the protein in rice is better absorbed. Rice, as it is easily digested, is better tolerated particularly by those having digestive problems.

Excess intake of either can cause a rise in blood sugar. Hence a diabetic should keep his intake of rice or wheat low each time and rather have it distributed throughout the day. Equal division of food, rich in carbohydrates, must be done and the total quantity consumed should be limited.

PLANNED DIET FOR THE SEDENTARY ELDERLY

An example of planned diet for largely sedentary elderly people for the whole day, covering all your meals and snacks would be:

Cereals *(rice/wheat)*: 300–350 gm. (Flour should be taken for a change, as it does not have much nutritive value being refined stuff although it may be filling; rice should be reduced to 150 gm by increasing the wheat content, if your energy level is low and you feel sleepy from time to time; otherwise, in normal cases, rice quantity may go up to 200 gm).

Pulses (*dal* or lentil, *chana* or gram, *badam* or peanuts, *matar* or dry peas, bean, soybean, *rajma*): 70 to 75 gm for non-vegetarians and 90-100 gm for vegetarians.

Roughages or *sag* or *green leafy vegetables*: 100 gm, as it gets digested quickly and helps in bowel movement.

Other green vegetables: 65–70 gm;

Roots and **tubers** (*potato, sweet potato, carrot, beet, radish, onion, ginger*): 60–70 gm.

Egg: 1 to 2 (optional for the elderly—those with high cholesterol should not take);

Fish, meat, chicken: 30 to 40 gm. and preferably of 'lean' variety;

Milk and **milk products** (like *curd, yoghurt, paneer*): 100 gm for vegetarians; 50–60 gm for non-vegetarians;

Oil, fat, butter, ghee: 30–35 gm including in cakes, pastries, sweets, chocolates, tea, coffee, dessert (saturated fat interferes with the brain's efficiency; the fat particles injure brain cells and hamper the ability of neurotransmitters to carry messages)

Fruits: Seasonal fruits; at least 1 banana per day.

Water: 3 to 4 litres of clean water (as unclean water may lead to jaundice or hepatitis especially during summer). Drinking plenty of fluids while suffering from a cold or respiratory infection could cause more harm than help.

A balanced diet should comprise the following groups of food - cereals, pulses, protein (meat, fish, egg, chicken), fats/oils, sugars, fruits and vegetables. Less than 30(thirty) percent of the total calories must come from fats. Vitamins must be obtained from natural sources (egg yolk, carrots, broccoli, fish, nuts, green leafy vegetables and citrus fruits) rather than from vitamin supplements. The distribution for a diet having an approximate 1800 calories count (which is suitable for the elderly) may be as follows:

WHOLE DAY'S DIET CHART

Early Morning (6.00–6.30 am): A cup of tea (with milk or herbal, if preferred and sugar-free if diabetic) and 2 biscuits. A handful of sprouted grams should be taken before taking up any vigorous physical activity, such as brisk walking, jogging, or physical fitness exercises.

Breakfast (9.00–9.30 am) (must have something for breakfast to prevent your body from going into the starvation mode and decreasing its metabolism): 2 to 3 *chapattis* with vegetable curry or 3 to 4 pieces of plain bread and 1 egg; or vegetable or egg sandwich; or semolina or sago porridge; 1 or 2 bananas (and, if possible, one additional serving of seasonal fresh fruit like mango, papaya, pineapple, orange, apple or grapes).

Lunch (1.15–1.45 pm): A combination of plain, boiled rice (50 gm) and *chapattis* (2 to 3); dal; fish; salad or *raita* (using plain curd).

Tea: A cup of tea with a small bowl full of puffed rice (*muri*) or flex rice (*chura*); or 2 biscuits.

Dinner (9.00–9.30 pm): 3 to 4 *chapattis* (or 1 to 2 chapattis plus a bowl of plain, boiled rice); dal; a light vegetable preparation; salad; a sweet dish.

There should be a gap of 4 to 5 hours between each meal. You must enjoy whatever you eat to help the digestive and metabolic processes. When you are consuming a lot of proteins, cereals should be taken as a small feature in your diet. And, you must consume cereals with dal and light vegetable curry. Oily, greasy, spicy food should be avoided to keep problems away. Take water at least 5 to 10 minutes after taking a heavy meal.

Saturated fats injure brain cells and hamper the ability of neurotransmitters to carry messages. Antioxidants such as vitamins A, E and C reduce the cell damage in the brain caused by free radicals, a byproduct of metabolism. Try to get vitamins from natural sources such as egg yolk, carrots, broccoli, fish, nuts, green leafy vegetables and citrus fruits, strawberries, grapes, red cabbage, plum and herbs such as *brahmi, tulsi* and *shankhpushpi*.

DIET FOR FAT PEOPLE

If you're 'fat' or 'obese', the guidelines that you should follow are: Don't eat more than four eggs a week; eat raw or steamed vegetables; eat more fish and poultry and less amount of red meat; limit alcohol, caffeine and salt in your diet; substitute whole milk by skimmed milk; drink as much water as you can and make it a habit to have a glassful before any meal; substitute sugar with low calorie sweetener; stop taking oily snacks frequently; daily exercise (bicycle riding, walking, swimming etc.)—30 minutes of activity, five times a week, should be the goal.

Home Remedies for Weight Loss: Spices like dry ginger, cinnamon, black pepper, etc. are good for losing weight; regular intake of carrot juice; vegetables like bitter gourd (*karela*) and bitter variety of drumstick are useful in losing weight; honey is an excellent home remedy for obesity—it mobilises the extra deposited fat in the body.

EFFECTS OF FASTING

Does periodic 'fasting' have a beneficial effect on general health and fitness? According to experts, going without food for a day, after a full meal 24–hour period, imposes mild stress on cells. The cells respond to the stress by increasing their ability to cope with more severe stress. The effect of fasting is similar to the effect of physical exercise on muscle cells. Fasting is expected to reduce the adverse impact of coronary artery disease (as the body is compelled to use up the cholesterol plaques deposited on the walls of blood vessels), high blood pressure (fasting thins the blood and interferes with the platelets which clot within the vessels and cause cerebral stroke), low blood sugar (fasting detoxifies the body and also cuts down the entry of protein into the body preventing excessive nitrogen deposition in addition to the nitrogen deposits caused by the low sugar problem), and migraine (fasting leads to detoxification which cools down the central nervous system).

MORE TIPS FOR DIET PLANNING

A few more practical tips about planning your diet follow.

There are three EFAs (Essential Fatty Acids): SFAs (Saturated Fatty Acids), MUFAs (Mono-Unsaturated Fatty Acids) and PUFAs (Poly-Unsaturated Fatty Acids). These must be present in the body in order to maintain fitness.

Omega-3 and *Omega-6* are two types of PUFAs and are considered EFAs for our body's fitness. Unfortunately, our bodies do not make them, they must come from outside through the right kind of diets.

Some fish varieties high in *Omega–3* are: herring, mackerel, salmon, sardine, swordfish, trout, tuna, hilsa, katla, pomfret and rohu. One 19-year long Japanese study has shown that men who eat fish regularly (once every two days) have a better chance of living longer. *Omega-3* fatty acids are thought to prevent heart disease by helping to reduce the inflammation involved in hardening of artery walls. They may also reduce blood pressure and chemically regulate the electrical impulses of the heart's rhythm. *Omega–3* is also important for brain development and may reduce the risk of Alzheimer's disease. Other sources of *Omega–3* are plant food like flaxseed oil, walnuts, canola oil and soybean oil, mayonnaise and salad dressing.

Garlic is very effective as a blood thinner. It can bring down cholesterol and stop blood clotting. Moreover, it has no side effects unlike aspirin, which has been recommended for more than 100 years for prevention of blood clots and heart attacks but has hazards like sudden strokes and gastrointestinal bleeding. 2 to 3 small nodules of raw garlic, in chopped off condition, should be swallowed like medicinal pills with a glass of water, every morning before taking breakfast.

Tea and coffee intake should be restricted to 3 to 4 cups per day. Tea and coffee contain caffeine, which acts as a stimulant, increases the blood pressure, reduces appetite and creates problems for the liver and the spleen. Therefore, raw tea and black coffee should be avoided; rather, to make it white, adequate quantity of milk should be added. However, those affected by diabetes, ulcer, and lactogen tolerance must avoid milk in tea. Likewise, those suffering from kidney problems, acidity and flatulence, must avoid lemon tea. Tea has another harmful chemical, tannin. Tannin is bitter in taste and it creates inflammation in the intestines. It also solidifies the iron contents of the food and makes it unproductive and useless. As a result, anaemia, duodenal ulcer, and digestive disorders develop.

Cola drinks should be avoided as they may also contain harmful chemicals (like pesticides).

Raw cocoa or fresh cocoa beans contain flavonoids (about 10000 mg per 100 gm). Flavonoids are plant-based compounds with protective antioxidants like those in green tea. The antioxidant may help decrease blood pressure and improve circulation. Processed chocolate products contain much less quantity of flavonoid.

EFFECTIVE FOOD PROCESSING

When different types of food inputs are properly combined, the body is able to do its job effectively, and digestion lasts for an average of three to four hours only, so you don't have to waste your energy on the digestive process. Improper combination of food affects the digestive process, which can take as much as eight, ten, twelve or fifteen hours even more and also leads to disturbed sleep and tiredness.

We consume two major food groups: proteins (meat, chicken, eggs, fish, vegetable proteins and dairy products) and starches or carbohydrates (potatoes, rice, *chapattis*, bread, pasta). Both proteins and starches are very concentrated foods requiring a significant energy output during digestion. Fruits and vegetables are not concentrated and so require far less energy for digestion.

When a protein enters the stomach, an acid-based digestive juice is required for digestion. On the other hand, when starch or carbohydrate enters the stomach, an alkaline-based digestive juice is required. Unfortunately, when an acid and an alkaline enzyme come into contact with each other, due to the fact that protein and starch/carbohydrate have been consumed at the same time in reasonable quantities (as we usually do while following our typical Indian food habits), they are neutralised.

So, if you were to eat meat and potatoes or fish and rice, or chicken and bread/chapattis, at the same meal, all combinations of protein and starch/carbohydrates, the digestive juices are neutralised causing the digestive process to be dragged out for too long. Therefore, eat protein and vegetable or starch and vegetable combination for effective food processing.

As further tips on effective digestion, one must not lose sight of the following ground rules:

Don't Overeat: To deal with the excess intake, if you overeat, the stomach has to expand. More acid will be secreted to cope with the excess. The sphincter muscles will open up backward under pressure to allow the acid to 'reflux' into the esophagus.

Chew the Food Well: Before swallowing, chew the food consciously. The mouth produces powerful enzymes to facilitate partial digestion.

Don't Lie Down Right after a Meal: In the lying position, the acid present inside the stomach can seep into the esophagus producing acidity.

Don't Eat when You're Not Hungry or when You're Extremely Tired: Resting your digestive system in between meals is one of the best ways to ensure enough digestive enzymes for the next meal.

Find out your food sensitivity, if any.

Don't eat on the run or under stress.

Don't smoke immediately before any meal as smoking may weaken your sphincter muscles.

Make it a point to lose excess weight if you have any.

If you tend to suffer from acne problem, avoid smoking, alcohol, eating chocolates, cakes, sweets, biscuits and chips as well as citrus fruits, sausages and cured meats (like bacon and smoked fish). Go easy on yeast products (beer, wine, bread and pizza) as well as fried foods. Cut down on your salt and coffee intake. Drink carrot, celery, apple and ginger juice and 6 to 8 glasses of water a day in between meals and say no to fizzy drinks.

If you have a dandruff problem, stop consumption of yeast containing products (like bread, pizza or nan roti). Say no to beer, cheese and butter.

If you feel stressed out, tired and listless, don't use caffeine, which tenses up muscles.

When you are tense, gut mobility changes and it can lead to cramps. So it's important to incorporate fibre in your diet. The best sources for fibre are fruits, vegetables and whole grains. Fatty and sugary foods are a strict no-no. Food high on sugar, say cakes and chocolates, can make you feel depressed. High fat food makes you sluggish. Spicy foods should be completely avoided because they induce laziness.

BODY AND EMOTIONS: AN EXERCISE FOR SELF-DISCOVERY FROM YOUR EATING HABITS

1. When you crave something to eat even if you're not terribly hungry, you go in for: (a) some specific food (such as sweets, cookies or potato chips); or, (b) not anything specific.

2. You often experience cravings: (a) when you're busy with some work and under pressure; or, (b) when you're lonely and bored.

3. When you crave something sweet, you usually choose: (a) an Indian sweet, a chocolate bar, a chewing gum; or, (b) a milkshake or an ice cream.

4. When you're not terribly hungry, you go for: (a) hot dogs, pizza, or an egg roll; or, (b) some homemade food.

5. The time of the day that you're most likely to experience cravings is: (a) in the middle of the afternoon when you're under work pressure earlier before retirement and now lonely after retirement; or, (b) late at night when you're tired and have nothing much to do and no one to talk to.

6. You just go crazy over: (a) potato chips, nuts, or other snack foods; or, (b) Indian sweets, cakes, pastries, chocolates, ice creams.

7. On a given day, you're likely to feel: (a) angry, frustrated, resentful, irritated, stressed or tense; or, (b) discouraged, lonely, bored, restless or fatigued.

8. Sometimes, you just go for snacks to avoid: (a) doing something (as eating is a great way to procrastinate); or, (b) food helps you to bury your emotions.

9. You eat mainly because: (a) it's fun; or, (b) it feels good.

10. For breakfast, you're more likely to choose: (a) a cereal (such as rice or *chapatti* or bread); or, (b) eggs or biscuits.

Scoring Method: If you chose more (a)'s, it means, your negative feelings of anger, stress, frustrations, resentment, burnout, bitterness, self-disgust or being overwhelmed and/or your desire for excitement are causing you to seek chewy, crunchy foods.

If you chose more (b)'s, it means you are probably struggling with feelings such as boredom, loneliness, sadness, depression, hopelessness or a lack of meaning in your life.

BLOOD SUGAR

Sugar and fat are our two energy sources. We organise them from outside in the form of food, beverages and drinks. We also produce them inside our body as we shall see now.

If you reduce your intake of sugars, you will need to replace those calories with the other energy source and, that is, fat. And high fat intake is by no means recommended. Thus diabetics who stop their sugar intake and go for fat input gain body weight and may become obese.

Let us talk about sugar now.

The Need for Sugar

We need a constant supply of sugar or glucose in our diets as our cells depend on sugar as their primary source of energy. Without it or when it is in short supply, they function at a very slow pace.

This is especially the case for our brain where a lack of sugar leads to lack of concentration. It gives us the kind of feeling when we skip lunch. While the body can organise a replacement for sugar for short periods through special biochemical synthesis, mental or physical exertion becomes very tiresome and, sometimes, indeed difficult without the supply of glucose.

Sugar "Highs" and "Lows"

Sugar "highs" come about when the brain suddenly has a fresh flow of energy such as a little while after drinking a cup of tea. Ten minutes after drinking cup of tea in which sugar has been added (such as early in the morning when you have your bed tea in empty stomach), the glucose gets into the bloodstream and circulates throughout the body being absorbed by the body cells which were hungry for energy. If you go for some vigorous physical activity at that time then the energy gets depleted and very little sugar goes to the brain. You need a fresh supply of food or a drink or some beverage (may be a health drink) to ensure flow of sugar into your brain.

But when you are physically not that active in early morning, the remaining blood glucose (after the body cells have been served) from the cup of tea that you had reaches the brain, you experience an intense energy flow. However, this sudden boost of energy is short-lived as how much energy can you get from one or two cups of bed tea and two or three biscuits; and very soon a fresh urge for energy develops and our system needs food and we become hungry.

Thus having a breakfast is essential to meet our natural urge for food following a long gap after the previous night's dinner. Skipping breakfast deprives us of energy supply which is harmful for our health.

When there is a high quantity of sugar in the blood, it leads to reduced appetite and we don't feel hungry. Our hunger is thus an empirical way of assessing the level of sugar in our blood.

When our pancreas detects a high quantity of sugar in the blood a little while after we have consumed something—a meal, a sugary drink or a beverage, it produces the hormone *insulin*. This stimulates cells in the muscles and liver to stop using fat as an energy source and take up sugar or glucose instead for use by the body thus reducing the quantity available to the brain. So the energy availability in the brain suffers and the high now turns into low.

Psychological Impact

Low blood sugar aggravates feelings of irritation and frustration. Our brain thus needs a constant supply of sugar to maintain its mood balance. Research studies have shown that people with higher blood sugar are better able to control their anger than those whose sugar levels are depleted. There may be an indirect link between *diabetes* and lack of self-control.

Details of the Process and how Diabetes Develops

Everything we eat, sooner or later, gets converted into glucose. Amongst various food items, starch or carbohydrates (the simple sugars like table sugar, honey, molasses, sweet syrups like sugarcane juice, *tal gur* etc.) and refined starches (like refined/milled rice, white bread, pasta, pizza, cakes, pastries and so on) are most rapidly converted into glucose, causing a sudden rise in the body's blood sugar level that demands immediate *insulin* action.

Now, what is *insulin*? Specialised cells in the pancreas, housed inside our abdomen, produce the hormone *insulin* that has the job of moving the blood glucose into cells where it can be used for energy or stored to meet future energy needs.

Insulin thus shuttles the sugars from food into body cells to be used for energy. Too much *insulin* also causes food to be converted into body fat, which leads to obesity. In addition, high *insulin* levels can cause cholesterol deposits in the arteries and high blood pressure.

Type 1 diabetes is an autoimmune disease where the cells of the pancreas fail to produce adequate amount of *insulin*. In the type 2 diabetes, the body typically produces enough *insulin* first, but unfortunately the body cells are resistant to the action. As blood sugar levels rise, the pancreas is forced to work overtime to produce even more *insulin*. Eventually, the pancreatic cells may wear out, causing an insufficiency of insulin. Most type 2 diabetics are found to be overweight. In type 2 diabetes, the body loses sensitivity to insulin. As a result, the amount of sugar, or glucose, in the blood remains high, leading to fatigue and blurred vision. Over the long term, excess blood sugar, can increase the risk of heart disease, kidney failure and blindness.

Eating sugary foods and other simple carbohydrates does not cause diabetes, but once a trace of the disease develops, it is usually necessary to limit, but not eliminate, consumption of such foods. Most extra calories come from sugary soft drinks and canned fruit juices. Sugar also, as we all know, promotes tooth decay.

Both kinds of diabetes greatly increase a person's risk of heart disease, kidney failure and blindness, as well as circulatory disorders. Type 2 diabetes can and often does result in debilitating, life-threatening disorders.

Diabetes can be prevented by regular physical fitness exercises that keep the body weight well within the permissible limits, control of consumption of fatty, greasy, starchy food and sugar.

As a preventive measure, have vegetables and whole fruits, which provide both bulk and fibre. Fruit juices, especially canned ones, are no good because they have extra fructose and added sweeteners. Cut down on refined cereals and sweetened drinks. Current findings suggest that a small amount of cinnamon can help protect diabetics from complications of their conditions. Diabetics could thus add a dash of cinnamon to their morning servings of coffee or orange juice or cereal. You can also make cinnamon tea by simply boiling water with stick cinnamon. Cinnamon may also help stave off the onset of type 2 diabetes.

Excess sugar in blood sucks up water in the body disrupting our internal waste-removal systems. Dry mouth, weight loss, lethargy, and dehydration can be common symptoms of diabetes. High blood sugar levels affect water in the eyes, actually reshaping the lens. Other symptoms of diabetes include blackened skin around the eyes and knuckles, gum disease and bad breath.

It would be virtually impossible to follow a healthful diet that didn't contain any sugar. Sugar is present in all fruits as well as in milk. In fact, milk has more of the milk sugar, lactose, than it does of protein. It's not sugar per se that has to be limited in the diets of diabetics. It's all carbohydrates, including not just simple sugar but the complex sugars, more commonly known as complex carbohydrates, found in all starchy foods (bread, chapattis, biscuits, cakes, pizzas, potatoes, rice, and so on). Carbohydrates in starchy items are just as capable of raising blood sugar to unhealthy levels in people with diabetes as the carbohydrates in sugar, honey, boiled sweets, *mithai* (Indian sweets) and the like. Thus when an eating plan is being worked out for a diabetic, sweet item can be included as long as total carbohydrate consumption remains below a certain level. This level, however, will differ from person to person depending upon lifestyle and severity of the disease.

www.ingramcontent.com/pod-product-compliance
Lightning Source LLC
Chambersburg PA
CBHW051818090426

42736CB00011B/1546